TRAFFIC IN THE ERA OF CLIMATE CHANGE

TRAFFIC IN THE ERA OF CLIMATE CHANGE

Walking, Cycling, Public Transport Need Priority

VIDYADHAR DATE

KALPAZ

Traffic in the Era of Climate Change : Walking, Cycling, Public Transport Need Priority

Rs. 890

ISBN: 978-81-7835-824-6

Published in 2010 in India by
Kalpaz Publications
C-30, Satyawati Nagar,
Delhi-110052
E-mail: kalpaz@hotmail.com
Phone : 9212729499

Laser Type Setting by: Rudra Computer Graphics, Delhi
Printed at : Chawla Offset Printers, Delhi

Contents

Preface

The deep injustice of India's transport system was best expressed by Mr Gopalkrishna Gandhi, former governor of West Bengal, in the Kalki Sadasivam memorial lecture in Chennai in March, 2010. He said nothing revealed the great divide in India as the divide between the motorists and the pedestrians.

But the pedestrian can no longer be taken for granted. In the urban areas the pedestrian suffers the constant humiliation meekly but in central India the pedestrian has acquired mobility in the armed Maoist movement. Beware of the fury of the patient man, Mr Gandhi said quoting India's former President K.R. Narayanan.

Of course, Mr Gandhi, grandson of the Mahatma, is no Maoist but what he says is most important and his words need to be taken even more seriously.

The pedestrian now suffers the same injustice as dalits. We have political democracy but no democracy on roads. Here the motorist is king and common people are treated like eighth rate citizens. The pedestrian should be at least treated with dignity and given enough space, especially because he or she leaves no carbon footprint which is of high importance in this era of climate change.

Raj Thackeray, leader of the right wing Maharashtra Navnirman Sena, typically represents the obsession with the motor car. He is crazy about cars, likes to drive fast and he does not like anyone even to touch his car. That is the issue. Cars monopolise road space, cause pollution, terrorise people day in and day out, maim and kill but the motorist becomes furious even if one touches the car. That is the new kind of untouchability and apartheid common people face.

This book makes a fervent plea for shifting the priority in transportation from cars to pedestrians and cyclists and public transport. It is possible to create a more humane and friendly environment on roads with imaginative planning and dedicated efforts. Terror now stalks the streets in the country as more people are killed in road crashes in India than anywhere else in the world and millions are injured each year. We shamefully expose our children to grave danger every day while they go to school. The streets can be made safe for children, old people, pedestrians in general, the physically challenged, women and other vulnerable sections. The book draws on the author's extensive walking and commuting for years in different parts of the country and some foreign countries to get a first hand experience of how harsh and humiliating life for ordinary people is.

The book is critical of the elitist policies catering mainly to motorists and the culture of highways, freeways and flyovers which completely ignore the needs of ordinary people. It is not against the motor cars as such. But the book argues that cars can co- exist peacefully with pedestrians, cyclists and other road users with better social and traffic engineering.

There should be true democracy on the roads. Roads are for people, not only for motorists. They should not be mere corridors for motorised traffic. Most road users are ordinary people, pedestrians. Planning has to shift in their favour. Even in Western countries they are widening footpaths providing more space for pedestrians and cyclists. There is more to it than social justice. It makes sense from the point of view of the environment and optimum use of space.

This is, I think, the only book of its kind in India arguing for a clean, green and humane transport and habitat. The growing environmental, climate crisis which threatens the very survival of the planet demands that we need transport that saves fuel and is friendly to the environment.

This makes the book even more relevant. The book should appeal to everyone. After all every one is affected by traffic jams or unbearable conditions of travel in buses and trains and while walking. The book should be of particular interest to activists, traffic and urban planners, engineers, bureaucrats, academics, police in fact everyone concerned with our urban and rural and social environment.

The book is also based on years of study as also interaction with experts from various fields including planners, activists, academics, engineers, government officials and politicians. The book looks at the sociology of transport and dwells on its political, economic, social implications drawing on examples from various fields including literature, cinema, theatre, philosophy, politics, history, economics and urban and rural development. I will be happy if this book stimulates fresh thinking and contribute towards making the world a better place to live in.

Inequality is growing in India and nowhere is the injustice to ordinary people more visible and obvious than on roads. It squarely hits you in the face if you look around. On the one hand you see luxury cars, highways and flyovers and the craze for speed. On the other hand one sees that merely crossing the road is a life and death struggle for people every day of their lives. While a few are becoming hypermobile, the vast majority are rendered immobile. Many people just do not dare stir out and travel in humiliating, overcrowded buses or walk on roads which do not have the basic facility of footpaths.

This is as serious a problem as hunger, malnutrition, housing shortage, pollution and communalism. Yet, it is so little studied and written about. What is happening in the transport sector is increasing social exclusion and apartheid.

The land of Mahatma Gandhi should have got its transport priorities right long ago. Gandhiji is best remembered for his long walks with the stick in his hand. So in a poor country with a vast population walking should have received the highest priority in the transport system. Yet, walking has become a nightmare in this country.

The problem is essentially one of political will. That is lacking because most political parties are obsessed with cars and highways and have forgotten the common people. Even the Communist party of India (Marxist) showed a very un-Maxist obsession with motorised transport, neglected public transport and made the Nano car project a prestige issue and in the process came to grief, suffering severe political reverses.

We have ideal conditions for promoting mass, public transport. We have a huge population with high density areas which makes public transport the natural and most economic choice. The economy of scale is completely in favour of mass transport. In Europe they promote public transport despite much lower ridership because it makes much more sense in terms of environment and land use and quality of life.

We have completely neglected the issue of quality of life. In promoting the car we have turned our streets and roads into an extremely dull, crowded, polluted, unhealthy arena with few public spaces, plazas, street furniture, street cafes. Streets can be fun if one looks at several European streets. There is no earthly reason why our streets cannot be made equally lively. It will cost very little money. A people-friendly environment makes economic sense. It costs much less money than fancy projects. The trouble is our planners and politicians are imitating the worst American models while ignoring the best practices in that country and elsewhere.

Instead of providing decent facilities for walking and public transport some of our elites talk of fancy projects which only invites international ridicule as in the award winning documentary film Age of Stupid of 2009.

As any decent planner would bear out massive changes are needed in land use planning so that housing is not far from the place of work. This would vastly reduce the need to travel long distance. It will also greatly cut down the use of cars. Public transport is essential but it cannot be an end in itself. There is no point in making people ride for hours in crowded conditions.

A forthcoming deluge of cars on roads threatens massive traffic jams. Besides there is the big problem of huge fuel bills and fuel shortage and economic and climate crisis. The issue requires radical solutions, not mere tinkering with problems. There is a serious need for enlightened people to interact with policy makers, politicians, bureaucrats, planners and others to convince them about the need for drastically curbing the number of cars. Measures like BRT (bus rapid transport), priority for public transport, walking, cycling are desperately needed but these will not be enough. The real need is to limit the manufacture and ownership of cars and driving and parking of private vehicles. There are powerful lobbies of motor car manufacturers, roads and highways to contend with. But it is in every one's interest to usher in a more democratic, people-friendly transport system. This will not only reduce congestion and pollution, it will also make our environment more healthy and friendly. Our land of Mahatma Gandhi and democracy should have long ago woken up to the problem and given priority to pedestrians, cyclists and public transport. Some of the Western countries have started doing that.

I have worked for several yeas on this book, reading numerous books and articles, meeting people. And above all, I have walked extensively and have experienced the hardships of people first hand, studied life on streets from close quarters.

I have drawn inspiration from numerous thinkers and activists including Jane Jacobs, Lewis Mumford and Jan Gehl.

I have benefited from my interaction with numerous scholars, architects, journalist colleagues, activists and academics including Praful Bidwai, Kumar Ketkar, Darryl D'Monte, Sujit Patwardhan, Terence Bendixson, Rahul Mehrotra, Ashok Datar, Sudhir Badami Shyamrao Joshi, P.K. Das, Kisan Mehta and P.G. Patankar, Dunu Roy, Akhtar Chauhan, Swapna Banerjee Guha, Bernard D'Mello, Sunita Narain, Dinesh Mohan, Geeetam Tiwari, R.V. Ranade and Pandharinath Ranade.

1

The Car is the Problem

The culture of the motor car, highways and freeways and flyovers is glamorous. But we now have to go beyond that. That culture is no longer environmentally sustainable or financially viable. We should have recognized this long ago. Western countries have now started to act.... We need to focus on public transport, on the mobility of ordinary people, not just of the elite. Moving away from the car may look like a step backward. Actually, it is a step forward especially when the world faces a serious threat of climate change and economic crisis. This is an idea whose time has come.

If we start giving priority to the interests of common people, we can easily start finding the right solutions. Even the car-dominated United States is learning its lessons. The American Congress, the legislative body, has a caucus for the promotion of bicycles for transport with no fewer than 165 members. It is headed by Earl Blumenauer who rides to Capitol Hill in a rusty red orange bicycle. A bicycle user with the wind at his back. That is how the New York Times described him. He points out that this is the right time to shift the focus to pedestrian paths and bicycles and rail transit and buses and public transport.

London, Paris, New York and several top cities in the world are devoting hundreds of km of road space to bicycles, widening their footpaths, treating pedestrians with dignity, giving them more time to cross at traffic signals, not treating them like criminals as we do in India.

If we are to be a true democracy we need to give much more space, much more respect to ordinary people on roads which are clogged, dominated, ruled by automobiles. The ordinary man feels totally alienated, overpowered, neglected, dwarfed by the whole culture of cars and skyscrapers and shopping malls and other centres of consumption.

It is ironical that in the land of Mahatma Gandhi the pedestrian is treated with such contempt. With the Mahatma's great tradition of long walks and padayatras India should have been a paradise for walking. But life becomes hell as soon as one steps out of the house onto the road which is completely dominated by automobiles.

The street has traditionally been a great social, public space all over the world. In many Western countries streets are being revitalized, rescued from domination by motor cars.

We have almost stopped thinking about these issues, such is the impact of the car culture. It is assumed that since there are more and more cars in the market, we must provide more space for them. But then the Western world has found that this just does not work. You may go on increasing space for cars. You will still be in a jam. The main solution is to severely restrict the number of cars. Our politicians, bureaucrats, planners need to become more sensitive to the problems of the people, not only of the car lobby and other vested interests.

The real issue which seldom figures in discussions is that there is a huge increase in the number of people who need to walk. The rulers only talk of providing for the needs of the car, not of the pedestrian.

Europe and some Latin American countries have come up with pro-people transport strategies. We should emulate them. First we have to sensitise politicians and bureaucrats and planners. They need to give up their obsession with cars.

For too long the system is treating common commuters with contempt. Just outside the area for visitors at the arrival section at Sahar international airport in Mumbai, stands an imposing multi-storey car park. And just by the side is a BEST bus shelter, shining and of stainless steel, but pathetically small and utterly unfriendly to users. It has just one bench and it is an insult to passengers. One just slides down, can't even rest one's butt, leave alone sit comfortably. It is almost as if they are treating common people with a vengeance. There are just six to seven seats for hundreds of people including visitors and thousands of airport, airline employees, who stand in the open in heat or rain. The space for the bus stop is not larger than the space for parking one car. There is parking for 3600 cars at present and the capacity is to be raised to 12,000 cars.

And outside Andheri railway station, the main access station to the Sahar airport, the steel bus stop is completely broken down and commuters are forced to stand on the road helplessly waiting for the bus. This is the kind of humiliation poured on millions of such people working hard for the economy. And yet, the authorities boast of making Mumbai a world class city.

Sometimes the wait for a bus outside Sahar airport can take one hour and the journey takes one more hour. By this time the privileged can reach from Mumbai to Delhi. So there is increasing hyper mobility for some people with air travel and fast cars while millions are stranded. Much of this mobility is gained at the expense of ordinary people. Literally. Private airlines have not paid dues of hundreds of crores to the public sector Indian Oil Corporation for aviation fuel. They tried to blackmail the government in August, 2009 by threatening to go on strike if they were not given a massive subsidy of thousands of crores of rupees. Surprisingly, the bluff was called by aviation minster Praful Patel who has been their biggest promoter all these years. Till only a couple of years ago he was talking of liberally giving licenses to private airline for the asking.

And the Maharashtra government amended the development control rules in 2009 so that the rich could build helipads on top of their buildings and fly at will. The immediate beneficiary would be the Ambanis living in Sea Wind building at Cuffe Parade. The move drew strong protests from activists including Sumaira Abdulali, an anti-noise campaigner of Awaaz foundation, and Swaran Kohli of the Nariman Point Churchgate Citizens Association.

The aviation privatization policy had proved a disaster. The airlines went on buying new aircraft, built excess capacity, indulged in cut throat competition in air fares and paid the price.

While the authorities constantly talk of building world class airports and allocate huge sums on this infrastructure, one seldom hears them talk of providing even basic facilities at state transport bus depots or railway stations. Instead of augmenting space at these crucial public spaces, they are depriving people of this asset by selling their land for shopping malls.

One of the exceptional bureaucrats is Sanjeev Sahai, chief executive of the Delhi Integrated Multi Modal Transit System. Referring to the neglect of passengers at bus depots and railway stations, he says this is how we disenfranchise the poor.

The congestion, chaos and dirt in and around the badly maintained inter state bus terminus in Delhi is shocking. Here multitudes of poor passengers can be seen sitting or sleeping on the floor offer a sharp contrast to the makeover of Delhi's airport. (Sudheendra Kulkarni in the article 're-enfranchise the poor in our cities' in Indian Express (9-8-09).

The callousness is visible all over. All norms are thrown to the winds in the construction of flyovers and highways. The new Delhi Gurgaon highway has been built without basic safety features, medical aid, foot-over bridges, underpasses, according to Rajendra Kataria, deputy commissioner for traffic, Gurgaon. The result is it has become a death trap for ordinary people. There were over 1500 serious accidents on the 21 km stretch in the first few months of its opening, according to information obtained under the Right to Information Act by K.S. Anand, a Delhi businessman, whose son was killed on the highway.

A high speed culture of fast cars and highways is being imposed on society without providing any safeguards to ordinary people who become their ultimate victims. Added to this is corruption and inefficiency in execution of projects. There is need to educate scientists and engineers in ethics, said E Sreedharan, the chairman of Delhi Metro Rail Corporation at the IIT in Mumbai in 2009. He attributed the recent mishaps on Metro projects in Delhi to the decline in moral values of professionals.

Poor urban planning and administration have meant that streets have lost their vitality as social spaces, have become mere corridors for motorized traffic. It is a nightmare merely to step outside the house onto the street. This is no exaggeration because India is now at the top of road fatalities in the world.

As most cities in India have a high density of population they can become financially and environmentally sustainable with strengthening of public transport and curbing of motor car use.

Our politicians and bureaucrats talk of making our cities world class but think mainly of flyovers and highways. They are not aware that New York is now priding itself as a world class walking city. The New York city department of transportation is reinforcing its green bonafides with several measures. It has produced a report called World Class Streets. Remaking New York city's Public Realm. It has prepared a strategy with the assistance of the noted Danish architect Jan Gehl who is a consultant to several cities including Sydney.

The famous Times Square and Broadway areas in New York are being pedestrianised, closed to vehicular traffic and being made social places. Chairs are put in main squares so that people can sit, talk, eat their lunch, relax. That is how cities can become vital, lively social spaces.

New York Mayor Bloomberg and traffic commissioner Janette Sadik Khan are going out of their way to make people aware that streets should become public spaces with safety, aesthetics, beauty, environment and community concerns. Rahul Mehrotra, noted architect and author on urban planning, points out that pedestrianisation was inexpensive and promoted social bonding.

In a car-dominated environment ordinary people feel completely neglected, dwarfed, isolated, alienated. Cities can function very well without cars as Venice and Fes, the heritage town in Morocco, show. They are very livable and enjoyable. We need not do away with cars from our cities, we only need to restrict the number. We should not allow cars or the car lobby to rule over us, dictate terms to us.

There is also need to have compact cities with major facilities within walking distance or easily approachable by public transport. This would involve proper land use planning. Public transport needs to be given top priority but this should not be an end in itself. It should not mean that people should be required to spend hours travelling long distance by public transport, rail or road. The ideal is to have houses and work places as near as possible so that long journeys are not necessary. This will require a new approach to urban planning and governance.

Politicians need to set an example by walking, promoting public transport and curbing cars. But they do not want to walk even a short distance. In Bangalore there is a proposal to purchase golf carts for going the very short distance in the legislature premises. The idea was mooted by transport minister R Ashok with support from assembly speaker Jagadish Shettar. In Mumbai special buses were run some years ago to carry legislators between their hostel and the legislature though the distance involves barely minutes of walking.

For ordinary people life becomes worse with fancy schemes for motor cars. A foot over bridge looks like a facility for pedestrians. But it is actually built for the convenience of the motor car so that the pedestrian does not come in the way. It actually makes the pedestrian's job much more difficult. It makes him or her go up and down and then walk further than he or she normally would have. This actually results in lengthening walking distance and causing much inconvenience to pedestrians, says Nishi Mittal, a transport expert working with the Central Road Research Institute in Delhi.

It is necessary to restore liveliness and humanity, social inter course of streets. The fact is people like to look at each other, we are fascinated by faces and bodies each face tells a story. This mingling and bonding can take place only by humanizing streets, reducing the number of cars.

Streets and squares are marketplaces for trade, discussion, demonstration, formal and informal meetings. Public spaces are democracy in essence. It is through public spaces that cities display their character, their generosity. Erosion of public spaces undermines the very fabric of society, says Richard Rogers, the eminent architect, designer of the Pompidou Centre in Paris. The motor car culture is destroying public spaces. Cynically, municipal authorities are giving away public spaces for car parking at ridiculously low rates to motorists depriving people of their basic rights. The municipal standing committee in Mumbai is refusing persistently to increase the car parking charges, according to R.A. Rajeev, additional municipal commissioner.

But in India streets are being increasingly made dreary by robbing them of their character as a social space and they are used mainly for motor car traffic.

I have always been fond of fast cars and own a Lamborgini and a Ferrari F 512. Among the new cars, I am now planning to buy a sports Mercedes. It is the speed that thrills me most - industrialist Lalit Suri quoted in Times of India in Mumbai on May 29, 2005.

That really shows that at least for a few the car is essentially an instrument of prestige and thrill. It is not so much a means of transport. Abiraj Rajan, a mechanical contractor, is a car fanatic. He says cars should never be used for the mere purpose of commuting. (Priyanka Desai in Hindustan Times 1-10-05)

Abiraj owns five cars and is planning to buy two more. The trouble is the society has to pay a heavy price for the comfort of a few. The damaging impact of the car is heavily documented.

The society is not adversely affected if every one has a fridge or a television set. But as more and more people buy cars, the problems are multiplying. The car grabs precious urban space, causes severe pollution and requires building of roads and highways and expressways which means more loss of greenery, farmland.

In India Status Comes with Four Wheels, was the apt headline of a report in the New York Times in December, 2005. A more interesting headline for the same story in the International Herald Tribune was India's New Money Culture, a Lust for Cars.

The report by Amy Waldman from Vishakhapatnam mentioned that 36-year-old Ram Reddy bought his fourth car a Toyota Innova, big as a luxury van that retails for a minimum of $23,000, many times India's per capita income. The Innova is the new plaything of the moneyed classes of Vishakhapatnam.

This is happening in a country which is home to the world's largest pool of poor people. But its middle class has gone up in the last decade to 250 million while the number of super rich has also increased substantially.

In a country where consumer goods were so limited some time ago that refrigerators were given pride of place in living rooms, people have even more wares to spend money on, cell phones, air-conditioners and washing machines and the biggest status symbol of all, cars.

Rajneesh, a self-proclaimed godman, calling himself Bhagwan, was known for his collection of some 97 Rolls Royce cars and advocacy of free sex in his ashrams. Columnist Malavika Sangghvi, who saw Rajneesh glide in his Phantom wondered whether the reverence aroused by the spectacle was for the vehicle or the guru (DNA 20-9-06).

In contrast the lot of poor Indians is miserable. They either have to walk or have to resort to an extraordinary array of contraptions for transport. They ride tractors and trailers, carts and crowded jeeps. What they cannot regularly rely on is public transport. Cars speed past people waiting patiently for long for buses.

India's growing material hunger, the craze for possessing cars, has another downside. It is largely being met by credit and debt.

In a rare case a poor man in search of glamour and mobility may look for other solutions. Desperate to buy a second-hand motor bike a young man tried to rob a couple seeking privacy on the rocks on the sea face behind Joggers Park in Mumbai and stabbed to death the young man in 2007. The alleged culprit Santosh Verma was ready to do anything for the bike, said Rakesh Maria, joint commissioner of police in Mumbai.

Vijay Mallya, seen as the ultimate pleasure seeker and flamboyant capitalist in social circles, owns a racing team for Formula I. Mallya is bound to give the rapidly increasing pool of speed junkies an adrenaline rush, observed the DNA (2-9-07).

Many people look upon the car as a girl friend or second wife, lavishing attention on it. They may talk with their car or be seen kissing its bonnet while leaving it in the parking area. Many spend enormous amounts on interior decoration of cars and fitting them with gadgets including DVD players. It is a home away from home for the rich. But the gadgets are posing a serious distraction for drivers and raising safety concerns. This is worrying psychologists, according to David Strayer, a leading researcher on distraction in cars. (International Herald Tribune 27-10-05).

A Mercedes Benz club has been formed in Mumbai since 1997, by enthusiasts like industrial photographer Sharad Apte and Kiran Shantaram, a film maker with the Gandhi cap, traditional churidar trousers and kurta. Son of the legendary film director V Shantaram, Kiran is active in the film society movement for promotion of good cinema. Freddy Turel owns some vintage cars one of which has a seat at the rear called the mother-in-law seat for a possessive mother who wanted to escort her daughter on a date.

No wonder, Vasundhara Raje, after becoming chief minister of Rajasthan, wanted a Mercedes car for official use after initially settling for the humble Ambassador car and then the Ford Endeavour.

For the rich walking is mainly a recreational activity or even a fashion statement. Vaundhara Raje created quite a flutter when she walked on the ramp in fashion shows in Jaipur and Bangalore in 2006 ostensibly to promote the state's weavers.

Her nephew Jyotiraditya Scindia, the glamorous young Congress minister and heir to the Scindia fortune, has a passion for fast and luxury cars. It runs in the family. He admits even his little son has the passion. When asked if he had done a course in the US in car racing, he laughed and replied with 'no comments.' (Rediff.com 18-2-02).

Today it is the mystique of Bollywood, India' Hollywood, which is often used to lure car buyers. GM hired film stars Saif Ali Khan and Rani Mukerhejee to advertise its Aveo as a vehicle for the young and sophisticated while Ford used Abhishek Bachchan, film star and son of superstar Amitabh Bachchan.

A few decades ago the hero in Hindi films often used the Cheverolet Impala to lure the heroine and the stars imported the car in real life too. Among the bigger collectors of American cars is lawyer Diljeet Titus whose cars are featured in Hindi films. He runs his own car museum in a sprawling farm house in Mehrauli near Delhi which is called pro bono publico, in public interest, which is ironical considering the elite image of the cars.

The car essentially provides an ego trip for the rich. So the rich and famous even get special vehicle registration numbers for their vehicles which add to admiration of the unthinking fans. So Amitabh Bachhan has the number 11 on his BMW, Ajay Devgan has 5000 on his BMW, Shahrukh Khan has 555 on his car, also a BMW. It cost Rs 10,000 to get the special number from the RTO (regional transport office) of the government in the year 2006. Two years later the amount had increased several times. Amitabh paid Rs 75,000 for the number 9000.

While the poor are stranded, immobolised, the rich enjoy tremendous mobility on roads and in the air. The rich, like kings of old think, they are God or close to God. I want to touch the face of God, industrialist-aviator Vijaypat Singhania said while announcing that he wanted to fly a hot air balloon to a record height of 70,000 ft above sea level.

The chairman emeritus of Raymond, the synthetic textile company, subsequently flew in a balloon as tall as a 30-storey building in November 2005 setting a world record. He is known for his flying across several countries in his single-engine light aircraft.

The rich can get away with anything. It is reported that once Mr Singhania flew his plane under the bridge across the river Ganga, a very dangerous thing to do indeed. When asked about this by Shekhar Gupta, senior journalist, Mr Singhania declined further comment saying he would get into serious trouble.

Mr Singhania also recalled that in his younger days he paid Rs 10 per hour for flying as in those days flying was heavily subsidized. This shows how the rich enjoy huge subsidies for their pleasure.

Gautam Singhania has a passion for cars and speed. He participated in 2005 in the Cannonball 8000, the popular international auto run from London to Rome by road with co-driver Hormzad Sorabjee. Singhania rode in his bright orange lamborgini Gallardo. This again shows that for the rich driving is an end in itself, it is not about going from one place to another for travel need. And when you like to drive at that speed, back home in India you naturally see pedestrians as a nuisance on the road and want all the road space to yourself.

Gujarat, which is synomous with trade and capitalism, has a number of young rich capitalists flaunting their new cars costing crores of rupees. So Modi of Cadila Pharma, Gautam Adani of Adani group and Pankaj and Amit Patel of Sintex group vie with one another to have a different brand of a car. People want something more special, said Javed Desai, a car dealer. A car is to a man what a diamond is to a woman, said Amit Patel. (TOI 30-9-07).

But who can enjoy more mobility at the cost of government funds than wives and officers of the IAF (Indian Air Force). A CAG report tabled in Parliament in 2007 made this clear. Nearly Rs 75 crore were spent in unauthorized use of VIP aircraft. Eight aircraft meant for transport for troops and supplies were converted into VIP aircraft though 19 other aircraft were earmarked already. This showed indifference to the primary role of the planes, the report said.

Nine of the modified planes were never used by the three entitled VIPs, the President of India, the vice-president and the Prime Minister.

The wives of Air Force and Army chiefs have come under particular criticism.

The Army used four times more vehicles than sanctioned and spent close to Rs 280 crore on hiring private vehicles during 2005-06.

This shows the tremendous mobility enjoyed by the privileged while the poor do not have proper space even to get a foothold in a suburban train or to walk on the footpath. In fact immobility for the poor is a major cause of child mortality and deaths of pregnant mothers in the country. They cannot reach public hospitals for health care.

That is why the West Bengal government has decided to pay transport costs to underprivileged pregnant women to reach state-run hospitals and health facilities in time for childbirth. (IE 12-6-07).

For the handicapped India is a nightmare whether on roads, buses, trains or even aeroplanes. The physically and mentally challenged are often denied a seat on flights. The civil aviation department sought an explanation from Sahara airline in 2007 after Rajiv Rajan, a cerebral palsy patient, was denied a seat in Chennai for a flight to Delhi. They even called in the police to show me the way out, he said in a complaint. It was only after a furore over the case that the directorate general of civil aviation framed adequate rules. Javid Abidi, convener, Disabilities Rights Group, says a lot more needs to be done for the mobility of people with disabilities. And footpaths are so uneven that even the strongest people cannot use them.

A motor cyclist was arrested some time ago for brushing against the car of industrialist Vijaypat Singhania. But what happens when vehicles brush dangerously past pedestrians, knock them down, cripple them, day in and day out and the number would run into millions ?

While people like Mr Singhania have all the air space to fly, roads to drive on, and the seas to navigate their yachts the poor lack even walking space. The Mahalaxmi race course with area of nearly 200 acres is one of the few public spaces where citizens can take a stroll in Mumbai. But Mr Singhania wants it to be converted into a luxury hotel and a theme park. His suggestion to the Maharashtra government on this drew widespread criticism in the media. (Mumbai Mirror 25-7-06)

As for son Gautam Singhania his private helicopter seems a metaphor of his world view as he poses with his cowboy hat against the aircraft. He hates life in the slow lane and enjoys being called a demon. (Bombay Times 9-9-06). If some people do not approve of his lifestyle, it is their problem, he says. His latest acquisition is a yacht, the first yacht entirely made of wood hand-crafted by traditional craftsmen from Gujarat known for their boat-building skills.

Then look at this. 'This may just be the right time to widen the roads. Over 20 beauties are ready to speed down the tarred tracks this year and take the Indian car bazaar by storm. Tighten your seat belts and get ready for a ride.' This is not an advertisement for cars. That is how the special report on cars in The Times of India begins. Not surprising since the boundary between newspaper reports and advertisement is being blurred because of the pressure from the rich and powerful and big industry. In this case, the pressure is from the world's most powerful industry.

Robert Walser in his famous book Walk says he cannot understand ever how it can be a pleasure for motorists to hurtle past all the images and objects which our earth displays. It is as if these people have gone mad.

He compared the car to a wild beast and says if someone keeps a wild beast that escapes the owner must take responsibility for the damages. Indeed a car on a road is a very dangerous public activity but it is seen as an essentially private activity. The fact that a car impinges on the freedom of others is seldom taken into account.

Despite the immense danger posed by the car to society, any effort by the common people to present any resistance to the car is viewed as a big crime by the establishment. There is the infamous case of the caning in Singapore of Michael Fay, an American teenager, for spray-painting, defacing motor cars in 1994. The punishment was thought to be too excessive but the Singapore government did not relent despite strong protests in the American media and appeals from President Clinton and others.

Trouble began in September, 1993 when judicial commissioner Amarjeet Singh, husband of nominated MP Kanwaljeet Singh found that his car had been sprayed with red paint. It was later noticed that several other cars had been painted.

In Europe a new form of protest, car vaulting, has emerged. People climb over cars blocking the footpath. But in Central Athens a young man Tassos Pauliassis, 29, was in trouble after he put his hand on a car that was blocking his way and set off an alarm. He was arrested faced the prospect of jail for four years, all for asserting his right to walk on the road in a country where pedestrian rights are widely disregarded and where per capita car ownership is highest in Europe. (IHT 11-11-07).

But in India many have become slaves of the car. The prominent architect Charles Correa has remarked that rich women would be gladly seen on the footpath on Fashion street in Mumbai buying clothes but they would never ever travel by a bus as this would be considered below their dignity.

Amitabh Bchchan wanted to cut down a 20-year-old 25-ft tall peltophorum tree because it came in the driveway of his new office. Imagine the office is just behind his bungalow at Juhu where many of his fans, assemble for his darshan. The best thing would be for him to walk the short distance. If that is not possible because of the attention of fans, he could very well be driven there and from the office. (TOI 19-6-05).

The superstar is said to have eleven luxury cars including one Lexus, two BMWs, a bulletproof car with sturdy tyres used for car races. One vehicle is redesigned by car stylist Dilip Chhabria from an Ashok Leyland bus to look like a Jet in which the star can relax in between shots during film shooting.

Another film star and former union minister of the Bharatiya Janata party, Shatrughan Sinha, wanted an exclusive access to one of the gates of the Lav Kush building at JVPD in Juhu. However, the Mumbai high court judge A.M. Khanvilkar overruled the move following objections from other residents that he was encroaching on a common passage.(DNA 13-8-06).

Film star Shahrukh Khan became unpopular among neighbours for sveral years because of the alleged illegal construction of his building on the Bandra seafront. The ceaseless grinding noise from construction of his underground car park has shattered the peace, especially in Retreat House where people assemble for meditation and introspection.

Mr Gajanan Kirtikar of Shiv Sena faced severe criticism some time ago for building a road in the green Aarey milk colony merely to; provide better access to a posh residential high rise colony and golf course in Goregaon which are built on much environmental destruction. And he is a former minister of state for home in Maharashtra.

Manohar Malgaonkar, a novelist, mentioned an interesting experience at the house of a friend. He was introduced to a non-resident Indian who had come to India on an annual visit. Out of nothing she asked me 'what car do you drive ? I drive a BMW, she revealed. Mr Malgaonkar said he could see that was the whole purpose of her question to be able to rub home the fact that she an NRI, was so much better off than myself and the others in the room. After all there is no point in your being rich if no one knows that you are rich, is there ?

The rich fork out for a single car the sort of sums most of us don't earn in a lifetime. Don't ask a man who owns a Toyota or Porsche or how much he paid for it. That is because foreign-made cars are outrageously expensive in India. And quite a few of these are imported illegally. The directorate of revenue intelligence seizes a number of high-end cars to unearth a huge duty evasion racket. One of the seized cars a Toyota Land Cruiser belonged to businessman Chandan Basu, son of West Bengal's former chief minister Jyoti Basu.

The main suspect in the import scandal, Sanjay Bhandari, was let off by the Supreme court in 2008 as the directorate of revenue intelligence failed to produce vital documents.

Chandan Basu reacted angrily to the seizures. 'One thing I realize now. It's becoming increasingly difficult to live in Bharat.' (Indian Express 10-9-05). That is the point. The rich want to live life without restrictions or obligations and they threaten to emigrate. The directorate of revenue intelligence seized eight cars including seven BMWs from top industrialists Industrialist Samir Thapar found two of his cars were seized, a lamborgini and a BMW.

Also implicated was television producer. Ekta Kapoor. But, when questioned by journalist Pranati Mehra she said No Comments.

And more and more names kept tumbling over the next few months including film stars Sunil Shetty and Sanjay Dutt. Shetty bought the monster Hummer vehicle, a civilian version of the Humvee used by the US army. The first Hummer went to Arnold Schwarzenegger, the right-wing body builder film star who now reportedly has eight of them. In fairness to him he later turned into a crusader for the environment as governor of California.

Just two days before Sunil Shetty's alleged duty evasion became public, he had hit the front page for cheering participants at the flag off of the Voltas Motoxtreme 2005 car rally in Mumbai along with Formula 1 driver Narain Karthikeyan.

Film star Saif Ali Khan and Sushmita Sen were similarly implicated in alleged irregularities in the import of luxury cars.

High profile civil aviation minister Praful Patel has faced court proceedings in a case of alleged cheating of Unit Trust of India for Rs 50 crore as chief of Autorider automobile company. (TOI 20-9-06).

Parliament member Ajay Chautala, son of the former chief minister of Haryana, got away after paying the duty of nearly Rs 19 lakh (Hindustan Times 4-9-06)

Princes Diana had to think twice before acquiring a Mercedes. In the end she compromised by hiring the car on a monthly rental of 1500 pounds per month.

But the car was not too expensive for the political head of a third world country, Pakistan. Ms Benazir Bhutto ordered from the manufacturers a model priced even higher than the one Diana hired Ms Bhutto paid some Rs 60 lakh in those days for the car in the nineties.

The manufacturers used Ms Bhutto's car for an advertising gimmick. They showed the car and its owner standing beside it. Under the photograph there was a caption in bold lettering 'A beautiful car for a beautiful lady.'

Many bigwigs in India import foreign cars through total fraud Used foreign cars come through the Mumbai docks. Passengers, who are not genuine owners of the cars, bring them under the transfer of residence rules.

There is something disturbing in the psychology of some car owners. A young man, not satisfied with three cars in his house in Karol Bagh, Delhi, drove away with a Toyota Camry car from a showroom. The youth allegedly threatened the showroom employee with a toy gun and tried to hijack the car. He then ran out of the car but was arrested. (TOI 18-12-07).

In the United States vehicles fitted with personal security devices make a new status symbol. As inequalities grow, there is fear of attack from the poor on the road and so you have armoured cars, bullet-proof windshield, tyres that will keep running even when flat and even a cylinder of tear gas to disperse your assailants.

That the car is seen as an instrument of dominance and aggression is best illustrated by a two-page advertisement of Hyundai's large-sized vehicle Terracan in 2003. The text goes like this 'Suddenly, there is no place on earth that isn't conquerable on four wheels. Roaring in as a true-blue SUV (sports utility vehicle) is the mighty Hyundai Terracan. Powered by a cutting-edge diesel engine that unleashing an awesome force, it makes mincemeat of every terrain under the sun. Climb inside and you are greeted by an overwhelming sense of authority. From the extravagant interiors, shift on the move four wheel drive. You are in absolute command. Go ahead, think wild, think city, think distance lands, think the impossible. It is your world after all. Rule it. (TOI Mumbai 5-8-03).

This is not fanciful. This kind of an approach is very much there in real life. Note the utter lack of concern not only for other road users but also the entire environment.

One advertisement said 'get ready to roar with the beastly Honda CR-V. The association of a car with a beast should not come as a surprise since environmentalists see the automobile as extremely uncivilized.

A committee appointed by the Maharashtra government recommended in 2009 that car parking should be banned in 430 public buildings in Mumbai for security reasons. This means it is all right to park on roads and other public spaces and to endanger the lives of common people.

Car parking wars are now a regular feature of life in various housing colonies. Now, the clashes have reached the corporate parking areas. The war between the Ambani brothers, Mukesh and Anil, India's top industrialists, has extended to car parking and food courts in the Dhirubhai Ambani Knowledge City in Navi Mumbai, new Bombay.

Cars are involved in various other forms of barbarism. An audio music system company displayed in Mumbai some time ago a music system with capacity to make as much as 149 decibels. Human ears start bleeding after 145 decibels. The system was displayed at various places including Carter Road, Bandra, not far from the office of the additional commissioner of police but the police did not seem to mind. It was only in 2008 that a concerted drive against honking was launched by the Mumbai police and flagged off by film star Amitabh Bachchan. The new traffic police commissioner Sanjay Barve has begun administering an oath to taxi drivers not to honk.

In 1950 a prominent California biochemist established that there was a definite link between automobile exhausts and smog conditions in Los Angeles, the car capital of the world with millions of cars. Dr Arlie Haagen-Smit stated that hydrcarbon compounds produced by the automobile exhaust react with oxides of nitrogen under sunlight to produce photochemical smog. It is significant that the fact was discovered by someone outside the automobile industry. For years the automobile manufacturers felt no obligation either to engage in research themselves or to support outside inquiry into the nature of pollution, points out Ralph Nader, the highly respected trenchant critic of automobile culture in his book Unsafe At Any Speed.

Nader has given many instances of the callousness of the American auto industry in causing pollution and numerous pedestrian deaths due to faulty designing of cars. Manufacturers put appearance and style of cars above safety. A common complaint by a driver who has struck a pedestrian or another vehicle is 'I did not see him.' This was because of defective design of the car.

Worse, with all the advances in technology, the average fuel economy of America's cars and trucks fell to its lowest level in 22 years in the 2002 models, the environment protection agency reported in 2003. The technology and engineering leaps of the last two decades have been poured into everything but fuel economy, the New York Times reported. Since 1981 the average vehicle has 93 per cent more horsepower and is 29 per cent faster in going from 0 to 60 miles an hour. It is also 24 per cent heavier reflecting surging sales of sports utility vehicles.

Over the same period fuel economy has stagnated contributing heavily to the nation's rising oil consumption. This is also a major contributor to global warming.

The report said fuel economy would have improved 33 per cent since 1981 if performance and weight of vehicles been held constant.

Various enlightened groups in the West are now revolting against the motor car. As far back as in 1969 a group of university of Minnesota students dragged an automobile engine in a wagon, dropped it into a grave, covered it with dirt and solemnly declared an end to the tyranny of the internal combustion engine over the lungs and lives of civilized people, World Watch, a staunch environment group, reported.

A young minister read the eulogy 'ashes to ashes, dust to dust, for the sake of mankind, iron to rust ......' Al Gore, who at the time of the burial was finishing his senior year at Harvard, had studied under Roger Revelle, one of the scientists who sounded the alarm about greenhouse warming.

Gore continued to follow the issue over the years and during his campaign for vice-presidency of the United States he suggested that the pollution-spewing internal combustion engine be phased out in another quarter century. In the film Inconvenient Truth he has argued that global warming is the greatest crisis in human history.

Not surprisingly the automobile industry, which is causing so much damage, spends more on advertising than any other industry to convince people that the sprawling development promoted by the car enhances freedom and prosperity.

The US spent six times more money on highways than on public transportation in 1988-99 and the trend continues.

The US consumes 43 per cent of of the world's gasoline with five per cent of its population.

The car lobby also has had a negative impact on Europe. Central and eastern Europe account for 45 per cent of the world's light rail system but was beginning to be replaced by cars and roads, says Molly O'Meara in her book City Limits published by World Watch Institute.

So serious is the threat posed by motor cars to the environment that the state of California sued the six largest car makers for contribution to global warming in 2006. The companies, Ford, General Motors, Toyota, Honda, Chrysler and Nissan have been held responsible for past and future cost of combating the pollution crisis. The law suit did not succeed but it made an important point.

Emissions from cars of the six companies have contributed to 30 per cent of all carbon dioxide emissions from the state, the complaint to the court said. Global warming has harmed California's environment and public health forcing the state to spend millions to respond to threats such as coastal erosion. The state's economy, health and agriculture were being harmed by global warming. Global warming has also reduced California's ice-pack, a vital source of fresh water, raised sea level and increased threat of wild fires.

Surprisingly California governor and body builder-film star Arnold Schwazzenegger has taken up the issue seriously. In Beijing, worried by the impact of air pollution during the Olympics, the authorities began imposing a ban on cars with odd and even numbers on certain days.

Seldom have cars been targets of public anger as during protests by of impoverished black Muslim youths in France in November 2005. Hundreds of cars were burnt. It was the biggest unrest in France since the student protests of 1968. In India buses and trains are often targets of attack during angry public demonstrations which is ironical because common people depend almost entirely upon public transport. In a rare attack on cars, 150 vehicles were damaged during the Shiv Sena's protest against land acquisition for Mukesh Ambani's special economic zone in Raigad district. The agitation was led by Mr Manohar Joshi, a former speaker of the lower house of Parliament.

In the 1968 Paris uprising the symbol of the insurgency was a paving stone which the protesters dug out of the streets by the hundreds to hurl at the truncheon-wielding police officers. No other country in Europe immolates cars with the same gusto and single minded efficiency of France.

Burning cars is typically French, said sociologist Michel Wieviorka. It is quite easy and spectacular. Set a fire and the whole world watches you. It calls the attention of the media and when the media comes, the politicians follow (Reuters 16-11-05).

The noted French philosopher Jean Baudrillard saw the burning of cars by protesting immigrants in 2005 as a sort of eternal flame as that under the Arc de Triumphe burning in honour of the unknown immigrant. Ninety cars are burnt on an average daily in this France of ours, he says. This shows that the whole Western model is disintegrating not due to terrorism or storming by African immigrants but from within.

The superiority of Western culture is sustained only by the desire of the rest of the world to join it, the philosopher says. When there is the least sign of refusal to join it, the West loses its seductive appeal in its own eyes. It is precisely the so-called best or most attractive creations of Western culture like motor cars and shopping centres which are torched by protesters, he says. (New Left Review Jan-Feb 2006).

Immobile jobless youth burn cars, the ultimate symbol of mobility, as an expression of their anger, helplessness, feels another French philosopher Paul Virilio. In his book Speed and Politics written in 1970 Virilio says that unemployed youths are subject to police repression which is intended to control their wandering. When they burn cars, the society begins to question its own values. The car is the most potent symbol of the destructive effects of state-led modernization processes. Cars monopolise streets, the most public of spaces but cars are themselves extremely private spaces, protected, insulated from external sounds, dangers.

In India the motorist can literally get away with murder. A motorist gets far more respect than a pedestrian or a cyclist as a car is a symbol of money, prestige, private property. It is not surprising to find that very often a car finds it much easier to breach security while a pedestrian would be harassed at every point.

Jane Jacobs, the celebrated urban planner, described the erosion of streets by automobiles as nibbling to begin with, then taking heavy bites and ultimately eating away the soul of the city. Surrendering of Paris to automobiles is particularly tragic because it has excellent street architecture. There are few blank walls on the road.

Automobiles themselves are a terror and a menace on the road. The companies, responsible for so many deaths, global pollution and warming, pretend that they are actually doing good for the society. So General Motors shows that it is doing something for cancer patients by partnership with the National Cancer Institute by working on breast cancer research trials. This move was strongly criticized by Corp Watch, a strong group exposing the corporate sector's crimes and campaigning against their misdeeds. A corporate polluter should not seek to enhance its image by working with a cancer institute, the group pointed out.

Automobile companies also very often display misleading advertisements which seek to suggest a close bond between Nature and motor cars. New car models zoom in fantastic, open natural surroundings as if they are part of nature. Another insidious idea is to create the impression among potential buyers that there is enough, huge open space for a car to move about when actually the opposite is true as roads are severely congested despite maniacal road construction activity to benefit the car lobby.

One television advertisement for Santro car shows film star Pretty Zinta as a European beauty in Europe standing amidst tulips. Shahrukh Khan zips past her in various car brands to impress her. It is with Santro that he succeeds. That apart, opposition from protest groups has had some effect. There is less display of large breasted women with cars in advertisements. Now, they are trying to show that cars are environment friendly, recyclable.

In India philistines want to put cars even in pristine areas. A concerted campaign launched by the hotel and builder lobby to open the hill station of Matheran to motor cars has been luckily foiled by environmentalists. The charm of Matheran in the Sahyadri hills near Mumbai lies precisely in its banning of the car from the town. One has to constantly maintain vigil against an anti-social lobby that is out to commercially exploit the lovely hill station to the detriment of the environment. The lovely, little hill train running between Neral and Matheran has proved to be a great tourist attraction and completed 100 years in 2007.

Unfortunately, politicians are abetting the car culture and doing little to promote public transport. The Times of India published in 2003 a list of luxury cars owned or driven by politicians. Udhav Thackeray, the Sena executive president and son of Bal Thackeray, is caught on the wrong foot in one picture in the media. He is seen getting down from his Toyota Landcruiser after championing the cause of train travelers. He had travelled ticketless the previous day by a local train to protest against fare hike. He was clever enough to undertake a short journey between Bandra and Churchgate and the ticket checking staff was wise enough to leave the ticketless Sainiks alone. While Raj Thackeray flaunts his luxury cars, his supporters burnt public transport buses during the agitation against North Indian migrants in Mumbai in 2008.

Far from promoting public transport, politicians are helping themselves to get loans with highly subsidized interest payment for buying cars. Even as Maharashtra reeled from a high debt of Rs 115,000 crore, the Maharashtra cabinet raised the limit for vehicle loans for state legislators from Rs 500,000 to Rs 10,00,000. They can avail of the loan for each term. (HT 10-2-06).

Mumbai's Mayor Datta Dalvi of the Shiv Sena ran up a bill of over Rs 450,000 for using his official red light Honda City car to make several trips to his home district Sindhudurg more than 400 km away in 2005. Another former Shiv Sena Mayor not only refused to pay for use of his car for private visits he wanted to suspend an employee for sending him the bills.

The politicians have no embarrassment in showing off their love for luxury cars while travelling becomes more and more difficult for ordinary people. Uddhav Thackeray is glad there are so many indigenous models in India now but he prefers the Land Cruiser, Raj Thackeray is known for his passion for foreign luxury cars.

MPs and MLAs enjoy great mobility, their travel bills paid for by the state. Fifty six legislators of the Nationalist Congress party flew from Nagpur to Delhi by a special aircraft of liquor baron Vijay Mallya to join the birthday celebrations of party boss and union agriculture minister Sharad Pawar in December, 2006. Mallya, owner of the Kingfisher airline, is known for his display of wealth and conspicuous consumption.

Mallya wants to convert Rajpath in Delhi, the venue of the nation's ceremonial parades and elite road, into a racetrack for an annual Formula One event. He discussed the issue with Delhi's chief minister Sheela Dixit and she was excited about it, he said. (Times of India 29-3-07). He also wanted other spacious roads in the nation's capital to be used for Monte Carlo type races. He proudly displayed a formula 1 car in the company of fashion models using the famous landmark of the Gateway of India in Mumbai in 2008.

Arun Jaitley, former union information minister of the Bharatiya Janata party, owns five cars including a BMW, according to the returns submitted by him while filing nomination for the Rajya Sabha in 2006. On the other hand, the high profile union civil aviation minister Praful Patel has assets of Rs 50 crores but does not own a single car according to his returns. Can one beat that ? And former Lok Sabha speaker Manohar Joshi is one of the richest politicians owning a chain of Kohinoor coaching classes for technical courses throughout Maharashtra and a luxury hotel. While filing returns for the Lok Sabha elections in 2004 he claimed he did not own a single car but claimed in 2006 that he owned only one car, a Honda Accord, for which he took a loan of Rs. 11 lakh from ICICI bank. (Maharashtra Times 14-5-06).

Relatives of powerful politicians too enjoy unlimited mobility. Sarangi Mahajan, sister-in-law of the slain high profile leader of the BJP, Pramod Mahajan, misses a life of business class travel, going to five star hotels and foreign trips. This life came to an end after her husband Pravin shot dead brother Pramod in Mumbai in 2006 (interview in Bombay Times 3-1-06).

Mr Pramod Mahajan's brother in law and senior BJP leader Gopinath Munde inaugurated a five-storey car park near Mandai market in the heart of old Pune. The Rs 4.55 crore park with a capacity for 300 cars and 2000 two-wheelers is incongruous in the historic part of the city.

An exceptional politician with no love of cars is Natesan Gounder Ramaswamy who as chief minister of Pondicherry was known for riding his Yamaha motor cycle, sipping tea at roadside stalls, talking to common people. (IE 17-4-06).

The motor car has often been touted as a symbol of freedom for many people. But in the U.S. many have been reduced to a miserable state because of the car. This is best exemplified in Arthur Miller's famous play Death of a Salesman written in the forties. The hero Willy Loman has to drive hundreds of miles as a salesman and life has become utterly monotonous and meaningless for him. After driving for nearly four decades for a living, he is tired and as he can no longer drive is immediately dismissed by his young boss whom he has known as a baby. It is an irony that Willy Loman kills himself by crashing his car.

In another famous play Raisin in the Sun by Lorraine Hansberry life as a chauffeur, of opening and shutting the car door for the boss is no life at all for the young black protagonist. Walter's relationship with the car is not of freedom and power but of servant of someone who has power and freedom.

The car needs to be condemned by ordinary people not only because it makes their life, their environment miserable, the car is mainly a status symbol, a toy for the rich. If mobility was the main motive, people would have gladly taken taxies and auto-rickshaws. But ironically they take cars even to joggers parks. They see nothing wrong in this.

Advertisers know the car is not really a necessity and they must lure buyers through tactics of all kinds. So one company advertises its car thus 'this is not a car. It's an aphrodisiac.

They have to do things like that because the car creates vicious traffic jams and it is no longer a pleasure to drive any longer. The Americans as part of their propaganda against the Soviet Union during the cold war always made fun of Russian women spending a long time in queues to buy food and other items. But then what about American women spending even longer time behind the wheel ?

While giving mobility to a few, the car denies mobility to many, particularly children. As public transport is neglected and walking and bicycling are highly reduced due to the car, children are particularly at a disadvantage. City and town squares, far from being democratic public spaces, are being reduced to sites for traffic jams in which there are so many people close to each other but they all feel isolated, and nurse a feeling of hostility to others. The traffic is used imaginatively as a symbol of the jam in the lives of many people in Makarand Sathe's Marathi play Chowk (square) directed by Atul Pethe.

It is a pity that even the few socially conscious architects amongst us have devoted little time to design for children. It is also a pity that the eminent Dutch architect Aldo van Eyeck should be so little-known in India where his work is particularly relevant since our children are crying out for space to play.

He put the needs of children and neighbourhood democracy at the centre of town planning and urban renewal. Every street corner should have a playground, he pointed out and he actually designed over 700 playgrounds in Amsterdam. If cities are not suitable for children, they are not suitable for others as well, Eyeck pointed out.

Only two out of ten British children now play in streets and parks close to homes compared to 7 out of ten when their parents were growing up. A similar pattern exists in India. Children who do not play outside do not eat well, do not sleep well, become obese, develop other problems.

Two British organizations the National Children's Bureau and Play England have taken up a campaign to make streets and public places friendly and safe for children.

Cars also make roads extremely unsafe for children but cruelly enough the onus of road safety is placed on children, not motorists. I was intrigued to find a traffic park for children at the Cooperage garden near Mantralaya in Mumbai. Here traffic police seek to inculcate a traffic sense into children by showing them how signals work and how they should cross only at pedestrian crossings. Ironically, just about a 100 metres away the pedestrian crossing in front of the state government headquarters at Mantralaya is the unsafest for pedestrians. VIP vehicles with red lights on top as a symbol of privilege and power routinely break traffic signals outside Mantralaya. The culprits include ministers, even the chief minister. No VIP thinks he needs to follow traffic signals.

The car culture promotes colonizing of more and more land and destruction of nature, especially of hills as one can see most noticeably in Powai, near the world-renowned Indian Institute of Technology, in Mumbai where one builder is notorious for desecration of entire hills. Such builders and architects should learn from the noted architect Frank Lloyd Wright who would tell his disciples 'No house should ever be built on a hill. It should be of the hill, Belonging to it.

Rocks from blasted hills once landed on the tennis court while children were playing, said a local resident S.K. Saxena. Debi Goenka, environmentalist of the Bombay Environment Act Group, who lives in the area, said though the hills are part of a no-development zone, mining and damage to the environment continues in the name of excavation and leveling if not quarrying. The order issued by former Mumbai collector C.S. Sangitrao to stop excavation were ignored. (Mumbai Newsline, Indian Express. 8-10-05).

India needs more people like Sunderlal Bahugunas, the leader of the Chipko movement (Hug the tree movement). The 79-year-old Gandhian started the movement with a trans-Himalayan march in the eighties to save trees.

He joined Mumbai's environmentalists in October, 2005, to embrace trees and save them from being felled for road widening of the Lal Bahadur Shastri Marg, a major artery of Mumbai, undertaken by MMRDA (Mumbai Metropolitan Regional Development Authroity).

Officials and engineers do not realize that even on widened roads trees should be retained. The environmental benefit apart, trees act as a check against overspeeding.

Mumbai's additional municipal commissioner R.A. Rajeev admonished affluent residents of Napeansea Road in Mumbai when they opposed cutting of trees during widening of the road. He told them there would be no need to cut trees if each of you guys did not park so many cars on the road. The rich want to buy more cars but do not want to provide for the parking.

The car is shown its place by enlightened citizens of Boston. Its pedestrians are notable for their assertive stance against the automobile. On foot, Bostonians bully the car. They slap the hoods of idling automobiles as if they were nasty children.

The car takes an enormous amount of scarce space, it needs three parking spaces in its daily rounds, one at home, one at work and a third at the shopping center. It makes a wasteful use of space both when it is in motion and when it is not.

Planning for the pedestrian is the DNA for design. That would make life much more livable. But our planning is for the car. A pedestrian requires five sq ft of space when standing and 10 sq ft when moving. A car requires 300 sq ft when standing and 3000 when moving at 30 miles an hour, more when it goes faster.

The car creates a negative impact on street life. As cars clog roads, pedestrians, assaulted by cars, pollution and noise, retreat into vehicles making street life more dull, lifeless, a mere corridor for vehicles to move, not the eminent social, lively space it should and can be.

The streetscape could become much more lively with facilities like benches on roadside as in cities like Pune where citizens sit down, relax, enjoy watching life on the street. There are also very comfortable steel chairs at bus stops in Pune which are very well-designed. We are so used to the dominance of the car that we think the benches would be an anomaly. But benches are provided in the West, in all civilized societies and there is increased need in India where most people walk long distances and need to rest for a while and have shelter in our hot and humid climate. But there is so much distrust of the poor in our country by our establishment that such ideas would be treated as bizarre. Even a World Bank official once told me that when he told Indian officials about the need to provide footpaths, he was looked upon as a strange animal.

The car damages the environment in three stages, during its making in the factory, its running on the road and in its disposal. The process of manufacturing a car itself produces 29 tonnes of waste and 1207 million cubic yards of polluted air. And once ready, the car causes more and more pollution. The study is based on conditions in Germany where recycling, smaller cars and conservation reduce the numbers compared to America known for its throway culture. In America 20 million cars are discarded each year leaving behind toxins and a huge debris.

The private car is an environmental fiscal and social disaster which would not pass any value-for-money test.

The car lobby is pampered at the cost of basic services like primary education and health for the poor. The Pune municipal corporation spent Rs 388 crore on road maintenance and construction in a year as against just Rs 58 crore on primary and secondary education and public healthcare.

A study of transport in Pune city shows that car and two wheeler users receive far higher subsidy than bus services (Unravelling myths about subsidies in urban transport by Ashok Srinivas and Girish Sant. Economic and Political Weekly 2-8-04).

The study also calls highlights the lack of transparency in municipal budgets. Pune's civic budget gives less money to public health in a year than to traffic signals at junctions and dividers on roads.

A car user, causing pollution, should attract the same stigma which is attached to a smoker, says Dr Vivek Monteiro, a nuclear physicist and Communist trade unionist in Mumbai. California became the first American state to declare secondhand smoke a toxic air pollutant putting tobacco fumes in the same category as diesel exhaust, arsenic and benzene because of its link to breast cancer.

But despite its most advanced and spectacular network of highways and freeways California remains one of the most polluted regions because of automobile exhausts. Yet, obviously the automobile lobby is much more powerful than the cigarette and tobacco lobby and it is seldom seen to be as nauseating.

Thousands are exposed to carbon monoxide released by automobiles which causes severe headache, nausea, dizziness, permanent visionary damage, coma and even death.

An extensive survey conducted in Mumbai by the Indian Society of Environmental Science and Technology has brought to the fore the evils of the car, according to Mr K.A. Khasgiwale, a retired scientist in the Bhabha Atomic Research Centre, the coordinator of the survey.

Trucks are quickly blamed for pollution because their black thick smoke is so visible. But pollution caused by cars is more dangerous.It is often invisible and odourless but is threatening. Carbon monoxide (CO), released by car exhnausts, has 200 times more affinity with blood than oxygen and is very quickly absorbed in the body causing extensive brain damage. CO is also the main component which causes suicide deaths as people suffocate themselves.

Sadly, among the major victims of car pollution are children. There has been a 30 to 40 per cent increase in children suffering from pollution related illnesses over the past few years, according to Dr Sanjeev Mehta, chest specialist at Lilavati hospital in Mumbai.

And young patients are developing resistance to routine medication with the result treatment is becoming more complicated, expensive. Children are particularly vulnerable to respiratory illnesses because they have narrow bronchial tubes, their lungs are not yet well-developed and their immunity is lower, said Dr Ashok Rathod, head of paediatrics at J.J. government hospital in Mumbai. Dr Sandip Rane, interventional cadiologist at Asian Heart Hospital, filed a public interest litigation on vehicular pollution in the Mumbai high court in 1999 which led to the formation of the V.M. Lal committee to recommend measures to clean up the air. One of the main suggestions was to reduce the number of vehicles on the road. It has not been implemented and will not be so long as the automobile lobby remains powerful.

The claim by West Bengal government in the state legislative assembly that Kolkata is the least polluted among Metro cities in India is strongly challenged by environmental activist Subhas Datta.

Laboratory tests have indeed shown that Kolkata is the lung cancer capital of India. The incidence is higher among women, according to Partha Basu, head of gynaecological oncology in the National Cancer Institute. Dipak Chakrabarty, chief scientist in the pollution control board in Kolkata told a government meeting at Writer's Building that pollution levels in Kolkata were far higher than permitted and with a high potential to cause deaths.

Fuel used in auto rickshaws in Kolkata contains a high level of kerosene, petrol and naptha due to rampant adulteration and corruption (Cancer cocktail on roads. Telegraph 14-7-08)

Children walking to school on roads congested with traffic are particularly vulnerable. The proper policy would be to reduce vehicular traffic near schools, both to reduce congestion and pollution. That is elementary. But this is never done.

In America a smoker is treated like a pariah but ironically car is king though it causes far more damage than cigarettes do.

Motorists are known to invade some wildlife sanctuaries in India at night, make a lot of noise and keep the headlights full on in search of animals. Poor cattle grazers and others are blamed for killing tigers but it is the rich and mighty who are the main killers of wildlife. A big board outside the Bharatpur bird sanctuary lists the thousands of birds killed in hunting expeditions by former; princely rulers and visiting British bigwigs during the days of the Raj, British rule.

The cost of the private consumption by motorists is paid by the masses. This was first demonstrated by the English economist A.C. Pigou as far back as 1920 when motorisation was still in its infancy, particularly in Britain where it lagged far behind the U.S. levels, points out author Daniel Lazare.

Pigou was unquestionably on the right track in noting that the public in general suffers incidental uncharged disservices from resources invested in the running of motor cars that wear out the surface of road and causes numerous other problems. This is a disservice, he added, that by rights should have been charged to the motorist or auto manufacturer responsible for such damage in the first place. What Pigou did not know at the time was the degree to which such disservices would pile up in the subsequent decades as motorisation accelerated.

John Kenneth Galbraith in his well-known book the Affluent Society grappled for the first time with the great paradox of post-war development, growth of private opulence and public poverty. India is very much witnessing this phenomenon.

In America as highways and cars multiplied private wealth was exploding. Yet, the more it exploded, the more the public sector seemed to wither. Commuter railroads were sliding into bankruptcy, city streets were rundown. As the Broadway drama West Side Story indicated the very word urban was becoming synonymous with crime, racial strife and decay.

Daniel Lazare, author of the book America's Undeclared War, points out that the old inner cities in America were much more efficient before the car dominance began. They were compact and walkable A worker was within easy reach of thousands of jobs. The car has enabled the ruling class to expand, to shift far out of cities with disastrous results for all.

In 1959 Soviet Premier Nikita Khrushev raised the issue with American president Eisenhower. He said the only impressive thing about the American highways was the waste. All that rushing about represented so much squandered time, money and labour. Americans do not seem to like the place where they live and always want to be on the move to go somewhere else. Khrushev's comments were not merely due to political differences. These made Eisenhower think and he did later realize that serious mistakes had been made but it was too late by then. He made known his misgivings when he told his highway advisers that running interstate routes through the congested parts of the cities was entirely against his original conception and wishes, according to biographer Ambrose.

In America both fuel and car are heavily subsidized. So a man thinks nothing of taking a five thousand pound sports utility vehicle to fetch a carton of milk. It is like using a sledgehammer to kill a fly. But who cares ? That is what makes the American system, the lifestyle so repugnant. It is so much against nature, so wasteful, so arrogant.

Subsidising cars, fuel thus lead to a form of Gresham's Law in which unsound practices drive out sound ones, Lazare points out. Because motor vehicles benefit from rising subsidies, they force off the road modes that do not, even though they may in fact be more efficient.

With the society straining to accommodate a rising tide of traffice, footpaths and bicycle paths are not given sufficient fund allocation.

As cities expand because cars make it easy to do so, others suffer. For those wanting to walk or cycle, the distance becomes a problem. You cannot walk such a long distance through fumes and congestion. In close-knit communities, cities, walking is easy and is a pleasure. America was also giving huge subsidies for luxurious housing for the rich in the suburbs who were enclosing themselves from ordinary people by living in heavily fortified colonies.

Americans cause 23 times more carbon di oxide emissions than does India. If India and China motorise to the level of America one can imagine the environmental damage to the earth. The result will be rising sea levels, global warming, and more and more hurricane damage like Katrina. India's environment minister Jairam Ramesh, IIT-educated engineer and economist, did well to confront American secretary of state Hillary Clinton during her visit to India in 2009. As a developing country, India could not jeopardize its growth and could not accept compulsory cuts in emissions. Actually, the

Americans themselves are at least partly responsible for the emissions in India as their car companies are increasingly selling their cars in India where the market for cars is going up while it is going down in the US. So the Americans and Japanese want to capture other markets and indirectly increase their pollution levels.

Though India is a poor country our elite unabashedly supports motor cars and modernization of airports and having modern airline fleet while neglecting trains and public transport. They talk of investing in highways and airports but when it comes to trains, they talk as if they are a burden and have to be tolerated. Actually, motor cars and air travel really burden the economy and environment while travel by rail and bus is cheaper and more environment- friendly. Despite the financial crisis of 2009 which left Japan 'battered and bowed' because of the crash in car exports, India and China continued to promote the cult of the car and its production with increased incentives. (Cars for Comrades. Forbes. 24-2-09).

While car culture destroys civic life and public spaces, railway stations are remarkable landmarks and excellent public spaces. Some of the best buildings in India are railway stations in metro cities and numerous other towns in India. Victoria Terminus, now Chhatrapati Shivaji Terminus, was recently declared as a world heritage site and is after Marine Drive perhaps the best-known landmark of Mumbai.

As in America, early motorable roads were a pleasant phenomenon which provided access to city dwellers to the charm of the countryside as old issues of the motoring magazine of the Western India Automobile Association show. But as the road and car lobbies grew stronger and gained a stranglehold over the transport system, the road and flyover network has assumed positively ugly proportions.

The car has increased anti-social behaviour of those who have always hated the poor. Now you can leave the luxury of your home, get into your car and reach your destination without coming into contact with ordinary people. But these elements are always afraid of poor people on the roadside and so the clamour for building highways and freeways without access to pedestrians.

Needless honking makes motorists among the most ill-mannered people in India. Horn blowing is often a deliberate act to harass people, especially pedestrians.

A little relief from the horn blowing menace is a Supreme court ruling banning the use of horns between 10 p.m. and 6 a.m. The question is how far it will be effective.

The municipal corporation in Mumbai failed to demarcate silence zones and use noise checking meters, lawyer Darius Khambatta told the Mumbai high court in 2009 in response to a petition filed by anti-noise activist Sumaira Abdullah.

The car is no longer a machine but a detachable room fitted with all kinds of luxuries. Many are proud that they can do their office work from the comfort of their cars.

Anti-social bastards is the expression used by George Monbiot, top columnist of the Guardian and environmentalist, about motorists who indulge in speeding, killing people, and opposing cameras which catch speeding offenders. Margaret Thatcher, former British Prime Minister and staunch opponent of socialism, glorified the car. She said any young man, who does not own a car at the age of 26, should be seen as a failure.

Surveys have shown that people like friendly streets with fewer cars. They like housing which is close to railways stations and bus stops. They do not want concrete islands or wide streets. What they do want are older places, the shaded sidewalks, house with detail, main streets with life and texture. Such vintage, pedestrian-friendly places are charming. Two things are mutually exclusive, sense of place and space for cars. The more parking space, the less sense of place. Less parking space means you have a graceful, easier life. Reducing the number of cars enlarges the richness of the environment, points out noted author Jane Holtz Kay. There is now increasing revolt against the car lobby and people are increasingly supporting public transport, railways and trams.

High cost of free parking is the apt title of an acclaimed 700-page book written by Donald Shoup, professor of planning in the university of California. The real problem, he says, is that there is too much free parking, not shortage of parking. Parking takes up huge spaces and increases costs which could far better be used for housing and schooling.

When parking is available, people prefer to drive and so they add to the problem of congestion. the main reason why parking fees are not charged at all or increased is political. No motorist, even in America, wants to pay for parking. Urban planning should plan for people, not for cars. But they are providing for cars rather than people.

Americans are now waking up to the damaging impact of the car. In Los Angeles the dismantled rail line was revived in 1996 to the delight of crowds.

In Gurgaon near Delhi, developers have realized that the car cannot cope with the runaway development of luxurious housing estates and the mall culture. So DLF, the top construction company, is planning its private railway service over 3.75 km. It has signed an agreement for a feasibility study with RITES and has sought concessions from the Haryana government. The rise of DLF on the share market shows how the construction industry has emerged as the leading capitalist enteprise in India.

In London the socialist mayor Ken Livingstone's move to levy congestion charge on cars entering the central area was opposed by the US embassy. It refused to pay the levy saying it was a kind of tax and diplomats should not be charged taxes. Livingstone responded with typical sarcasm saying 'it would be nice if the US ambassador pays and does not avoid the payment like some little crook. (Guardian 28-4-06).

Just 40 km from Mumbai, children die of malnutrition and many are denied water which is grabbed by a Coca Cola plant. But this does not prevent the media from singing the glories of new car models. Says one report 'if you just look at the Indian rich list, there are more people in India who can afford Ferraris than in the whole of Europe. This market has not been tapped fully, says Audi's Delhi rep Amit Burman. And that is just what these high profile car makers intend to do with their mean machines.

Just over a decade ago the market was dominated by the stodgy Ambassador from Hindustan Motors and boxy Padminis from Premier Automobiles.

The craze for cars is fuelled by easy availability of loans at low rate of interest. Just go to the market and come back with a car, declares one advertisement. It is that easy to buy a car now even for ordinary people. It is not easy for the poor to get loan for a bicycle though. Mr Jan Nijman, a geographer, during a recent visit to India, was perplexed by this fascination for the car among the consuming class in India. He hails from Amsterdam and teaches at the university of Miami in the US.

Though people in Amsterdam are far better off than those in Mumbai, in Amsterdam everyone owns a bicycle and rides daily for work, going to school and college, market and to meet friends. But in Mumbai, where he spent months doing research in 2005, people are crazy about buying cars though driving over long distance is quite burdensome. It is all a question of prestige. These people would be much better off traveling in trains and demanding a better train service, he feels.

The motor car is not only bad for the environment, it causes pollution, guzzles fuel, and causes congestion, it is bad for the user. It turns the motorist into a paraplegic, says Daniel Behrman in his book 'The Man Who Loved Bicycles.' And he could not have put it better.

We model ourselves not on humble farmers on horsebacks but military men riding the horse holding the sword high with the right hand. Just think how popular is the image in Maharashtra of Shivaji, the 17th century, ruler, on horseback.

He has also been converted into an icon of Hinduism. In neighbouring Pakistan, General Musharaff conducted his 'election campaign' for presidentship with pictures loudly proclaiming his as a military hero on horseback lifting his rifle proudly.

The motorist is like the military man on horseback. The military man is contemptuous of people without horses, the 'unmounted rabble.' The motorist too looks down upon pedestrians. The military man did not clean and water his horse. That was for the groom, the people on foot. Similarly, the mechanic does the work for the motorist who seldom dirties his hands. The motorist does not come into contact with the street or the people, he reaches others only through the glass from the comfort of his air-conditioned vehicle.

The arrogance of motorists grows as they protect themselves in their cars. With the air conditioning the motorists do not have to smell the stink, feel the dust or hear the excruciating decibel. And the motorist can look away from misery with the tinted windows. (Gautam Adhikari, DNA 12-2-06).

In a deeply unequal society any rider thinks he is superior to the person on the street.

In China one of the biggest betrayals of Mao's revolution comes in the form of rapid motorisation. The Chinese society and government seem to learn nothing from the disastrous consequences of motorisation in America.

The semi-rural expanse 30 km from Shanghai, once a mosquito-infested wasteland, is now dotted with factories. It also has a formula one racing track. In October 2004 the inaugural races drew a crowd of 150,000 people, some paying as much as 215 dollars per ticket. That is the average monthly wage of a factory worker. Much of the rest of the time the track is empty but it is mainly a showpiece. A few elitist Chinese say that Detroit, is the former car capital but it does not have a race track, we have it. Strange for a nation which was once looked upon as the harbinger of a people's revolution.

And the crazy construction going on on the outskirts of Shanghai is being guided by an architect who is the son of Hitler's architect Albert Speer. And cars now dominate a streetscape which previously was a river of bicycles. The government is now not so liberal with soft credit for car buying. China is already paying a huge price for the madness. Daily hundreds people die in road accidents and 45,000 injured in China.

Air pollution in Asia's worst-hit cities is five times as bad as in Paris, London and New York and five to six times above levels prescribed by the World Health Organisation (WHO).

Tokyo is an exception. Its Metro area with a population of 35 million people the pollution are well below those of European and American cities. Beijing and New Delhi are years away from bringing down pollution levels safer levels, according to Anumita Roychowdhury, associate director of Centre for Science and Environment in India.

The car-friendly Left Front government in office for over three decades in West Bengal, has after persistent denials accepted that Kolkata is a highly polluted city and its air quality is alarming. Nearly 10,000 people die in Kolkata each year because of pollution-related ailments, said Dipak Chakraborty, chief scientist of the West Bengal pollution board, in a meeting with ministers and bureaucrats in 2008. Transport minister Subhas Chakraborty had to eat a humble pie. He had claimed in the legislature only a few days earlier that Kolkata's air was much cleaner than in other cities.

Singapore has shown the way in reducing pollution, said Jitendra Shah, coordinator for social and environmental issues for the World Bank. Neighbouring Jakarta is three times more polluted.

China accounts for about 12 per cent of the world's energy demand but its consumption is growing more than four times global rate, sending Chinese oil company executives on an increasingly frantic search for overseas supplies.

Even during the world economic crisis of 2009, the Chinese bought more cars than the previous year while those in much richer countries bought much fewer cars. In fact it became the world's largest car market outstripping the US as the government gave increased tax cuts and rebates for buying cars.

Even Venezuela under its left-wing anti-American president finds the roads of its capital Caracas jammed as the country rich with oil gets more and more cars. As motorways and sidestreets are clogged from early morning to late in the night, road rage and shoot-outs are occurring. So psychologists advise motorists to eat a snack, read a book, solve a crossword, listen to music and try not to shoot anyone when in a traffic jam. A 16 mile trip to the airport becomes an Odyssey. People drive from 5 a.m. to avoid jams and suffer from sleep deprivation.(Guardian 23-11-07).

The eminent French film maker Jean Luc Godard uses the road traffic jam as a symbol of the failure of capitalism in his 1967 film Weekend. I think it is a terrific allegory.

The film is a dark, comic, apocalyptic vision of the end of capitalist society.

The consumer society destroys itself in automobile wrecks. It depicts how a failed materialistic society rushes headlong into angry, violent anarchy. The ten-minute tracking shot of the automobiles, the traffic jam, fuelling of anger, honking of horns the burning of cars, motorists attacking each other is considered one of the greatest in cinema history. The film is a biting, raucous satire on capitalism and consumer society.

A hysterical woman runs back to her car, not to help the dying but to rescue her Hermes handbag. People revert to a nasty primitivism, resort to violence. The bored and apathetic heart of the bourgeois is never far from acting out its most homicidal fantasies. This is an over-consuming bourgeoisie (filmworld.com).

A section of the elite wants to convert Mumbai into Shanghai because of Shanghai's glitz and its anti-democratic character, its curbs on entry into the city, its ruthless demolition of dwellings of the poor.

A few years ago the judiciary had supported such moves towards making Mumbai habitable only for the rich. So it was a pleasant surprise to find Mr Dalveer Bhandari, the then chief justice of the Mumbai high court, and judge S.J. Vajifdar warn the Maharashtra government counsel that the poor have their place in Mumbai and said they could not be thrown to the winds. The court asked the government to provide rapid mass transit to the poor who are being made to live further and further away from the city center.

But the point is the poor need to stay near their place of work, livelihood. The real need of the hour is to orient the cities in such a way that people do not have to commute long distances. Mass transport is needed but it should not be used as a pretext to throw the poor to far off places while the rich grab prime areas after ousting the poor.

Though cars impose a very heavy burden on the society in terms of pollution and road congestion, they are very lightly taxed in India. There is a strong case for a steep increase in road tax for motor cars, argues Ashok Datar, a transportation analyst. He also points out that cars are heavily subsidized. Several corporate houses give free cars to officers with the result they use them indiscriminately, even when they are not needed at all. That also explains why prominent politicians claim in their statements before the election commission that they do not own a single car. The obvious reason is they float companies which own the cars these people use for their personal work. Same with businesspersons.

Tobacco companies are now being fined millions of dollars for causing deaths. They have a highly negative image at least among civilized people. But in comparison car manufacturers bear no social stigma though they contribute so much to global warming and to ill-health through pollution.

The unbridled colonization by cars creates numerous problems. There is no planning for various amenities required for cars like repair garages or showrooms. So garages spring up everywhere on the road causing a big nuisance with their oil, fumes and noise of welding and cutting. Car showrooms are among the biggest encroachers on the road. Even the Nehru Centre complex in Mumbai has not been free from this problem. But worse are some second hand car dealers who do not even bother to hire showrooms. They put all their cars on the roadside, cars worth tens of millions of rupees enjoying free access to scarce urban space and making life miserable for citizens of those areas.

Upper class residents, themselves heavy car users, are also victims of the car culture. As posh restaurants and malls, gyms and cinema multiplexes do not provide any car parking space in their premises, cars are parked in lanes and by lanes making life miserable for the residents leading to conflicts day and night.

Some restaurants offer valet parking and park the cars of visitors on roads as if these are their own property. Sometime ago, Mr Ramdas Athavale, an MP: from the Republican Party of India, parked his car in front of a restaurant. His personal assistant was beaten up by the restaurant staff as they claimed the public space as their own. As for valets what a terrible waste of human power to make people perform the meaningless task just to satisfy the vanity of a few. Then cars are parked far away from restaurants and here again security guards are provided to look after the vehicles. There is no end to the wastefulness.

Rampant corruption in the municipal corporation in Mumbai ensures that huge shopping complexes and multiplex theatres can come up without any parking facility at all. In Bandra one shopping complex lets its customers park their cars on the footpath. Never mind the inconvenience to pedestrians.

But the real question is why bring cars to restaurants and banks close to one's house ? This is done merely because some people have huge egoes, false ideas of self-importance.

Though Delhi has much more land area in Mumbai it faces a land crisis for parking as nearly 1000 cars are added to the city daily disrupting the peace of posh housing colonies like Defence Colony and Greater Kailash. Fights over car parking are among the commonest complaints at police stations. Private cars are parked even in the premises of the Delhi fire brigade and other cars obstruct fire brigade vehicles, says, the fire brigade chief R.C. Sharma (Down to Earth 27-5-07).

A mob of rich people attacked police officers from the Malabar Hill police station in Mumbai in March 2006 as towing vans began taking away cars parked on Walkeshwar road in an area known for ministerial bungalows.

Several buildings in the area do not have any car parking space but residents own more than three and four cars which are all parked on the road creating a major nuisance. The police should have acted years earlier. An even greater injustice in the area is the complete absence of footpath all along the road from Chowpatty sea face to Malabar Hill. At least this area with top ministers should have had had a more democratic road system with proper footpaths. But this has never bothered either the politicians or the police.

It is only when the parked cars clogged VIP traffic that the police acted. For once, they acted against the rich. Police commissioner A.N. Roy rightly said the rich and powerful living in the area could not be allowed to take the law into their own hands.

At the same time the motorist lobby was crying for the blood of melody queen Lata Mangeshkar because she opposed the proposed flyover in the posh Pedder Road nearby.

Indeed, intrusion of privacy is a major issue in the case of the Mohammad Ali road or J.J. hospital flyover which looks into the dwellings of many Muslim families on upper storeys on the road. Motorists on a flyover also look with disdain upon people down below at street-level, humorist Bachi Karkaria noted some time ago. When the flyover was closed for a few days for repairs, motorists were forced to travel on the road below into the raucous proximity with the sellers of plumbing hardware and ready- to- wear pajamas. The flyover has narrowed the road below. People should have pelted us with stones instead of letting us pass. Not only had we narrowed their space we had taken away their privacy, turning cloistered four floor flats into public spaces open to our whiz-past gaze. But they let us pass unmolested. Khali Pili tension nahin lena, live and let stare,' Bachi wrote. (TOI 4-4-07).

Mr Shirish Patel, one of the few socially conscious civil engineers and urban planners, has demonstrated through studies that the Pedder Road flyover may ease traffic on the flyover but would make it worse on the road below. He opposes the American culture of sprawl, highways and flyovers. The worse scenario, he says, will be when the view from Marine Drive will be altered with the bridge linking Bandra and Nariman Point. 'When we look out from Marine Drive, do we really want a horizon of motor cars ? Or the present horizon of sea and sky and setting Sun?'

Peddar Road residents are rich and influential and a special consultation meeting was held to explain the flyover project to them and to listen to their grievances. Such a privilege was denied to the less influential residents of Mohammad Ali Road who are hit badly by the J.J. flyover. Worse, the residents suffered terrible noise from vehicles as advertisement posters were allowed to be put up on sound absorbers. The authorities would not have dared do this in an affluent area. Public works minister Anil Deshmukh himself made a power point presentation on the Pedder Road flyover. The Pedder Road Residents Association, headed by Veena Singhal, argued that instead of a flyover, there should be an underground, under-sea traffic tunnel from Worli to Nariman Point. The flyover jutting into the Chowpatty beach would spoil the beauty of the historic area, argued Mr B.A. Desai, a former minister of state for urban development and former additional solicitor general of India. Underwater, underground transporation tunnels are working well in several places in the West. The Rotterdam Harbour tunnel in the Netherlands has different levels for cars, pedestrians and cyclists.

Stringent steps are being taken in several countries to curb the use of cars, but the municipal administration in Mumbai is aggravating the situation by giving generous incentives to builders under the pretext of providing car parking space.

For several years builders were allowed to get away with murder as far as car parking provisions was concerned. The result was all the cars are parked on the road as there is no car parking in the building at all. This is done at the cost of pedestrians they are left without space to walk. And when they are run over, killed and injured, the traffic police and others are quick to blame pedestrians for being careless. In the West not only are roads being pedestrianised and cars excluded, entire residential areas without use of cars are being built.

But in India because of the pressure of the automobile lobby and corrupt politicians and bureaucrats more and more concessions are being offered to the lobby to the detriment of the city.

Besides, it is not the basic function of the civic body to create car parking spaces. It should rather concentrate on its obligatory functions like maintaining cleanliness, providing healthcare and primary education and roads including footpaths.

In the process it is gifting away precious open spaces to cars at ridiculously low rates and disfiguring the city. Many do not realize it but car parking does disfigure civic space. Just think of open spaces without cars and what a relief it is to the eye. Of course, there is the invisible pressure, tremendous pressure, from the car manufacturing lobby, to provide more and more car parking. Getting rid of cars from the car park near Jehangir Art gallery and surrounding areas during the Kala Ghoda festival gives an idea of the visually delightful landscape one can have.

Some of the car parks are scandalous. Many motorists simply bribe the employees manning the car parks and park virtually free. So the civic body loses revenue even while valuable urban space is lost, misused by people who have no business to park their cars in the area in the first place because many car trips are simply redundant.

And the civic body for years charged such a ridiculous low rate of just Rs five for the first hour and Rs three for every hour after that. If one calculates the market price of land, the motorists get a cheap bargain if they pay the official rate, many do not do even that. The municipal standing committee refuses to increase the parking fee despite frequent proposals sent to it, according to additional municipal commissioner R.A. Rajeev. One can imagine the influence of the car lobby.

Now the corporation is providing food parks and repair facilities at car parks. The question is why is even a fraction of this enthusiasm not shown in providing elementary facilities to pedestrians ? Bologna in Italy may be an exception but it has an ancient covered walk way of 23 miles. Surely such a facility is badly needed in our hot climate.

The corporate sector is one of the biggest violators of civic norms. Some big corporate companies including those running five star hotels have openly flouted norms by using car-parking basements for commercial activities. One can smell the aroma of hot bread being baked in one such basement of a prestigious five-star hotel with a long history in Mumbai. Now, multinational hotel chains have demanded relaxation of car parking norms in Mumbai. So, all those cars will be parked on the roads causing more and more inconvenience to ordinary people. What is more the big corporates will be increasing their profits by using the car parking space for more hotel room.

Cars parked on road are not seen as a nuisance but hawkers earning their livelihood are because they are poor.

Municipal authorities in Mumbai, who commit the atrocity of allowing car parking on footpaths, are surprisingly hostile to selling of books on footpaths. There is nothing so lovely as books out in the open.

The Darya Ganj Sunday book bazaar in Delhi has a 40-year-old tradition offering an array of books at unbelievably low prices. Many look forward to Sundays to browse through these books. But the book selles are harassed by the police and the municipal staff, according to writer Khushwant Singh who loved to look for books on pavements in every city in the world he visited.

The attack on the book culture by the authorities hits the serious reader in different ways.

The wealthy flaunt their luxury cars without embarrassment in a society in which a vast majority is immobilized or suffers grave handicaps for travel needs. So Mukesh Ambani, the most influential Indian industrialist, drives the 20-ft behemoth because this is all-out opulence, an extravagant show of wealth The younger Ambani, who is close to film superstar Amitabh Bachchan and socialite party-loving politician and power broker Amar Singh, uses the Mercedes which can dash to 100 km in a few seconds.

A car-free day in a week or so would be ideal in metros in a poor country. It will work wonders, save fuel, bring down accident rate, reduce congestion and it would create such a wonderful feeling that you can walk freely without fear. But some motorists would not accept any restrictions even for one day in a year. A resident of Marine Drive in Mumbai, Dilip Shah, went to high court complaining against the closure of the road to cars for the Mumbai Marathon of January, 2006.

Posh cars is the new status symbol in sugarcane-rich Kolhapur in southern Maharashtra. There were 65 Mercedes cars in the town in 2005. The former princely ruler Chhatrapati

Shahu Maharaj, who pioneered low-caste reservations in his state a hundred years ago, was also among the first owners of the Maybach car in the country.

There is now a choice of several brands of cars for the upper class unlike a few years ago when the choice was limited to Fiat, Ambassador and Maruti. A car fitted with all gadgets is a home away from home for the rich. The big Caravan vehicle is the home for Shahrukh Khan in Ashutosh Gowariker's film Swades.

Sachin Tendulkar may endorse the Fiat Palio but for his own use he will have nothing less than the the most luxurious of cars. And then of course he also has that ultimate status symbol – the Ferrari.

He has a number of cars and it is not surprising that his garage is bigger than two houses, as Indiatimes Auto section reported some time ago. His collection includes a Ferrari, two Mercedes cars, a BMW and a Maruti, in memory of early days.

When Tendulkar met Brian Lara, another star batsman, in Mumbai in 2006 they discussed not only cricket but fast cars. Both of us love fast cars, said Tendulkar after he drove up in a metallic blue Mercedes. (DNA 7-4-06)

Sourav Ganguly lives upto his undemocratic nickname Maharaja. He is reported to have 36 cars.

Rahul Dravid, more sober and cultured, is content with two cars, a Santro and Honda City.

The rich also flaunt their old vintage cars with rallies. Mumbai's police commissioner A.N. Roy, accompanied by his wife and family drove a 1952 Chrysler Convertible belonging to Nitin Dossa, chairperson of the Vintage and Classic Car Club of India during a rally held in Mumbai splashed on the front page of Hindustan Times (27-2-06).

H Cama, owner of a 1937 Buick Road Master in the rally, said he owned 20 vintage cars. Mr Moin Akram, president of the Vintage Car Club of Pakistan, came from Karachi the rally and plans to organize an India-Pak vintage car rally.

The rich can go anywhere at any time in their cars but ordinary people are denied even proper connections of public transport from important railway junctions like Kasara on the Mumbai-Nashik section. There is no bus stand in the town, surely space cannot be a constraint in this semi-urban area. Buses stand haphazardly anywhere on the road near the railway station. You never know which bus will come from where.

Even while leading a high life politicians want to present a simple image. Mr Sharad Pawar is one of the richest politicians in the country but on his birthday on December 12 in 2005 he was projected in special newspaper supplement editions with pictures showing him standing in a bullock cart holding the reins in his hands. Ironically, on this day he also launched Pune as an international airport with the starting of a flight to Dubai. Though a mass leader, he is basically a highly elitist politician and the earliest and staunchest supporter of globalisation.

One of his close supporters Baba Kalyani of Pune has emerged as one of the leading auto ancillary manufacturers in the world. Bharat Forge, the Pune-based company headed by Kalyani, recently took over the German company Carl Dan Peddinghaus to become the second biggest auto ancillary company in the world.

The company is increasing its profits by 30 per cent a year even as Delphi, the world's biggest ancillary producer, has run into heavy losses.

The opening of India's economy has forced its manufacturers to reinvent themselves. Chennai's auto component firms have done this almost maniacally, the Washington Post reported in a news item headlined Detroit's Next Big Threat. (WP 5-12-05).

The quality of work has improved rapidly and won awards from international auto manufacturers. The TVS group, the largest of India's auto components firms, now exports around a third of its production.

The car lobby met its ultimate humiliation in 2008 when the big three of Detroit Chrysler, Ford and General Motors sought a financial bailout after running into heavy losses. Yet, the top executives flew to Washington in private jets arousing widespread condemnation. The bailout idea was universally criicised. Subsiding private profit with public risk and money is a terrible idea, the Wall Street Journal noted (8-9-08). The New York Times called the executives blue suited beggars in a report titled Beggars Banquet. (9-11-08).

Detroit, once a cult of hypermobility, is now a poor city, half its population cannot read, 22 per cent of the people are unemployed. Dogs roam empty streets and winds howl through empty shops. The love child of America's greatest post-War passion is preparing to die. (Guardian 20-3-09).

During its days of arrogance and prosperity pedestrians killed by cars on roads were mocked at in Detroit. Packard motor company mimicked memorials to children killed by cars. It built a giant tombstone which redirected blame for the deaths away from cars to pedestrians. Erected in memory of Mr Jaywalker. He stepped from the kerb without looking, the epitaph said.

Nothing came to symbolize the American Century as the American car. American cars were about freedom, sexual liberation, confident patriotism, it was claimed. That prized possession is now made in Korea, Japan or Germany and America's car industry is in serious trouble.

America was thought to be the best in the world, its cars too were thought to be the best. The dream ended in 1970s with the oil crisis. And then Chrysler was taken over by Daimler, Toyota and Honda are opening more and more car plants in the US while Ford shuts down its plants. Hollywod's car of choice now is not American, but a Toyota Prius, energy efficient hybrid driven by Cameron Diaz and Leonardo Di Caprio.

The Chrysler Le Baron Imperial car was a a massive yacht of an automobile in 1974 whose interior was literally larger than the kitchen of my apartment in Manhattan, wrote

Michael Tomasky in the Guardian (18-5-07) The US car makers woke up to the harsh reality of the oil crisis much later. Besides the Americans were arrogant. They initially made fun of Japanese cars. Made in Japan was a punchline in American television sit-coms.

Unlike America Japan showed no imperial ambition or arrogance and quietly overtook America in which management failure was to blame, though unions and workers are the usual scapegoat.

But the US, which has 30 per cent of the world's vehicles, causes more than half of car-caused green house gas emissions in the world. This is because in the US cars are driven over more miles, have lower fuel economy standards and use fuel with more carbon. General Motors is a big culprit.

General Motors has aroused anger with its closure of plants not only in the US but also in other countries. The car manufacturer's announcement of cutting 12,000 jobs in Germany was greeted by the popular magazine Stern with a telling cover page cartoon. It showed a big cowboy boot with GM branded on its sole which is about to crush hundreds of small people.

Strangely, the Communist party of India (Marxist) vigorously pursued the car culture instead of focusing on mass transport and needs of pedestrians.

The CPM-led West Bengal government made the Tata car manufacturing project at Singur near Kolkata into a prestige issue before the company decided to shift to Gujarat following strong public resistance. The government acquired fertile, agricultural land amidst strong opposition from several sections including the Communist party of India. The car project is a serious departure from Marxism. The best refutation of the car culture came more than 30 years ago from two eminent Marxist economists :Paul Baran and Paul Sweezy. They argued how the automobile industry, the biggest in the US, played a disastrous role in shaping cities to suit its own interests, hampering the interests of the people.

The Tatas are producing what is being called a people's car, a small car, so the name Nano, for Rs 100,000, producing 100,000 cars annually. The Bengal government brazenly acquired fertile, green land from farmers without their consent under an outdated land acquisition Act of 1894. and the land is irrigated both by canal water of the Damodar Valley project as well as groundwater. The government showed shocking apathy in answers given to questions on issues like the land use map, the number of affected people, projected employment. The land was acquired allegedly in public interest but the land transaction with the Tatas was brazenly kept a secret. (Parthasarathi Banerjee EPW 18-11-06).

Mamata Banerjee, a fire-eating leader of Trinamul Congress of West Bengal, and Medha Patkar, the leader of the victims of big dams, strongly opposed the project.

Women blew conch shells and men have pelted stones at policemen setting up a base in the Singur area. Ravi Kant, the then managing director of Tata Motors, swore by the clean record of the house of Tatas and the environment in its automobile plant near Pune.

Several farmers were reduced to working as watchmen for the Singur plant after giving their land for the project and were not even paid their wages by government agencies. When they asked for wages, they were asked to keep quiet. (HT 14-5-08)

But a people's car is seen as a misnomer. Even assuming that the car would be low-priced, it would still be a disaster from the point of view of urban planning, space and environment.

The Left Front chairperson Biman Bose and industries minister Nirupam Sen brazenly defended the Rs 1000-crore project. The minister even ridiculed the demand of the project victims to get jobs in the plant on the ground that they had no expertise.

The prospect of Renault-Nissan challenging the small car project with their own venture does not deter the Tatas We are not afraid of European carmakers, they don't make cheap cars, Ratan Tata, chairperson Tata Motors, told shareholders, in Mumbai in 2007. But he sees Chinese companies coming to the Indian market as a bigger threat. (TOI 11-7-07).

Mr Jyoti Basu, former chief minister for nearly two decades, led a major agitation against a small fare increase of one paisa for trams in Kolkata, in 1953. The agitation had spread like wild fire as the Communists gave a call 'ride the trams but do not pay the increased fare.' Hundreds were arrested and many became martyrs, Jyoti Basu has said in his autobiography serialized in the CPM mouthpiece in Bengali Ganashakti. The agitation will be written in gold letters in the nation's history of mass struggles, Mr Basu wrote. He was supportive of the Nano project saying it would spark an industrial revival in Bengal.

It is ironical that the CPM has espoused the cause of the private car while sadly neglecting public transport. Kolkata's public transport buses are old and decrepit. Fortunately, it has retained the tram which is enjoying a major revival in several countries and Kolkata has an expensively built underground Metro rail. But sadly as a policy the Communists have not opposed the car lobby and not taken up the cause of public transport. This should have been part of a major class struggle.

Government must facilitate the era of mass motoring, the Times of India said in a gushing editorial on the car project (9-1-08). Once the commercial production of the car picks up it would change the face of the Indian automobile industry the way Reliance and Air Deccan have revolutionized telecom and aviation respectively, the editorial noted. It saw the car as the epitome of what the free market can accomplish. Tatas' venture has already fuelled competition in the market with players like Bajaj-Renault and Maruti-Suzuki jumping into the fray to develop low-cost cars.

Mr Ratan Tata, chairperson of the Tata Group, said he produced the car after seeing a typical sight on the road. A man on a two-wheeler with a child standing in front, his wife sitting behind, add to that the wet roads – a family in potential danger. Fine, but then there are more disturbing sights of people hanging out of overcrowded buses, trains, jeeps and other vehicles, sitting dangerously on roof tops. So investment in public transport is far more urgent than in motor cars whether they are branded as people's cars or small cars. The Tata car named Nano in Gujarati means small.

Mr Tata says 'I have two passions in life. Cars and aircraft. I have always dreamed of being a fighter pilot.' He flagged off a Ferrari promotion India tour in Mumbai in 2008 which took two cars to 57 cities in 72 days with a team of 50 journalists. The hospitality and fuel expenses were borne by the Tata group.

Ratan Tata,71 then, is a bachelor who does not drink or smoke. His vices revolve around speed, driving fast cars and flying jets and racing his speed boat across the Mumbai harbour. (Randeep Ramesh, Guardian 28-3-08).

The take-over by Tata Motors of the global consumer brands Jaguar and Land Rover in March, 2008, was hailed by some as reverse colonialism since the cars are produced in England. Jaguar is now on Indian beast, declared the Times of India in an eight-column headline on top of the front page, followed by a claim that Tatas now rule Britannia. By the end of the same year the project proved to be both ill-timed and costly and the Tatas were desperately seeking financial help from the British government and facing strong opposition from the media and politicians. It was a reversal of fortunes, as Business Week commented. A year earlier Tatas were riding high, on top of the world.

Earlier Ford's 1989 acquisition of Jaguar and 2000 purchase of Land Rover had been absolute stinkers. It is hard to fathom what is in it for the Tatas, asked the Times (27-3-08).

Investors too were skeptical and Tata Motors' stock fell by 13 per cent as Jaguar was known to be loss making, the US market was slowing down and the two brands do not fit into the Tata stable of low-cost vehicles.

Ashok Mitra, a respected former finance minister of the Left Front in West Bengal and economist, has strongly criticized the Singur car project as a sell-out to the Tatas with subsidy of hundreds of crores being given to the industrial house when the state government was heavily in debt. CPM cadres were brought out on the streets to extol the virtue of Nano. Some went to the extent of shouting the chant Ratan Tata Lal Salam. (Economic and Political Weekly EPW 25-7-09) Mr D Bandopadhya, a reputed retired bureaucrat of West Bengal and former executive director of the Asian Development Bank, demanded that since the Tatas had shifted from Singur, they should meet the cost of land acquisition, development and the police protection that was provided for two years. The Tatas did not pay a single rupee for the land acquisition as farmers were compelled to give their fertile land at a low price. It was totally illegal, a fraud, as land can be acquired only for public purpose, not for a company's benefit.

The government could have given land in the Durgarpur and Kharagpur industrial areas where the Tatas already have their factories. But the idea in giving the Singur land was partly to take revenge on the local people for defeating the CPM in two legislative assembly elections, Mr Bandopadhyaya said. (Mainstream, 2-4-09).

And such acquired land is then permitted by the Left Front government to be used for real estate allowing companies to make a hefty profit. A couple of years ago Hindustan Motors at Uttarpara assigned the lease for 314 acres of land for a real estate venture, pointed out Nirmal Kumar Chandra, a respected retired professor of economics in the Indian Institute of Management, Kolkata, in a sharply worded article Tata Motors in Singur : A Step Towards Industrialisation or Pauperisation ? (EPW 13-12-08).

The handling of the transfer of the Nano project to Gujarat too completely lacked transparency. Even the political and bureaucratic executive in Gujarat had no inkling of the deal till they saw a beaming Narendra Modi, chief minister, and Ratan Tata, at a widely televised news conference on October 7 in 2008. The decision of the Tatas disappointed many as they have a liberal, clean image while Modi has a very negative image because of the communal carnage conducted in Gujarat against Muslims in 2002. Mr Tata, who had earlier been a critic of the massacre, now lavishly praised Mr Modi as a dynamic leader and corporate leaders began hailing the chief minister as the future Prime Minister.

It was finally revealed that the Gujarat government had given huge benefits at common people's expense to Tatas which include an astonishingly high Rs 9500 crore at an interest rate of only 0.1 rate of interest repayable in 20 years, 1100 acres of land 35 km from the state capital of Ahmedabad whose cost can be paid in eight instalments. Here is a classic case of subsidizing a private vehicle which will contribute to congestion and adversely affect the poor.

Each Nano car will mean a loss of Rs 60,000 to Gujarat's treasury, said Shaktisinh Gohil, leader of the opposition in the legislature.

Curiously, the Nano car was driven to the Golden Temple in Amritsar and the Chisti dargah in Ajmer under instructions from Ratan Tata to seek divine blessings in February 2009.

The Nano became Mr Modi's vehicle for seeking foreign investment in Gujarat. The project falls in the Gandhinagar constituency of Mr L.K. Advani, the ultra right wing leader of the BJP.

The commissioner for the Mumbai Metropolitan Region Development Authority T Chandrashekhar reacted with uncharacteristic radicalism to the Singur project in 2007 saying he would file a public interest litigation in the high court as the low priced cars would choke the streets and all the new flyovers and roads would be rendered inadequate.

Nine years before the Singur project, the CPM-led government showed an utterly un-Marxist fascination for formula one car racing which was revealed only in 2007. In 1998. Mr Bhattacharjee had pushed for the project like his own baby (Telegraph 24-6-07) Land for the project had been identified, land acquisition had started and a memorandum of understanding had been signed for the elitist project involving creation of various luxury facilities including 5,000 five star hotel rooms and special tracks for trailers to carry racing cars. It was only the Central government's ban on tobacco advertising which aborted the proposal as the main sponsors were multinational tobacco companies.

The project would have been a financial disaster as even rich countries and giant automobile companies are now finding it difficult to support this wasteful, elite sport. But even at the height of the world financial crisis and their own severe financial difficulties Tatas were sponsoring a Ferrari team in Formula 1 while flamboyant liquor manufacturer and airline owner Vijay Mallya continued to field a team in the races which had a poor run. And Rolls Royce advertised its Rs four crore new model Phantom with seven column story on the front page of the Sunday edition of the Hindustan Times (22-2-09).

It is not surprising that the car lobby has a free run even in the Sahyadri hills of Shivaji, the 17th century hero adopted by the Hindu Right as its icon. A whole new township Amby Valley for the super rich and film and cricket stars has been built by the Sahara group here with its own runway for aeroplanes. The runway became the driving track for BMW to show off its cars in a two day camp for grateful journalists and others. (Indian Express 16-12-07).

The Bus Riders Union in Los Angeles could win a major victory in mass transport in 1994 and it is strange that the

Communists never launched any struggle of that kind. The union forced the Metropolitan Transport Authority to allot more funds for bus transport which is the main mode of transport for the poor, Afro-Americans, Hispanics and others.
A CPM leader Benoy Konar used Marxist phrases in the party mouthpiece People's Democracy to defend the Nano project.

Life would be much better for the farmers if they become industrial workers and there is reduced dependence on agriculture as in the US, he said. Industrial workers in the US do not have to toil barefoot, bare bodied in water and dirty their hands like our farmers. He also supported the CPM's welcoming massive investment by the Salim group in Indonesia which has close ties with former dictator General Suharto. The general's hands were soaked with the blood of thousands of Communists in the worst massacre of Communists anywhere in the world.

Ironically at the height of the agitation against the car plant in December, 2006, West Bengal outlawed hand-pulled rickshaws with the legislative assembly passing a bill depriving thousands of poor people of their means of livelihood without offering any compensation.

It is true pulling the vehicle is physically tough but this can be compensated by paying more money for this eco-friendly ride. And the government's main idea was not humanitarian but driven by the interests of the car lobby, providing more space for cars on the roads.

In Delhi cycle rickshaws are being phased out with imposing of restrictions like only the man in whose name the vehicle is registered can ride it. Would the police put such a restriction on a car owner, asks Madhu Kishwar, editor of the feminist magazine Manushi and campaigner for the right of rickshaws and hawkers. A migrant who through hard work expands his cycle rickshaw network is hounded out by the police but an airline chief is hailed for expanding his fleet.

Small cars would increase congestion and emission levels. Transportation systems and green house gas emissions are interlinked, we need increased public transport, said Rajendra Pachauri, chairperson of the Inter-Governmental panel on Climate Change and co-winner of the 2007 Nobel Peace prize, in response to the launch of the Nano car.

Another real fear is that a lot of ordinary people with aspirations will spend their scarce resources on buying the Nano car while depriving their children of basics like food, clothes and education. This is already happening in drought-prone areas where farmers hold on to their motor bikes but sell utensils. These vehicles have disturbed the socio-psycho-economic cycle of life, said Kishore Tiwari of the Vidarbha Jana Andolan Samiti which has focused on suicides by debt-ridden farmers in the region. Vehicle dealers and bankers get a commission in the purchase of vehicles but they do not know how the vehicle takes away the money of the family, said Tiwari. (Times of India 20-4-09).

Since Nano has aroused strong protests from environmentalists, directors of the Tata group of companies began an environmental tour of Europe to catch up with the environment protection moves. The group has realized that it has not concentrated on environment friendly products (Financial Times 19-4-09).

Unfortunately the Left in India seems completely oblivious of liberating voices in the West on urban planning and transport. Brian Richards, a noted British architect, who collaborated with Charles Correa on transport study for New Bombay (Navi Mumbai) in its early stages, envisioned cities free of cars. He bicycled in London till his death at 76 in 2005 and public transport was his passion (Guardian 14-1-05). In his book Future of Transport in Cities Richards strongly advocated restraint on car use. This could be achieved with a strong political will but then transport is politically a hot potato and politicians do not want to displease the car lobby.

It seems incredible now but two automobile giant companies had their assembly plants in the heart of Mumbai in the 1940s, General Motors in Opera House area and Ford in Sewree, recalled Sumant Moolgaokar, a veteran of the Tata Telco truck manufacturing company, while talking to me. (Times of India 6-6-1989).

The anti-car movement is picking up strongly in the West. An organization Street : Panthers has sold 25,000 stickers against cars in Athens. These declare 'I am a donkey so I park wherever I want to.' These are pasted on offending cars.

Novelist Milan Kundera expresses his revulsion towards the omnipresence of car in his work Immortality and says the noise of cars corrodes every moment of contemplation like acid.

In another novel Slowness, Kundera celebrates slowness and wonders why the pleasure of slowness disappeared. Real freedom is not jettisoning of restraint. A speeding motor cyclist is cut off completely from reality, he is unaware of his age, wife, children and he knows no fear as he is cut off from the past and future. Speed is a form of ecstasy technology has given us. But it does not help. A character in the novel, a young man speeding on a motor cycle, finds that his penis fails to cooperate during love making.

The great architecture critic and historian Lewis Mumford deserves to be read daily like Chomsky but is surprisingly ignored. He put the issue of motor cars and the highway beautifully way back in 1963. He was right to warn the Americans against the 26 billion dollar highway program. By the time the American people realize the folly, it will be too late to correct all the damage to our cities and our countryside. His writing applies to other countries as well in our present times.

The American has sacrificed his life as a whole to the motor car, like someone who demented with passion wrecks his home in order to lavish his income on a capricious mistress who promises delights he can only occasionally enjoy.

The Times of India, typically representing high society views, argues for promoting the culture of speed when speed was sought to be curbed following serious road crashes in New Delhi. Why should cities crawl ? was the headline (18-3-09). With better roads new cars must increase speed. Then why build flyovers and then criminalize drivers for fast driving said the daily without showing any concern for pedestrians who are the victims of the new callous road culture and reckless driving. Delhi's police commissioner S.N. Srivastava said the speed limit on the Delhi-Gurgaon highway had been raised to 80 km. But it now take upto one hour for pedestrians simply to cross the highway at one point because there are no pedestrian crossings. Special buses are being run to ferry passengers over a long distance and then transported across on the other side. What a monstrous waste of time of ordinary people to save the time of the affluent.

In Mumbai a number of subways or underground pedestrian passageways were promised to provide relief from the onslaught of cars following the construction of the flyovers but were not built as the civic corporation later discovered that it would be very costly to shift the water and electricity cables underground. In effect, flyovers have helped cars run faster while making life extremely hazardous for common people as it is difficult to walk on the road or cross it.

Worse, MSRDC has allowed vehicles to be parked beneath the flyovers despite the warning by the then chief minister Vilasrao Deshmukh that these were a security threat. Mr M.N. Singh, former police commissioner, says these are indeed a hazard and the space must be used for much needed greenery.

Advertisements for cars and motor cycles continuously glorify speed and violence coupled with sex. In 2009 the television advertisement of a Bajaj motor cycle showed two sisters fighting a deadly war against each other so that one can go out and ride a sexy motor cycle driven by a young man. The vehicle also makes sexually provocative gestures. In another advertisement the rider of Bajaj bike defeats another rider and throws mud in his face before going away.

The close connection between speed, fascism and the motor car is brought out by Martinetti in his Futuristic manifesto with fiery prose that talks of a racing car whose hood is adorned with pipes like serpents of explosive growth, a roaring car. The manifesto glorifies militarism, pours scorn on women, libraries, death, feminism.

Lewis Mumford, the eminent architecture critic condemned the car and the cult of speed as a sacred cow of the American way of life, overfed, bloated, poisonous, turning land into waste, trampling down vegetation, depleting wildlife, burning areas into wastelands. (review of Ralph Nader's classic book Unsafe at any speed. New York Times Review of Books 28-4-1966).

We must treat the pedestrian with the same respect we give to the car. Where walking is exciting and visually stimulating people will be perfectly ready to walk. The legs will come into their own again why should anyone have to take a car and drive a couple of miles to get a package of cigarettes or a loaf of bread ?

We have met the enemy and it is we motorists, declares Dom Nozzi in his book Road to Ruin. The book is about a culture gone mad. Until 1945 the focus of design in American cities was on people, pedestrians, bicyclists, kids, neighbourhood streets where people walked, socialized, kids played, kicked the can and cycled. There were sidewalks, people greeted strangers, conducted business, window-shopped, warmed to acquaintances through shops and restaurant windows. Now city planning is mainly about cars and wide roads. A higher standard of living has not resulted in a better quality of life. Livability is what people want. What is important is the public realm.

Of the ten most livable cities in the world seven are in Europe and one each in Australia, Canada and New Zealand

Not one is in the United States or India. No Indian city figures even among the first 100.

One of the most perceptive criticisms of the car comes from the French philosopher Andre Gorz who committed suicide with his wife in 2007. Gorz, a friend of Sartre, said the car industry has diverted resources, labour and capital from priority tasks like housing, education, public health, public transport, city planning and rural services. Roads are built instead of houses and public transport is sacrificed.

The road lobby's claim that the problem of pollution and congestion can be solved by building more roads has been proved wrong. Studies in the US show that cities like Phoenix, Denver and Detroit are most polluted though they have proportionately a much bigger area under roads than other cities. Houston is thinly populated but has high emissions because of a large number of cars.

A sustainable city without cars is being built by noted architect Lord Norman Foster on the outskirts of Abu Dhabi. It will channelise oil wealth into a livable, nice city, self-sufficient and with renewable energy. No one will live more than 200 metres from public transport, the roads will be only three metres wide and 70 metres long. Building will huddle together as in the traditional casbah lane.

Delhi Metro asks commuters to use the lifts at railway stations less often so that they can stay fit. It will be a good exercise, they are told. Why is such advice not given to motorists, that they should walk more often and drive less ?

Aravind Adiga's Booker award winning novel The White Tiger offers some interesting insights into the car culture. The novel's anti-hero Balaram Halwai is a car driver who murders his exploitative master with a broken liquor bottle. His master's wife kills a child on the road under the wheels of her car, drivers routinely go to jail for driving crimes committed by the owners. Ironically, Balaram, the driver, himself becomes the owner of a car rental service after bribing the police and when one of his drivers runs over someone, he suppresses the case.

The trouble is even a planned economy like the Soviet Union made the same mistake like the capitalist ones in promoting the car. 'I am appalled that a planned economy should have no goal except to rival the worst mistakes of a capitalist one, 'said the famous economist John K Galbraith in his autobiography' A Life in Our Times.

He had warned against the automobilisation of the Soviet Union way back in 1981. But no lessons were learnt even by the Indian Communists as the CPM's craze for Tata's Nano car shows. The book Cars for Comrades by Lewis Siselbaum of 2008 portrays the Soviet rulers' fascination for cars.

The disadvantages of the car far outweigh the benefits. Cars are very big killers on roads, they cause congestion and pollution, obesity, drain our foreign exchange and so on.

Worse, all these objects advertised as marvels of engineering and modernity are actually quite inefficient. Sixty per cent of the cars produced in India fail the fuel efficiency norm completely which is shocking particularly because of the rising fuel prices. The bigger the car, worse is its technological rating. (Nitin Sethi TOI 16-3-08).

It is often better to walk and take public transport than your car. Staying put in the comfort of air-conditioned cars can even spell death. It proved to be a fatal mistake for several motorists caught in heavy flooding in Mumbai in July, 2005. They were not swept away. They faced a more horrifying death.

Cars turned into death traps for 16 people as water entered their vehicles and the doors could not be opened. This was partly due to modern technology with automatic door opening system which failed due to the floods. Some of these people could have easily saved their lives as they were not going far from their homes and need not have taken their cars out.

Most cars now have sturdy glass windows which are hard to open, according to automobile interior decorator and designer Dilip Chhabria. Poor quality locking systems are also to blame, said Adil Darukhanawala, editor of Car India magazine. (Times of India 29-7-05).

In a shocking incident the Mumbai police picked up four children and asked them to pay a fine of Rs 1200 for disturbing neighbours with their game of cricket in the building compound in 2006. so the danger posed by cars, their air and noise pollution is acceptable but children are not given even a little freedom. (TOI 20-12-06). In the upscale Bandra (west) suburb in Mumbai some older housing societies charge as little as Rs 50 per month per car for parking which is a fraction of the cost of land in Mumbai. The rich are heavily subsidized for their land use, while the poor are denied land even for a shelter over their head. Now even the sea beach is being used for car parking in Dadar, Mumbai, depriving people of their scarce open space.

Even little spaces for just coming together and little games are not available even in posh localities, not to speak of poorer areas totally starved of public spaces.

Physical activity, games are essential for physical and mental growth. On the other hand video games dull mental and visual acuity, says Hemant Thakkar, physician at Jaslok hospital in Mumbai.

But then obsession with cars seems to make people simply insensitive. So when there is a parking crunch, not only do people do away with children's playing space but also trees.

Lack of car parking space does not dampen the craze for car buying as illustrated by a cartoon by R.K. Laxman. It shows a man who has just bought his car from a show-room. He says to the salesman 'Could I keep the car here till I find a parking place and the road to drive it on ?'

Playing spaces for children are under attack because of the car.

A playground for children was sought to be converted into a parking lot or a multi-storied car parking for visitors to the Siddhi Vinayak Ganapati temple at Prabhadevi in Mumbai.

A parking lot for visitors to a temple seems a contradiction in terms because normally temple visitors are expected to come with all humility, preferably by walking, not taking cars. The very essence of pilgrimage and worship is that you come as a common human being, not flaunt your money. Since the number of devotees and income is going up dramatically, it is seen as an easy target for terrorist attack. So, a huge security wall has been built around the temple which has encroached on the road, has caused great inconvenience to people in the neighbourhood and a strong rebuke from the Mumbai high court. Mr J.N. Patel, judge of Mumbai high court, asked during a hearing in 2007 why the temple itself cannot be relocated provoking strong reactions from the Shiv Sena and others. (TOI 22-9-07) The wall has created more problems of access, especially for school children in this area.

Look at the double standards. While a wall has been built on the road outside the temple, the authorities sought to demolish a part of several heritage sites including a Parsi fire temple, the St Andrew's church, a school, a cemetery and a playground to widen Hill Road in Bandra in Mumbai. It is one of the most cynical exercises undertaken to benefit the real estate and automobile lobby. Cynically,the municipal corporation has tolerated intrusions by several big shops on the road, grabbing vital public space. St Stanislaus school, whose playground, has helped create Olympic hockey players, has among others, refused to part with its space. Leading Hindi film star Shahrukh Khan figured in a controversy over his opulent building at Bandra Band Stand intruding on the road leading to the popular Mount Mary Church.

Similar to Siddhi Vinayak, the annual traffic mess that arises during the Mount Mary fair in Bandra can be easily handled by closing the road to vehicles and providing enough walking space for pilgrims. People will gladly walk if a proper environment is provided.

While poor children are major victims of the car culture, richer kids have their chauffers leave their seat and open the door for them and drop them at the school, points out Dr P.S. Pasricha, traffic expert and former director general of the Maharashtra police. This is in contrast to the Walk to School Campaign in England which is getting very good response.

Dropping of children at the school door by car creates huge traffic jams in front of elite schools. The elite Cathedral and John Connon in cooperation with parents and children pioneered the system of introducing school buses. The initiative was taken by principal Meera Issac and Indrani Malkani along with the then deputy commissioner for traffic Himanshu Roy in 2002. Only children under security threat such as children of politicians are allowed to come by car. And they must arrive early and leave after the buses carrying other children have left. This experiment has worked well and been followed by many other high profile schools including Bombay Scottish at Mahim.

DPN Prasad, principal of Bombay Scottish, said earlier there used to be almost 2,000 cars outside the school at 8.30 a.m. and 3.30 p.m. There used to be mayhem and ambulances headed for Hinduja hospital nearby often were delayed due to traffic congestion. The school also now has staggered timings for different classes so that all the children do not enter and leave at the same time.

The Bangalore traffic police begun in July, 2005, imposing a fine of Rs 800 per day for dropping and; picking a child by car at the school gate. The police have banned car parking within 200 metres of 16 upper class schools.

Unlike the kids driven to school, many other kids face severe hardships to reach school in crowded buses or auto-rickshaws or walking in hazardous conditions on roads. In Pune, the main centre of education, it is common to find as many as 16 school children packed into an auto-rickshaw which is designed for three people.

That apart riding to school is not good for the health of children. They grow up with heart disease and brittle bones, according to a study done by the Institute of Child Health in England. Besides there is the huge problem of obesity. Failure to walk to school has other negative consequences. Such children are less likely to participate in games and they grow up being unhealthy.

Children, who are continuously protected from the outside world by riding in cars, later find it difficult to adjust to the real world outside, the rough and tumble of life. The car insulates them from real life. You cannot understand the harsh realities of life sitting protected in the backside of the car.

The American model is the worst to follow especially for a poor country like India. Half the total area of US towns and 65 per cent in Los Angeles is occupied by roads, garages and car parks. And yet congestion is chronic in America. It is now well proved beyond doubt that building more roads results in more congestion. In many places cars take more space than homes, wrote Daniele Stewart bitterly in the prestigious French newspaper Le Monde Diplomatique. (July, 2000)

Malini Akerkar, who spent two decades in the US, says it is more important to reduce the need for cars than to promote highways and flyovers which ultimately result in more congestion. Mumbai has a high density of 700 cars per km of road against Delhi's 127. Architect Bina Balakrishnan and corporate executive Ashok Datar have formed NETRA, a network of transportation alternatives which has come up with various traffic restraint measures.

The fact is the government imposes much more tax on public transport buses than cars. In Delhi a car pays only Rs 300 a year as tax while a bus is charged more than Rs 13,000, nearly 43 times more. Shockingly, the share of buses in the total vehicle fleet in India has dwindled from 11 per cent in 1950 to 1.1 per cent in 2008. the personal car has not replaced the bus, it has only marginalized it. The message is loud and cler. Cars do meet our aspirations but they cannot meet our needs. Our needs must be met by public transport. (Down to Earth Supplement 15-3-08).

Mr Uttam Khobragade, general manager of the BEST bus undertaking in Mumbai blames auto-rickshaws and taxis for congestion on roads rather than private cars which are far more in numbers. Preditctably, he was condemned as an agent of the car lobby by Sharad Rao, the leader of the workers' union in BEST.

An excess of cars disfigures a city so much that Jim Kuntsler, an eminent critic of the urban environment, calls America an automobile slum. And because cars are parked everywhere he calls the US the United Parking Lot of America.

In Kolkata a proposal for a car park in the prime area at Dalhousie beneath the Lal Dighi lake has aroused strong protests and even governor Gopalkrishna Gandhi has had to intervene in what is seen as an environmental and aesthetic disaster. The Rs 35 crore project will create commercial space of 115,000 sq ft to park just 600 cars. The emptying of the lake of the water for the car park is also feared to pose a fire hazard to Writer's Building, the state government headquarter, as it is the main source of water in the area.

A Rs 32 crore parking plaza to mark a maximum of 284 cars at New Market in Kolkata remains highly underutilized after it was opened amidst much fanfare by West Bengal chief minister Buddhadeb Bhattacharjee in 2007. People will not pay and park here unless free roadside parking is banned, said B.K. Mundra, chief of Simplex, a sponsor of the park. This pampering of the car goes on in the Marxist-ruled state, often at the cost of pedestrians. In Park Circus an underground car park is proposed encroaching on the footpath.

The century-old Taj Mahal Hotel, a major landmark opposite the Gateway of India in Mumbai, has a big reputation that people do not realize it is a source of nuisance. A large number of cars of the hotel's guests and customers parked in the open space in the vicinity block the space which should belong to pedestrians who throng the Gateway.

This situation would be completely unacceptable in any European city where pedestrian spaces, open space take precedence over car parking.

A redevelopment plan for the Gateway area devised by architect P.K. Das says it is not the government's job to provide space for car parking and the hotel is obliged to create the space for its guests, Das said.

Some of the money for luxury cars comes from financial swindlers, corporate criminals and crooks. Harshad Mehta, who was known as the big bull, and who was prosecuted for manipulating the stock exchange to the tune of thousands of crores, had a fleet of cars. Eighteen of his cars including eleven imported ones were put up for auction. In 1995. The cars included six models of Toyota, two Honda Accords, a Mazda and a Lexus car.

It is not just big businesspersons and film and cricket stars who love luxury cars A senior Maharashtra bureaucrat Bhupati Prasad Pandey had in his possession five official cars and four cellphones in 2005 (Prafulla Marpakwar, Times of India June 5, environment day). And he headed the environment and energy department.

The car lobby knows this and so advertises cars as a status symbol, even a sex symbol. An advertisement of the Skoda Octavia car in India showed a couple kissing in the boot of the vehicle and the caption says 'the boot unfolds a double bed.' It promises bed-room space with self-activating door locks for privacy. (Hindu Business Line 13-1-05).

A front page picture in the Times of India showed a number of scantily clad models showing off cars at the auto show in New Delhi.

While pedestrians, the main victims of motor cars, have no organization worth the name, the motorists in Mumbai have a very old organization the Western India Automobile Association with its office in the prime Churchgate area.

It celebrated its 75th anniversary in 1984. Mr Ram Gandhi, convenor of the platinum jubilee celebration committee, described the motor owners as poor rich motorists who are constantly obstructed by taxies, hawkers and pedestrians. Mr Gandhi wants liberalization of imports and cutting of duties. The domestic car industry, he feels, was too protected.

The WIAA's complaints since the beginning have been the same, inadequate roads and fuel prices. This is clear from a report in the Times of India of 16-10-1919 It sought reduction in the price of petrol which then sold at 12 annas or 75 paise per gallon. Till a couple of decades ago there were only two brands of cars in India, the Ambassador of Birlas and Premier Padmini of Premier Automobiles founded by the nationalist Walchand Hirachand. Premier fell into bad times subsequently and for many years did not pay dividend to investors. The two companies enjoyed a monopoly but provided little technological improvement in their cars for decades.

There used to be a long waiting list for cars and Bajaj scooters as demand heavily outstripped supply. It was considered quite an achievement to obtain a vehicle out of turn through acquaintance in the management or the government.

Even in 1990 there were 250,000 applicants for the Maruti 1000 model, ten times more than the cars that were to become available at an unspecified price. It showed the pent up demand for such transport from several thousand urbanites with disposal incomes was tremendous (Darryl D'Monte TOI 6-3-1990).

The Indian car industry' record is far from impressive. There is a joke in fact about the Ambassador car which the upper crust spiritual guru J Krishnamurthi used to tell. When Mr Birla, the Ambassador car maker, died St Peter would not open the gate for him. When asked what he had done for God, Mr Birla thought for a while and then came up with an answer 'When people open the door of an Ambassador car, they always exclaim Oh My God.

But the joke apart, the Ambassador is found to be a reliable and sturdy vehicle by government ministers and bureaucrats. Even my senior colleague in the Times of India the famous cartoonist R.K. Laxman, would never use any car other than an Ambassador, and that too with black colour.

A prominent car manufacturer in Mumbai failed to pay dividend to shareholders for decades though it had a large share of the market in a highly protected licence permit regime. He also had to rush to court to avoid arrest after courts in different parts of the country were flooded with complaints that cars were not being delivered though big deposits were taken when orders were booked.

Haresh Sampat, a businessman, booked a PAL Peugeot car in 1995 after paying a deposit of Rs 25,000 After 11 years he had not got either the car or the deposit despite an order of a refund from the consumer court. Directors Vinod Doshi, Maitreya Doshi and Arvind Doshi contested the case in the high court. (TOI 21-8-06).

Bajaj Scooters enjoyed a virtual monopoly of the two-wheeler scooter market for decades until the motor-cycle market made scooters irrelevant by 2005. The last Chetak scooter of Bajaj rolled out of the Akurdi plant near Pune in December, that year.

The scooter was for years an inseparable part of the dowry in marriage. Many fathers booked the scooter in advance for the dowry. There used to be a long waiting list for the vehicle on which the dealers made a fast buck.

The car is now considered essential for upward mobility and people who do not have even a rental house now want to acquire a car. Their task is much easier with liberal loans for cars.

The car has become an article of dress without which we feel unclad, uncertain and incomplete in the urban compound, said Marshall McLuhan in his essay on the motor car in the book Understanding Media.

Like Sachin Tendulkar some politicians are also overtaken by the craze for formula one car racing. Chandrababu Naidu, former chief minister of Andhra Pradesh, wanted to set up a formula one racing track in his state. It was a ghastly decision in a state known for its poverty and armed resistance by Communist Naxalites, and it is not surprising that the electorate comprehensively defeated Naidu's party Telugu Desam in the 2004 and 2009 state assembly elections. Oddly, the symbol of the party is the bicycle which is also the symbol of the Samajwadi party.

Maharashtra government commissioned a feasibility study for a formula racing car project even as children suffered from malnutrition in Mumbai and hundreds of farmers committed suicide in June, 2006. A warning against the project was sounded by Mr Sanjay Sharma of JK Tyres'. Motor sports division who was involved in conducting a feasibility study for the Andhra government. He said 'It is easy to construct a track if the government decides to pump in big money. But where is the infrastructure to sustain it ? One of the basic requirements for hosting an FI race is to make available 5,000 five-star hotel rooms for a week. Where are these rooms ? FI projects in Malaysia, China and Bahrain are loss-making units and will continue to be so for at least another decade, Mr Sharma warned. (HT 15-6-06).

Amidst the global crunch, formula one organizers eye Asia but here the sport is not popular. China has not pierced the market much with its very expensive track in Shanghai. The boss of formula one in China was jailed for corruption in 2008. China is building its own version of America when its model might as well be Europe which is much more environment-friendly, less greedy.

The whole cult of the car and motor-cycles is promoted by stars and even the religious establishment. Sachin Tendulkar appeared in one television commercial riding a motor bike driving through fire, a tunnel and a road completely free of traffic. Pope John Paul blessed 41 Ferrari cars at St Peter's Square, one of the most important open spaces in the world. (picture in TOI 11-7-04).

Two three-wheelers manufactured by Italian auto maker Piaggio in Baramati in Pune district were presented to the Pope in 2008 at the Vatican, according to Ravi Chopra, managing director of the company's Indian subsidiary. The vehicles carry a special insignia of Vatican city and are white in colour in keeping with Papal requirements.

Far from discouraging private cars, the government is actually encouraging them, says Kisan Mehta, a champions of pedestrians in India, and a staunch critic of motorisation. He says wheel tax has remained constant at Rs 140 for sixty years. During the same period bus fares have gone up 96 times.

On the other hand the government is openly discriminating against public transport with heavy taxes on buses. In some states buses pay 270 times more as road tax than cars.

The industry has used beautiful, skimpily-clad women with inviting smiles to literally hook potential buyers. What do these women have to do with crucial features like fuel efficiency or safety of an automobile ? Not surprisingly the auto-expo held in Delhi in 1998 had numerous teeny-boppers dressed in a minimalist fashion draped all over their models. Korean Hyundai tried to cut Japanese giant Honda to size by scaling up the length of its hostess's dresses and Audi opted to clothe its hostesses in red minis.

Many loathe the car. Yashdeep Srivastava, architect and critic of a system of beautifying cities at the expense of the poor, says we continue to feed the automobile with improved concrete roads, flyovers, multi-storeyed car parks all of which fly in the face of the rationale to develop an efficient, non-polluting public transport system and other forms non-polluting personal transport.

It is not difficult to give up the car. Jane Holtz Kay, the author of the excellent anti-car culture book Asphalt Nation has given it up and is enjoying it. If this can be done in America, it would be much easier to do that in India where car dependence is much less. In many cities in America because of the vast sprawl with low density housing one has to go by car far away just to buy a litre of milk. Not so in India where land use is not so distorted.

Pico Iyer, a celebrated author, who can afford to live in comfort anywhere, choses to live in a two room flat in rural Japan with no car, no bicycle, no printer, no high-speed internet, no television. Happiness, peace and respect come only when they are not being pursued, he says.

But by and large the car has become a nuisance to everyone, only people have no option given the way the transport and cities are designed.

People, who give up cars or never owned one, are much happier. They save money, they require less space for their houses as there is no question of space for a garage and drive-way.

A car or a motorcycle make the family reduce expenditure on basic needs like food, nutrition, education and housing so that they can spend on the vehicle.

Public sector banks, which should be focusing on lending money to small farmers and poor people, have for years been ironically vying with each other to give cheap loans for car buying.

The State Bank of India, the oldest, biggest and most prestigious among commercial banks, gave a front page advertisement in leading papers sometime ago announcing attractive car loans. Its hoarding on the Western Express highway near Mr Bal Thackeray's bungalow declared 'No more trampled shoes at work. Car loans at lowest interest rates. How long can you postpone your first drive ?

The Bank of India in a front page advertisement offered loans for Indian as well as imported cars. A picture in the ad showed a young man wearing a tie and standing alone at a bus stop. A board atop the bus stand carries a message 'wish you had an affordable vehicle loan? (Hindustan Times 16-1-06).

The banks are now penetrating the small towns in search of customers for car loans as if this is the most important task for them.

Union Bank, resorted to a barrage of television advertisements in 2008. These showed a little girl burying a tooth hoping it would turn into gold so that her father would be able to buy a racing car.

Many people will never admit this but the fact is they buy cars mainly for their ego, to impress others, many succumb to peer pressure. I have seen people spending huge amounts on motor cars which drains them so much they travel second class in local trains in Mumbai in extremely crowded conditions. It is far more comfortable and economical in Mumbai to buy a first class pass for suburban train travel than to bear the huge expenses of operating and maintaining a motor car.

Automobile pollution is responsible for asthma affecting 50 per cent of the children in Bangalore. A 25-year-long study by Dr H.B. Parmesh, a WHO consultant, has shown asthma is the main cause of a high level of absence in schools.

There are two major crises of our times, terrorism and global warming. There is no disputing that America's excess oil consumption is fostering both, declared an editorial in the International Herald Tribune (25-10-06). And how true it is.

Vested interests in the US think environmental concern, making the country energy-efficient through lower consumption is some unmanly, girly talk. It is not environmentalists who are sissies, says Friedman. Those who fail to take tough decisions to reduce oil consumption are sissies, he says.

Bio-diesel is now being seen as an alternative but the project is fraught with grave consequences for the environment and food security for millions. Oil is extracted from maize, jatropha, soya and other plants but this requires using millions of acres and in the process huge forests will be cut to provide land for these crops as is already happening in Indonesia and Malaysia. The U.N. has expressed fears that this will increase global poverty. (Guardian 9-5-07). India's home minister P. Chidambaram too has strongly criticized rich countries for endangering the food security of many nations.

Fossil fuel companies's appalling record in causing pollution and climate change has forced a top scientist James Hansen demand that they be put on trial for high crimes against humanity and nature. The companies were also spreading doubts about global warming in the same way the tobacco companies blurred links between smoking and cancer, the scientist said. (Guardian 23-6-08).

Till the second world war America was the main oil supplier to the world but then as its energy needs grew, it realized it must look for oil elsewhere. It went out of its way to cultivate Saudi Arabia which was then an ordinary country though with huge oil reserves.

American involvement with the Saudi kingdom grew to new levels in 1979 after the Soviet Union invaded Afghanistan, the Shah of Iran was overthrown and Islamic militants staged a brief rebellion in the holy city of Mecca. The Americans wanted to protect their oil interests at any cost. President Carter warned against any attempt to gain control of the region.

In 2008 following the shock of a steep rise in the price of oil American president Bush was reduced to begging the Saudi king in Riyadh to increase OPEC production of oil so that the oil price could come down.

The Americans cynically overthrew the Iranian government in 1953 for nationalizing its oil resources. The coup was engineered by American and British intelligence agencies.

For developing nations achieving majority national control over oil was the defining victory of the anti-colonial struggle. The Americans could never tolerate this. They now control Iraq's oil though it is illegal for invading countries to seize natural resources under the Geneva convention, as Naomi Klein, the young and eminent author of Disaster Capitalism, points out.

The oil price shocks were correctly forecast by an NRI Arjun Narayan Murti, a star analyst of Goldman Sachs. He was sneered at when in 2003-04 he forecast that oil prices would breach $80 a barrel when it was only $30 a barrel. He was again mocked for his forecasts but again he proved right with the surge in prices in 2008.

In a trenchant testimony before the U.S. House Committee on Energy in 2004 he had said that the country was up shit creek, in serious trouble, if it did not wean away from the petrol-guzzling SUVs (sports utility vehicles) and other wasteful uses of energy. (Chidanand Rajghatta TOI 10-5-08).

It is an indication of India's growing craving for oil that the Saudi King was invited as the chief guest for the prestigious Republic Day parade in 2006 and Prime Minister Manmohan Singh broke protocol to receive the king.

The world should emulate Japan which has dropped oil usage by 15 per cent over the past dozen years and produces half of global solar power, points out Dilip Hiro, author of Blood of Earth. Battle for World's Vanishing Oil Reserves.

In the 1930s, the US produced 64 per cent of world oil, last year it produced only eight per cent. Nixon had declared in 1973 that America will be free of oil imports by 1979. but America has been rampantly wasting oil through its consumerism and even while President Bush talked of funding research in alternate fuel, people from the national renewable energy laboratory were being sacked.

The former Soviet Union went in for motorization after observing considerable restraint in the early years. Communist leaders since the seventies were quite fond of luxury cars. When Henry Kissinger visited the Dacha of President Brezhnev he was surprised to find a number of posh cars.

There is growing revulsion against the motor car in the West. Los Angeles artiste Craig Stecyk set fire to his Cadillac while another artiste Schuler ran a big nail right through an automobile as a form of protest against car culture.

But most politicians are as fascinated by cars as with film stars. While they are not bothered about providing basic facilities for walking, they are going out of the way to attract foreign car manufacturers to their states.

The Congress government in Andhra Pradesh was desperate to locate a Volkswagen plant in the state in 2005. Fearing competition from Tamil Nadu, the Andhra government hurriedly transferred two million Euros to an HSBC bank account of a company. This was done even before a memorandum of understanding with Volkswagen. And later, it was found that the company to whom the money was paid was not even the representative of the German firm.

Congress chief minister Y.S. Rajshekhara Reddy initially defended the deal but then dumped industries minister Botsa Satyanarayana and announced investigation by the Central Bureau of Investigation.

Is it a coincidence that two officials involved in this dubious deal were also connected with a formula 1 car racing project during the previous regime of the Telugu Desam party?

The officials paid 2.5 million euros and allotted 1500 acres of prime land without proper verification. A middleman wanted speedy allocation saying otherwise F1 could consider other locations. Fortunately, a senior officer smelled a rat, ordered an investigation into the antecedents into the middleman through a British firm and found him to be unreliable. Subsequently, the project fell through for various reasons.

VW was involved in a sex and bribery scandal only a few months earlier. So desperate was Andhra to get the Rs 5800 crore project that a politician said 'we did everything except touch their feet.' And the company representatives whom they so flattered turned out to be big racketeers. The Andhra government suffered a loss of nearly Rs 29 crore in the failed adventure and got some compensation from VW.

With bureaucrats and politicians like that fuel economy is far from the agenda of the power elites. They talk about patriotism all the time but do not mind busting so much foreign exchange on fuel on motor cars. In such an atmosphere it is not surprising that oil agents are threatening our very national security by supplying water instead of oil for battle tanks in the crucial Northern sector including Leh, Ladakh and Siachen. The then army spokesman Col. R.K. Sen said in 2005 that the army had detected the fraud. (TOI 18-7-05).

The very word automobility is questioned by some experts. It is equated with the car. But this is acceptance of a dominant ideology. John Whitlegg, transport expert, points out that the dictionary meaning of auto is oneself, not the motor car. So true automobility would be movement of one self, that is a human body, not the motor car. A person depending upon walking for mobility is a real automobile. He or she is the pedestrian and deserves the highest priority in the transport system. But gets the worst treatment.

The only true automobility is provided by walking. Cycling comes pretty close. In the West freeways have already become objects of joke. They are very expensive linear car parks. And that is not far from truth.

Death is too great a cost to be paid for so adolescent a thrill as speeding (No need for speed. NYT 7-9-08).

Nothing shows the connection between luxury car, arrogance of wealth, male chauvinism, sex, violence and speed as the widely reported case of alleged rape committed by Abhishek Kasliwal, 27, son of a textile mill magnate, on a woman double his age in his Mercedes car in the premises of the Sriram mill Mumbai in March, 2006.

The incident was another reminder of the rash and often violent life style of Mumbai's rich youths (Hindustan Times 14-3-06). Young men and women emerge heavily drunk from pubs late in the night after brawls. Sometimes the police drop them home as they are in no condition to drive. This also shows the class character of the police, heavily tilted towards the rich. In contrast, the police are often brutal towards the poor. The rape also underlines everything that has gone wrong with the fabric of Mumbai in the era of globalisation. The area where once Mumbai's proud textile workers were at work is now a site of fancy construction projects and rape.

In socialist Cuba cars are widely shared and hitch hikers are given a free ride in true socialist spirit (Christian Science Monitor 31-8-06). The island has only 32 cars per one thousand people and many vehicles are of the period prior to the 1959 revolution. But it shows that transport solutions need to be and can be creative.

Any Cuban with a car is required to pick up a hitch hiker. It is a way of life. Hitch hiking stations have been set up like bus stops for the elderly on main roads.

2

Politics of Transport

We will have to make a massive shift to public transport and clean fuel to deal with the twin challenge of pollution and road congestion. The committee headed by Bhure Lal, an enlightened bureaucrat, and appointed by the Supreme court has made this important recommendation.

It is high time it is taken seriously and we curb private cars. The EPCA environment pollution prevention and control authority has made its report after studying the environment in various cities. The committee included noted environmentalist Sunita Narain who says we now have an opportunity to reform and reinvent mobility, our transport system.

In the 1990s when Delhi's air was dark and dirty, the Centre for Science and Environment in Delhi ran a campaign. It called upon the Prime Minister 'Roll down the window of your bullet-proof, the security threat is not from the gun but it is in the air in Delhi.

A cost benefit analysis of streets would show that utilization of streets is enormously biased towards the rich. This means we are delivering a gigantic subsidy to the rich, according to Douglas Lee of Cambridge, Massachusetts, who has done calculations on the value of streets. This would apply even more to Indian streets.

Most subsidies in urban transport go to the rich, not the poor, points out Rinki Sarkar, a transport researcher. It is shocking that the American pattern with its senseless predominance of the motor car and freeways is being followed in other parts of the world. The pattern has proved to be a disaster for America but at least it is a rich country, though heavily in debt. Poor countries like India simply cannot afford the wasteful practices of America.

But the whole system is geared to building highways and expressways and widening of roads. The municipal corporation in Mumbai, which has been callous in vastly reducing health and education facilities for the poor goes out of its way to help the car lobby.

That is the real issue. Roads are built on a priority basis because these are essential for the builder and car lobby and corrupt politicians. In Mumbai perfectly good roads are dug up and reconstructed. It is a big scandal. So, other more vital sectors like education, health and sanitation are shamefully ignored.

What is worse the quality of life will be ruined for countries like India with the adopting of the American model. We need to reject that and instead follow the traditional European model with its emphasis on planning cities in such a way that they can be more accessible by walking and cycling and mass transit like train and bus services.

As Mayor of London Ken Livingstone strengthened public transport and pedestrian facilities with a commitment which drove him to comment that capitalism was a monstrosity close to fascism.

It took another socialist Mayor Enrique Penalosa to transform the Columbian city of Bogota into a paradise for walking and public transport with several km of footpaths and public spaces and dedicated busways and elimination of motor cars during certain hours.

When you build a sidewalk you are constructing democracy, it is a symbol of equality, Mr Penalosa says. We are now building roads for cars, cars, cars and cars without a thought for pedestrians. This is the picture in the developing world. The rich in these countries do not walk on the road as they see the city as a threatening space. Lack of footpaths is an indication of the lack of respect for people, Mr Penalosa says. The situation is like the one in France before the revolution of 1789, he says.

In Paris the car-hating socialist Mayor Bertrand Delanoe made a huge success of closing the city's busiest Georges Pompidouexpressway as part of improving the beachside resort on the Seine river's right bank. The project attracted millions of visitors immediately.

The most praised aspect was that it offered holiday for thousands of poor families and their children to play and enjoy themselves. By opening up the banks of the Seine in the heart of Paris to pedestrians, Delanoe gave Parisians back not only their river but also part of their city. This repossession is important despite its small scale. It ushers in a new relationship between citizens and their city involving a better quality of life, less traffic congestion, greater friendship, cleaner air and less noise. The project may turn out to have heralded an era of more humane city planning, the Guardian observed.

The Mayor successfully turned his back on the disastrous policy of former President Pompidou who in 1967 said he wanted to adapt the city to the automobile.

Our politicians, on the other hand, are obsessed with fancy, costly transport projects which will be a drain on our scarce resources and worsen the environment. A former chief minister, enthusiastically sought to make Mumbai a venue for Formula 1 racing in competition with globalisation's poster boy the then Andhra chief minister Chandrababu Naidu. But Naidu bit the dust in the assembly elections in 2004 and again in 2009 because of his decidedly anti-poor policies.

He would not have gone ahead had it not been for the support of others including heavyweight Sharad Pawar of Nationalist Congress party, Mr B.G. Deshmukh, former cabinet secretary, and Mr Ajit Nimbalkar, the then chief secretary.

Look at the enormous requirements for Formula 1. Land of 400 to 500 acres, investment of more than 250 million dollars, airport capacity to allow 50 Boeing jets to land in a single night, six to eight lane highways connecting the race track and the main grand prix track approximately 5.5 km. long.

The proposal was strongly supported by Bombay First, an organization of business and industry which seeks to make Mumbai fit to serve the interests of international finance.

Car-driven development has disfigured much of the landscape. Some of the heritage conservation campaigners like Rahul Mehrotra, Sharada Dwivedi, Shyam Chainani, Abha Narain Lambna and Tasneem Mehta are doing good work.

What makes a place feel public ? Moshe Safdie points out that in pre-automobile cities public funds were spent to build post offices, courthouses, libraries and places of governances and to maintain streets, markets and parks and squares. These were the places for spontaneous interaction, a distinct realm, maintained by the public. Street faces were embellished and treated with decorum. The principal streets and squares were landscaped with grand trees and flowering gardens. There was a consensus that architecture should be for the public at large, not to serve a few vested interests.

Under the automobile-driven city development, traditional streets of shops and local businesses have been replaced by super-block commercial towers, parking lots and interior-oriented malls. Streets empty of pedestrians and of street-level entrances and windows became increasingly unsafe.

The automobile experience taken as a whole is full of anxiety, there is the tension of traffic jams and gridlock, the cycle of searching for parking, walking through desolate parking garages, relocating cars, their getting towed and getting parking tickets.

There are some solutions, suggests Safdie. One is offered by Amsterdam city which embarked on a great experiment some years ago. Thousands of white bicycles were distributed throughout the city to be used free by any citizen. A person could pick up a bike when he or she needed it and when through, leave it at a sidewalk bike standing waiting for the next rider.

Imagine having a car when we wanted one but being free from worrying about it when we did not.

Ordinary people travel in the most suffocating, physically crushing conditions and often fall from trains. But a motorist would not tolerate even a scratch on the vehicle. Ordinary metal is valued far above human life in India. Since the motorist has spent a lot of money on the car he or she expects special privileges and sees others as a nuisance.

The municipal corporation of Mumbai has come up with bankrupt schemes like converting a part of Azad Maidan, the historic ground in Mumbai's Fort area, and gardens and other open spaces into car parks.

Far from making Azad Maidan more attractive to pedestrians and other common people, the corporation wanted to use the Maidan, bang opposite its headquarters exclusively for parking for corporators. Azad Maidan has now been literally locked out for pedestrians as preserving cricket pitches for the money-spinning game is considered far more important.

The Corporation area with the rail terminus nearby is most accessible by public transport and corporators should be setting an example by traveling by public transport.

The city desperately needs more space for public transport and it is an irony that available space is being thoughtlessly given away for paltry amounts for the benefit of commercial interests. In Delhi property interests were eyeing 42 terminals of the Delhi Transport corporation occupying some 200 acres of land estimated to cost Rs 25,000 crore in 2007 for constructing luxury hotels. It is proposed to push the bus parking underground. Noted architects K.T. Ravindran and Gautam Bhatia expressed skepticism over the move. (Asian Age 7-12-07).

The BEST deals are widely thought to be shady. BEST leased out 60,000 sq ft of area in the Seven Bungalows depot in the high-priced area in Versova for a paltry Rs 775,000 per year. Shockingly, no agreement had been reached for more than two years. Even an ordinary housing flat is not sold without a proper agreement. A shopping mall has already come up and the owner wanted to construct a beer bar on the site. BEST should be acquiring more land to meet growing demand, not scandalously disposing of existing land. (Times of India 28-9-06).

A plot of land was gifted away to the Ajay Piramal group, bang opposite the state legislature building Vidhan Bhavan at Nariman Point in Mumbai for a multi-storied car parking. In return, it was allowed to develop a multiplex cinema theatre and an expensive shopping center whose opulence overwhelms an ordinary pedestrian walking by.

And to top it all, the car parking has for a long time remained empty. Sucheta Dalal, a no-nonsense financial analyst, has argued that this is deeply wasteful. Because of poor response the parking charge for the first hour was reduced from Rs 30 to Rs 15 and remained at Rs 10 for every subsequent hour which is quite cheap and subsidized, if you like, considering the fancy property prices at Nariman Point.

Taxies can be a far better alternative to private cars. But the elite would not do that because it does not like to ride a vehicle used by commoners. Besides, many taxies are owned by ordinary people with little education. So, the corporate sector wants to take over the taxi trade and convert taxi vehicle owners into employed drivers. The taximen's union is being offered inducements like free trips to Singapore and other glitzy cities on the pretext of study tours.

Taximen have much simpler demands like easier loans. If industry can get concessional loans why can't we, asks Mr Prem Singh, president of the Mumbai Taxi Union. Just as bus depots provide rest rooms for bus drivers, there should be rest rooms for taxies as well, says A.L. Quadros, the moustachiod, president of the more militant Mumbai Taximen's Union. But then even existing taxi stands, where taxi drivers can park the vehicles and wait for customers are being reduced. So there is more and more parking space for cars, catering to the luxury of a few, while taxies, which cater to many more people, are being discriminated against.

The Central government took 58 years to recognize that cars need to be discouraged and bicycles and public transport need to be encouraged. The new transport policy was unveiled by union transport minister Gulam Nabi Azad at a meeting with chief ministers and transport ministers in New Delhi in 2005. But in practice the government is encouraging motor car dominance.

It was proposed to tax private car owners to fund non-motorised public transport systems. The government will support the development and sale of lighter, more efficient bicycles. There will be 50 km of segregated cycle tracks in all million-; plus cities and 100 km in three million plus cities. The idea is that the market is flooded with chic, lighter bikes with gears and tubeless tyres and electric bikes of international standard so that you can travel longer distances.

Dedicated taxes are also proposed to be collected for funding the more expensive urban rail projects. It is felt that dedicated taxes are paid more willingly since the benefits are visible soon.

Delhi's chief minister Sheila Dixit made a good suggestion that people buying a second car should be taxed heavily to deter people from buying more cars. She also wanted setting up of smaller haats, bazaars, for hawkers to induce them to shift from footpaths and cycleways. But little is done in practice.

What the country needs are regular bicycles for daily use by ordinary people as a means of transport, not recreation. Even a rich car-dominated country like the US is realizing the importance of bicycles. The Los Angeles city council has voted a bill approving the rights of cyclists in the city. There are 9 million active cyclists in the US. A former Olympian Bob Mionske, the author of the Bicycle and the Law – Your Rights as a Cyclist, gives free legal advice to cyclists. He runs his legal practice exclusively to defend cyclists.

Fortunately, the Mumbai high court has taken a more understanding view of the need to curb motor cars. The court's then chief justice Dalveer Bhandari and justice S.J. Vajifdar rebuked the state government in 2005 for giving excuses for not taking steps to curb the use of cars. Do not give excuses, if you have the will you can do it, the court told the government.

The court was responding to a public interest litigation filed by Debi Goenka and the Bombay Environment Action Group urging the court to direct the state government to implement the traffic restraint scheme as recommended by the committee headed by the then transport commissioner V.M. Lal.

According to the scheme vehicles will not be allowed to enter the island city on certain days depending upon the last number on their number plates.

Usually, our engineers and planners blindly, unthinkingly imitate irrelevant Western models. But they do not care for the really relevant models. For example, see the details with which the transport policy has been prepared by the U.K. department of environment, transport and the regions. There is one big chapter on the strategy of walking which considers various angles including the reason why people walk, why walking is declining, the dominance of motorized transport, road lighting being unsympathetic to walking, speed of vehicles deterring walking, and the impact of highway design and signals.

I do not recall even a fraction of such consideration shown towards pedestrians in our official literature on transport even though we have a far higher number of walking people than in the U.K. That apart the extent of walking in our society is also much higher because walking is the predominant mode of walking, partly due to less motorisation, many people do not have enough money even to take public transport and there is the cultural factor of a tradition of walking over long distances. Yet, there is a scandalous, unforgivable neglect of pedestrians in our system.

Kill one and frighten ten thousand,' a Chinese proverb says. Street violence plays precisely this role. Cars terrorise people all the time, deliberately so that cars enjoy an overriding priority on roads.

There is also need to provide a safe environment for women who are subjected to molestation. Even the capital city of Delhi is notorious for incidents of rape, women are abducted by anti-social motorists from the streets and raped in cars. Urvashi Butalia, a leading feminist writer and publisher, has mentioned her going through the molestation in buses in Delhi early in her life.

Another big contradiction is here. The draft policy wants to reduce the number of vehicles on the road and conserve fossil fuel but the government's industrial policy sees the automobile as the cutting edge industry in India's overall growth, points out analyst Praful Bidwai.

India's elite enjoys huge mobility while depriving the poor of even walking space. Shiv Sena's executive president Uddhav Thackeray flew for hours by helicopter above Mumbai to take photographs of the colourful Ganapati immersion procession in September, 2005 even as lakhs of people, like true devotees, walked several km. He made three trips the whole day, each lasting about two hours hovering over wide area from Juhu to Girgaum Chowpatty. Who paid for the flying, is not clear.

The cult and futility of speed has been thoroughly analysed and exposed by the eminent thinker Ivan Illich in his book Energy and Equity. The whole culture of speed gives tremendous mobility to the rich, allows them to travel great distances in a short time while this makes life more miserable for the poor who cannot afford to spend so much time and money in travel. We have industrialized travel widening the gulf between the rich and the poor.

When car trips increase, all other kinds of trips decrease by the same amount. So others actually suffer.

The duty of urban planners is to minimize trip lengths by making available places of work and other activities closer to homes. Moreover, energy consumption increases with increased speed.

Anyone using more public space like roads per capita must pay more for it. Herman Knoflacher, traffic experet, argues that motorization can be close to zero if cars are used only for emergency purposes or for disabled people etc. European cities can exist without facing any serious problems and decreased quality of life with between 50-200 cars per 1000 inhabitants. The transport system cannot be a means to exploit the majority of people for the benefit of a few. It also must not make people ill from noise and air pollution. But invariably there is a large investment in car transport.

Public transport needs to be more visible. Then it will attract more people, unlike the hidden and expensive underground system. When public transport is underground or elevated, it means the battle of the city against the terror of car traffic has been lost. There are many reasons why ground level public transport is more successful than elevated or underground.

Public transport on the ground is cheaper to build, maintain and operate, it becomes more accessible and more efficient. The entire transport system on the street level is under public and social control and so is more safe. There is an inter-releationship between public transport users and shop-keepers, pedestrians, cyclists and residents. They are able to view each other and assess the transport system.

The experience of European cities shows that replacing street level public transport by underground system has a negative effect on local shops.

Traditionally experts are obviously slaves or servants of the car traffic system. This must change if urban life is to become more livable, points out Knoflacher. A sharper comment comes from Harry Dimitriou, professor in the Barlett school of planning, London. He says there is a tyranny of the transport experts who impose highly structured motorized transport systems on very unstructured land use patterns.

Geetam Tiwari, transport expert from IIT Delhi, points out that in Delhi 80 per cent of the funds for transport recently were allocated for road widening schemes which mainly helped car traffic and there was little allocation for other road users. Road widening is done often by reducing the space for pedestrians.

Most plans for cities do not include facilities for pedestrian trips though pedestrians are a large majority of road users.

Geetam Tiwari has demonstrated that flyoves cannot provide long term solution because they improve journey time for a very small length of the road for private vehicles. Little thought is given for traffic further on. On the other hand flyovers adversely affect common people as bus stop locations are shifted away increasing the walking ditance by at least 400 m for changing buses.

Metro rail is not the best solution. It is heavily subsidized but even then the fares are often too high for low income people nor is the Metro the best system given our widely spread out cities with multiple nodes, centers. So Kolkata, Delhi and Chennai metro systems were carrying less than 20 per cent of their available capacity in the year 2007. Mexico city has the cheapest metro fares but attracts only 14 per cent trips because it is not very convenient for many. Metro system, which is ideal for European cities with strong city centers is not ideal for our cities.

The Indian decision makers who visit cities like Paris, London or New York and want to copy their underground or elevated Metro system do so out of context. They forget that these systems succeed to the extent they do only because those cities have the old settlement patterns where a large number of people have to travel towards the centre. Since these patterns of living will not be duplicated in modern Indian cities any Metro built there is likely to be grossly underutilized, says Dinesh Mohan, eminent transport expert and professor in IIT, Delhi.

What Indian cities need instead are systems that operate on every road and go from everywhere to everywhere, instead of converging towards the centre. If public transport is to be made more appealing it has to come closer to home than underground or elevated systems can. With cheap cars with air-conditioning and music the Indian middle class is enjoying comfort levels which the Europeans did not experience till the late 20th century, points out Dinesh Mohan. As a result, such vehicle owners will rather travel in congestion than walk in the Sun to reach overcrowded public transport and jostle for space.

The bus system is much cheaper. Metro is capital intensive and costs nearly Rs 300 crore per km. So for the cost of one km of Metro one can build nearly 30 to 50 km of bus network.

In India there is less and less concern for common people in transportation planning. In the first master plan for Delhi of 1962 there was a specific mention of bicycles and bicycle paths. This disappeared completely in the plan for the year 2001.

There is clear discrimination against public transport at every stage. In Delhi with very high level of private car ownership, private vehicles pay a measly amount as road tax while buses, which are much fewer, pay three times more tax.

The rates and pattern of motor vehicles tax for private vehicles as well as buses are archaic and arbitrary, says K.C.

Sivaramakrishnan, former urban development secretary of the Central government. Besides financing a car purchase is easy and quick while it is tough for buses and taxis.

Private sector money goes mainly into the production and distribution of private vehicles. There were only six lakh buses in India in 2000 as against 48 million private vehicles, mainly motor cars. In many states of India private vehicles pay a one time registration tax ranging between Rs 1000 to Rs 4000. On the other hand buses pay a tax calculated on the basis of passengers, including standing passengers which is quite stiff.

India's tallest luxury buildings are coming up land reserved for a road for ordinary people in Tardeo Hill in Mumbai. The hill had been excavated to build the twin towers creating panic among the super rich living on Carmichael Road.

So while providing greater access to the airport, access to state transport buses is being reduced. In Pune it is proposed to shift all the three State Transport bus depots outside the city to facilitate private car traffic. So common people will have to commute a long distance both while leaving the city and reaching it. (Loksatta 24-12-07). While the authorities are obsessed with building airports, the proposal for an inter state bus terminal in Mumbai is languishing for the last several years. It is scandalous that the bus stand for the busy Mumbai-Pune 24-hour service is located on the busy main thoroughfare in Dadar. Benches have been put up for passengers on the footpath.

An improved bus system would be far lower in cost and would reach many many more localities and serve a much wider, more number of people than rail.

The Delhi Metro has indeed become a glamour symbol because it is sleek, neat, clean and exclusive – like a multiplex cinema.Current tariffs are double the comprable bus fares. These tariffs are subsidized and will rise as the project's true costs unfold. The Metro will exclude the poor and can never be a mas transport system in the way the Mumbai and Chennai suburban rail systems are. It is meant to reach economic viability only when its first phase carries some 25 lakh passengers a day. Currently less than a tenth this number travel on it.

So sanitized is the Metro that the Metro's managing director E Sreedharan could not even tolerate anti-terrorist posters put by the police. He threatened the Delhi police with action if they did not remove the posters which, he said, defaced Metro stations. In a strongly worded letter Mr Sreedharan said action would be taken under a clause which involves penalty of six months jail.

The Metro is cool literally with its air-conditioning and is very popular among Delhi university students. A lot of dating goes on there (TOI 4-4-06). For girls, the Metro is also safer than the bus where they are vulnerable to eve teasing, molestation etc. Here all are of the same class.

The Metro is suitable in high-income societies where there is a large concentration of jobs in a high-rise central business district. In low-income low-rise Indian cities with their dispersed/multiple business districts, it is a problem.

The Delhi Metro also needs to be channelised in such a way that it does not destroy areas of great historic, archaeological and ecological importance. The pahadi area in the Delhi-Haryana axis of the rocky Arawalli ranges is an area in which ancient relics of all kinds are scattered, warns archaeologist Nayanjot Lahiri of Delhi university. Had it not been for caution from experts the Metro train would have gone close past the historic Qutub Minar tower.

Architect Kuldip Singh and others have cautioned the Prime Minister that the overhead Metro would deface the city, overwhelm people, buildings, trees, monuments.

Our car lobby should learn something from New York which has much less car ownership than other cities in the US. It has 120 miles of bicycle tracks, nearly 112,000 people ride bicycles daily and New York has the largest rail subway network extending over 600 miles.

New York is famous for its pedestrian culture and bustling street life which has given rise to break-dancing. More than half of New Yorkers do not own cars. It is the most populous city in the US and the most energy-efficient because of less dependence on the motor car.

The subway trains and railways stations play a big role in the social and political life of the city. Campaigning at railways stations is the signature of New York politics. Musicians and entertainers who make their livelihood on the subway are legendary. They come from all continents, African drummers and opera singes, Tai Chi performers and jazz players and Harlem break-dancing troupes. (Wikepedia).

Many subway musicians have made successful careers above ground and in foreign countries. Subways are a staple of New York's cultural life. Subways reduce dependence on cars to such an extent that a vast majority of shoppers in Manhattam do not use cars.

Moreover, look at the tremendous mobility the rich enjoy while the poor suffer more and more hardships in transport. Top industrialists in India are acquiring more and more jet aeroplanes for mobility and status value. Mukesh Ambani and Vijay Mallya, the ultimate pleasure seeker and liquor manufacturer, have gone in for a Rs 250 crore Airbus corporate jet each. Vijaypat Singhania, the high-flier who enjoys publicity through solo flying adventures, has a Rs 15 crore Hawker Siddley, Ratan Tata, a trained pilot, Kumar Mangalam Birla and Anil Ambani are among other jet setters with own planes. The Ambanis in fact have a fleet of planes There are more privately owned aircraft flying around than regular commercial aircraft, according to the director general of civil aviation (DNA 28-6-07).

Not to be left behind corporate leaders, Maharashtra's VVIps chartered private planes in 2007 when state government planes were not available. Governor S.M. Krishna, chief minister Vilasrao Deshmukh and deputy chief minister R.R. Patil used planes for places which could be comfortably reached by overnight trains. (Mumbai Mirror 9-7-07). Governor Krishna faced criticism over making frequent trips to Bangalore, his home town, by government plane and later offered to pay for his travel. Obviously, his trips Bangalore were not for official use.

Mr Deshmukh called upon government officers to travel by airlines rather than trains in an obvious bid to promote the interests of the airline lobby. He was speaking at the launch of the Mumbai-Nanded-Latur air service launched by Kingfisher. Pack the flights so that the services do not have to be closed down, he said. (MT 5-1-08).

Mukesh Ambani's high rise building for his exclusive use coming up in the posh Altamount Road will have several floors for car parking and repairs and proposes to have a helipad on top. The Ambanis also began building a helipad on top of their Seawind building at Cuffe Parad in 2008 without authorization or without consulting neighbouring buildings whose residents are up in arms.

The fire brigade chief A.V. Sawant has posed several questions to the Ambanis regarding the stability of the building, permissions from the defence, civil aviation and municipal authorities. Manoj Mirchandani, a lawyer living nearby and others have strongly opposed the move since helicopter movement so close to them will cause tremendous noise. The municipality has imposed a fine of Rs 234,000 on the Ambanis.

The Ambanis were unauthorisedly allowed to use the helipad at Raj Bhavan in Mumbai in 1988, as mentioned in former union home secretary Madhav Godbole's autobiography. Tax evasion plays an important though little-known part in the import of luxury cars and jets. Concessions are obtained under the pretext of chartering the cars or jets when in fact they are for personal use.

A blanket permission for helipads on top of buildings was granted by chief minister Ashok Chavan soon after taking over as chief minister in 2009 and soon there was a flood of applicants including Ratan Tata, builders Vickey Oberoi and Mayur Shah, Asian Heart Institute and Reliance Hospital. Ministers and bureaucrats are eager to build a helipad on the proposed twin towers of the government at Nariman Point. The development control rules were specially amended for the work, said T.C. Benjamin, urban development secretary.

Two aircraft of Reliance Industries were seized by customs in July, 2008 for alleged evasion of customs duty to the tune of nearly Rs 54 crore. Show cause notices were also issued to East India Hotels, Raymonds, Taj Air and others.

The customs department has unearthhed tax evasion of more than Rs 9,000 crore in the import of aircraft and the list of wrong doers reads like a who's who of Indian business (DNA7-7-08). The seizure of Nita Ambani's birthday gift is not a one-off instance. As many as 270 aircraft imported under the scheme to run passenger services have been diverted for; private use. With Rs 9,000 crores, given as virtual subsidy, for private luxury, would help several ailing State Transport Corporations to revive themselves. Besides, these bus companies serve a great social need, subsidise students and several disadvantaged sections.

Prior to the Parliamentary elections of 2009 the government's poll campaign in newspapers throughout the country was dominated by advertisements glorifying the aviation sector with pictures of a beaming high-flying civil aviation minister Praful Patel. It is as if flying by aeroplanes is much more important than providing drinking water, jobs and education to people. The minister was laying the foundation of an airport or inaugurating the building of an airport every other day before the elections. Not a single advertisement showed a model public transport bus depot because there is none to showcase. A clear case of misplaced priorities in the transport sector.

This at a time when the world was seriously concerned about the growing ecological damage caused by air travel as highlighted in the film Stupid made by Franny Armstrong. The film shows Jeh Wadia, promoter of Go Air showing utter disregard for the environment when saying every one should now travel by air because of low fares. fares. And Air India, the public sector airline, was being bled dry through sabotage. So its business class was always shown as full when the seats went empty and rivals got the business. Managing director V Thulasidas blamed software problems which sounds odd considering India's leading role in the software industry.

It is to the credit of union finance minister Pranab Mukherjee that he initiated the process of making ministers travel by economy class as he has been doing quite frequently for years. While a number of chief ministers are known for frequent and needless use of state government planes, West Bengal's chief minister is averse to using the state government helicopter which lay unused for five years and was ultimately sold off.

In pursuit of its mobility, the elite has stopped at nothing. It has not hesitated to destroy mangroves which provide a natural barrier against sea waves. The Maharashtra government's has proposed destruction of nearly 300 acres of mangroves for building a second airport at Panvel near Mumbai. The central government's refusal to give environmental clearance was opposed by chief minister Vilasrao Deshmukh and the concerned bureaucrat G.S. Gill.

While seeking to expand airports, the government was seeking to reduce space at depots of Maharashtra state road transport corporation (MSRTC). They were being robbed of vital space to provide space for shopping malls for Reliance, a major corporate house.

At the same time the Bombay Electric Supply and Transport Undertaking (BEST), which caters to 45,00,000 passengers per day, had to keep 385 buses off the road because of traffic congestion. Ten per cent of our buses lie unused in depots, said Sanjay Potnis, chairperson of BEST, in 2008.

Spanking new airports were built in Hyderabad and Bangalore in 2008 with several facilities. Hyderabad airport has a 17-bed medical entre, a 25-room lounge with showers and nap rooms, a luxury hotel and a clinic run by the big hospital chain Apollo.

State Transport bus depots cater to many more passengers than do airports and no one expects posh facilities there. But why can't they have usable toilets, facilities for drinking water, basic cleanliness, First Aid equipment, rest rooms, taking a bath and a shower ?. But often they do not even have a wash basin to clean one's hands and face. So far from acquiring more land for providing basic amenities, the government is taking land away from these depots. Formerly the slogan of ST was 'an ST bus on every road.' Now, unofficially, it has become 'a mall at every ST depot'.

The rich are traveling faster and over longer distances by planes and cars taking a heavy toll of the environment, causing pollution and consuming enormous chunks of land, points out transport expert John Adams. The world's car population has increased ten times since 1950 to 500 million but the number of people without cars has risen to 5.5 billion, a staggering figure.

Even if we devise pollution-free cars and have the most sophisticated road networks and signal system it will not work and life will be unbearable with the growth in traffic, points out John Adams, an authority on hypermobility.

He talks of an 800 pound gorilla at a cocktail party. Every one can see him, he makes them all nervous, he has a voracious appetite and disgusting excretionary habits. He smashes furniture and crockery every time he moves. But no one can do anything. Adams is talking about traffic growth but he might as well be talking about the deadly impact of the motor car.

Former World Bank president James Wolfesonhn was said to have bought two seats on airplane flights so that he could carry his cello with him on his travels.

So Mallya gives a party 30,000 ft above ground on board Airbus 380, widely touted as the largest aircraft and a fashion show is held on the luxury train Deccan Odyessy even as ordinary people struggle to get a foothold in overcrowded trains so that they do not fall down.

Much of this mobility for the rich comes at the expense of common people. Jet Airways had defaulted on bills of Rs 359 crore to public sector oil companies in 2008, according to the government's petroleum secretary R Pandey. At the same time the management upheld a flamboyant lifestyle and sacked 1900 staff members before the move was thwarted by a public outcry.

It is not just that public transport is so inadequate. Access to railway stations and bus depots is so poor. In Mumbai private cars are parked outside railway stations but BEST buses are not allowed to halt even for a few seconds to help passengers alight and run to catch the local train.

Even after reaching the station, it takes long to reach the train, in Borivli station in Mumbai one has to walk almost one km to catch a train to Churchgate. Such callousness frequently leads to protests and disruptions by thousands of people. After a disruption in 2009, the police arrested 32 railway commuters and produced before the magistrate amidst tight security and released on a personal bond of Rs 5,000. All the lawyers stood in the court in solidarity with the commuters. It was a moment of pride for us, said lawyers Vijay Singh and Ashok Sutrale. The protesters were taken in a police van, photographed and fingerprinted and locked up like common criminals.

Officialdom is so insensitive that instead of improving facilities they decided to post policemen at platforms to push commuters and help them get into crowded compartments.

At Vikhroli station thousands have to risk their lives daily and cross the railway tracks to go from one platform to another in the absence of a bridge. And this at a station nearest to the Indian Institute of Technology, Powai, a symbol of India's technological progress and excellence. It shows how much technology has failed to reach common people.

It Is Easier To Reach Heaven Than The End of the Street is the apt title of a recent book on the issue written by Emma Williams. She describes the daily Palestinian ordeal of long delays, arbitrary refusals, young soldiers' capricious judgements and the sometimes lethal consequences when a sick or pregnant person is being rushed to the hospital or is stopped or rejected at a checkpoint.

In India for ordinary people it is difficult even to walk across the road. It is worse for the blind and the crippled. It has become a nightmare for students of the Happy Home for the Blind since a Mall came up nearby and their bus stop was shifted far away. They now have to walk a long distance and tackle speeding vehicles which even the able-bodied cannot cope with. Besides vehicles are parked on the footpath, said an angry principal Meher Banaji. (Supriya Thanawala DNA 1-3—06).

Life is equally difficult for the physically handicapped students attending the Institute for the Physically handicapped at Worli near the Mahalaxmi Race Course, said parent Pratima Joshi. There is no proper access for the handicapped from the main artery. In Delhi two physically handicapped people Anjalee Agarwal and Sanjeev Sachadeva are vigorously working for making the city more accessible to the disabled. Both suffer from muscular dystrophy and are confined to the wheel chair but they constantly lobby for the cause.

They have helped upgrade Delhi Haat, the popular market, and design the Delhi metro stations and Delhi Transport corporation buses to make them suitable for the handicapped.

They will later look at banks, shopping malls and post-offices. (Delhi express newsline 26-3-06). The NGO Action Aid is working on sensitizing public transport authorities in Bangalore to think of the disabled, says activist Nithila Baskaran.

Though the US system is heavily biased against pedestrians and cyclists, it is friendly towards the physically challenged. Rustom Irani, a young wheel-chair bound film maker of Mumbai says he travelled in the US for hundreds of miles on his own and was able to access any public or private building. In India he found that even the newly built posh multiplex theatres had no facilities for the handicapped. He was told he will have to be physically lifted up the stairs. It was not possible to reach Marine Drive as well as the footpath was a good ten inches above the road without access. (IE 16-8-06).

India's national policy for persons with disabilities framed in 1993 promises a barrier-free access to the physically challenged. But this is only on paper. Life is hell even for the able-bodied. India is a signatory to a United Nations resolution to provide facilities for movement of the handicapped including warning blocks at the edge of pavements, placement of signs above the head level to avoid injuries and for crossing the road at traffic signals.

Life on the streets is hell for most non-motorists. It is getting worse with misguided government policies. Mr Shirish Patel, noted city planner and structural engineer, says the Maharashtra governement's poicy of giving a high FSI of four is ruinous for common people. It will allow builders to build high rise buildings without any concern for street life. The policy will greatly increase the number of cars without any increase in space for walking, for public amenities like gardens and schools and hospitals. It will be hell.

People are not bodies to be stacked one above another. They need to move about, go to work, walk, shop, go to a restaurant, meet friends. The more people you have in your vertically stacked plot, more space you need for other amenities.

This crucial space is not being provided. This has disastrous implications. Housing is not just buildings on a plot. To service we need roads, footpaths, gardens, schools and hospitals. A similar pattern is being more or less followed in other cities. There is total disregard for footpaths and other infrastructure. (Economic and Political Weekly 18-8-07).

Mr R.C. Sinha, a senior Maharashtra bureaucrat, showed his drive as a builder of the Mumbai Pune highway as vice president of the Maharashtra State Road Development Corporation (MSRDC) in the nineties. One wished bureaucrats were as committed to pedestrians as they are to motorists. As chief of the Maharashtra Airport Development Corporation he wanted to build airports even in small towns when what they need on priority basis is a good connectivity by state transport buses.

He resigned as non executive chairperson of Maytas Infrastructure after it was involved in the Rs 7000 crore Satyam Computer scandal in 2009 saying he was unaware of the fraud. He has known Maytas for a long time and the company had constructed part of the Mumbai Pune expressway when he headed the project. He was alleged to have shown favours to Maytas in allotment of 130 acres of land in Nagpur.

Serious questions about links between Maytas, the Hyderabad Metro railway and the politics of real estate have been raised by Mr C Ramachandraiah of the Centre for Economic and Social Studies, Hyderabad. (Economic and Political Weekly EPW 17-1-09).

Questions were raised by Mr E Sreedharan, the competent and non-corrupt managing director of the Delhi Metro Corporation, in a letter to Mr Montek Singh Ahluwalia, deputy chairperson of the planning commission, two months before the Satyam scandal broke out.

One of he points raised was the lack of transparency in awarding the contract to Maytas which has no experience in Metro construction and which has wide interest in real estate which it sought to promote with the railway line. The project, now suspended, would have resulted in the demolition of prominent buildings including the state archives and defacement of historic heritage precincts.

The state government was making available 296 acres of prime land to Maytas which was like selling family silver. Mr Sreedharan said worldwide no metro project had succeeded so far on a build and operate basis. Later state finance minister K Rosaiah and Hyderabad Metro managing director N.V.S. Reddyh threatened to sue Sreedharan at a joint press conference if he did not apologise. His stand is obviously vindicated.

Investigating Satyam and Maytas affairs cannot be complete without investigating politicians who facilitated the frauds, said E.A.S. Sarma, former secretary in the union finance ministry. (Frontline 13-2-09).

In Delhi the Metro goes underground in areas with important government buildings for security reasons and the Bangalore Metro is also planned to go underground in areas around the Vidhan Soudha, the legislature. But in Hyderabad it will also require demolition of pedestrian shopping areas and historical landmarks like Sultan Bazar and Badi Chawdi. These are also high density residential areas the contract signed with Maytas places the future of the city, its lands and its people in the hands of the company for almost 67 years.

Some legislators in Maharashtra do not want to walk even the little distance from the gate of Vidhan Bhavan to occupy their seats in the legislature. They are angry if their vehicles are stopped at the gate and some including Dr Deepak Sawant of the Shiv Sena and Shobhatai Phadnavis, a former minister, sat in protest outside the Council Hall. Deputy chief minister R.R. Patil assured the members that they would be provided vehicles from the entrance to the steps of the legislature. (Samnaa, Shiv Sena mouthpiece, 11-3-08).

Many bureaucrats do not think very differently. Mr Jagdish Khattar, a former IAS officer and managing director of Maruti Udyog, wants every Indian to become a car owner including the mechanic and the gardener. That would be empowerment, he said while talking to the Indian Express in the India Empowered series (17-11-05).

3

Plight of Pedestrians

A female lawyer Armin Wandrewala had this experience right outside the Maharashtra state police headqauarters in Mumbai in 2009. She was walking on the pedestrian crossing and found it blocked by a motor cyclist. When she asked him to move away he beat her up badly in full view of the public. So pedestrians are denied the right to walk safely even at pedestrian crossings and face assault when they assert that right. And they get little protection from the police. Instead, pedestrians are often seen by the police as a nuisance.

The problem is motor vehicles come speeding to traffic junctions even when they see red and cause quite a few crashes. In one such incident an old woman was fatally hit by a car driven by a doctor Parul Kolhe 33, near the Kanjur Marg traffic signal in Mumbai in 2009.

But the traffic police routinely wink at motorists' speeding because they want fast movement of vehicles. To hell with pedestrians, who are not influential anyway.

Instead the traffic police chose to target pedestrians and in fact conducted a drive against pedestrians, accusing them of being jaywalkers, in association with Hindustan Times in September, 2009 in Mumbai.

'I don't mean that the stupid pedestrian who comes in the way of the motor car deserves to die but the trouble is that a car driver has to suddenly apply his brake and break his neck in the process'. That is from motorist Roshan Thakkar in the daily DNA, Mumbai, (25-9-06).

That represents the general view of the motorists towards pedestrians. It is as if the roads belong entirely to motorists and no one else must walk on the road even if footpaths are either not there or are so badly built, they are unusable. Pedestrians seem to have no right to the road and they must pay with death, nothing less.

Motorists seem to believe that they are justified in killing or injuring pedestrians coming in their way. They blame the pedestrian. Fortunately, in an important judgement Nishita Mhatre, judge of the Mumbai high, ruled in 2009 that a person, considered a jaywalker, too is entitled to compensation in a road crash.

Wing commander Jitendra Nath was killed when knocked down by a car while he was crossing Marine Drive in Mumbai near the pedestrian crossing in 1986. The judge ruled that even if he was in error, the motorist should have seen him, honked and tried to save his life. (TOI 20-9-09).

Motorists forget that even in the best of times conditions on the road in India are not perfect. A person crossing the road may be deaf, blind, weak, mentally fragile, old and vulnerable. The person is not able to exercise the best judgement. And the motorist has to take all this into consideration, not assume the right to kill or maim the victim.

In the capital city of Delhi itself there are no pedestrian crossings at 45 per cent of the intersections and only five per cent pedestrian signals function, according to a study by the

Central Road Research Institute in 2008. Ninety per cent pedestrians in Delhi feel unsafe on roads and conditions have worsened in the last five years.

So it was quite a pleasant surprise to hear union home minister P Chidambaram take up the cause of pedestrians with Delhi's police commissioner Y.S. Dadwal and speak in the upper house of Parliament in 2009 in response to the issue raised by Ranjit Prasad, a veteran socialist who does not own a car.

The minister asked the police to give more time to pedestrians to cross roads and said it was unfair to ask pedestrians to use subways or underground passages. Roads have to be planned keeping in mind the pedestrians, he said.

Mr S.S. Ahluwalia, BJP MP, sought bicycle paths and skywalks.There are no traffic signals at some of busiest junctions in Delhi like the one near the GPO, General Post Office, where pedestrians have to run for their lives while crossing the road.

It is true that pedestrians need to observe more discipline and could face reduced risks if they walk on the right side of the road so that they see the incoming traffic. But by and large conditions are extremely hostile to pedestrians in the country.

This led Prime Minister Manmohan Singh to express his disappointment that many roads do not provide space for pedestrians or cyclists. He was speaking at the 95th Indian Science Congress at Vishakhapatnam in 2008 on the theme of environmentally sustainable science and technology.

Pedestrians and cyclists were pushed off the road by policemen when former chief secretary of the Uttar Pradesh government, Mr T.S.R. Subramaniam drove in his official vehicle. The former cabinet secretary notes this with some regret in his autobiography Journeys Through Babudom and Neta Land.

There seems to be a conspiracy against pedestrians, according to Mr J.B. D'souza, a respected critic of urban planning. He should know because he was the former municipal commissioner in Mumbai and former union urban development secretary.

Even in proven murder cases, judges give the death penalty only in the rarest of rare cases. But in India the mere act of a pedestrian's crossing the road is seen fit by some motorists to knock the person down, if not kill him or her. So the poor are blamed for living in slums, women are blamed for being raped and pedestrians for being killed or coming in the way of motor cars.

Mr O.P. Agarwal, a former joint secretary in the Urban Development department in Delhi, who was instrumental in framing the country's transport policy, has this observation. He lives in a posh area in Delhi but even here the footpath is so high. It is beautiful to look at but no one can use it. So people are forced to walk on the road.

Engineers mechanically do their job without any consideration for the needs and convenience of the users. Clearly there is need to involve social scientists, economists, sociologists and others to make it more humane, user-friendly, Mr Agarwal feels.

The pedestrian is unsafe everywhere. And most unsafe in India's famous public space, Marine Drive waterfront even with the green signal in operation. There are multiple hazards. Motorists come racing down and halt on the pedestrian crossing or often move beyond. This happens right under the nose of the police. The municipal corporation has constructed a cement barrier in the middle of the road on the pedestrian crossing. And climbing on the high footpath or getting down is an uphill task. The situation has worsened since Marine Drive was 'beautified' in 2007 with the state government footing a bill of Rs 30 crore.

Ironically, the rich come to the Joggers Park in their cars instead of walking from their homes which are not far away. So before and after their pleasure of walking they scare pedestrians on the road, blow the horn, spew fumes and heat and grab precious public space outside the garden for parking. Moreover, there are no footpaths outside the Joggers Park for ordinary people to walk on. They must submit themselves to the mercy of motorists while the ruling class talks of making Mumbai into a world class city.

London, is one of the world's greatest walking cities. Tourists too can cover some of the most prominent parts on foot. Besides, there are 67 miles of pathways on either side of the Thames river and 45,000 acres of green, open spaces, from royal parks to commons, woods and forest. And there are 80,000 streets (TOI. 30-10-05).

In India while the upper class has created recreational walk spaces for itself it has for decades consistently neglected the most basic problem of walking for common people for their daily activities.

In Kolkata the upper class has turned the large premises of the Victoria Memorial into a morning walking space.

Strangely, the lot of pedestrians is worsening in West Bengal though the Communist party of India (Marxist) is in power for the last three decades. The width of footpaths has been reduced from 4.5 metres to 2 metres to provide more space for parking for cars on the road. It is criminal to do so, said transport engineering expert Dinesh Mohan of IIT, Delhi. The cutting of footpaths is justified by the municipal authorities with the argument that in any case hawkers grab space there. It is like cutting your leg because it is paining, said activist Subhash Datta (TOI 25-4-08).

Bachi Karkaria, a well-known journalist, wrote succinctly about her walking experience 'My resolve battles vainly against the unending hurdles. The tempo of my stride has never risen. Only my temper. Defeated, I stagger home. Head bowed. It has to be. For if I don't watch out, I'll fall into another ditch.

Bachi was walking around Five Gardens, one of Mumbai's greenest and poshest areas near the beautiful Parsi colony in Dadar, Mumbai. One can imagine how much worse must be the conditions in other areas.

Facilities for pedestrians are better even in countries like Mozambiaque, Myanmar or Mauritius, asserts Mr P.V. Indiresan, former director of the prestigious Indian Institute of Technology. We must construct footpaths everywhere and widen existing footpaths instead of roads. That is one way of empowering the poor, cutting their travel costs and alleviating urban poverty, he says.

It is an irony that in techno-savvy Bangalore conditions for pedestrians are worsening while the city has a brand new airport and the rich clamour for more road space for cars reflecting the widening gap between the globalised elite and the common people.

Bangalore ranks 12th among 30 cities in India in terms of walkability, according to a study conducted by the union urban affairs ministry. The city ranks below Ahmedabad, Chennai, Kolkata and other cities. Surely, the city needs a better infrastructure for pedestrians, said traffic expert N Sreehari. Bangalore's municipal commissioner Dr S Subramanya said even able bodied soldiers cannot cross the roads with safety. The infrastructure has focused on vehicles, not pedestrians. Even pedestrian crossings are not safe, he said.

For pedestrians Bangalore is a thundering valley of death, a lunatic aslym. Even God would not be able to grant a boon to cross the road safely, said P Anantha Krishnan.

Madhav Badami, a transport expert in the school of urban planning in McGill university, Montreal, finds it odd that while the government spends hundreds of crores on the Metro railway, it is not concerned about basic amenities for pedestrians.

Mr Badami cites a short story titled Interurban Queen by R.A. Lafferty. In it a character testifies to the socially destructive power of motor cars. Every man on horseback is an arrogant man, however gentle he may be on foot. A man in an automobile is one thousand times as dangerous. The kindest man in the world assumes an incredible arrogance when he drives an automobile. It creates absolute selfishness in the driver. The car will destroy the sense of neighbourhood and true sense of nations. It will make very man a tyrant.

The arrogance of motorists towards pedestrians, seeing them as inferior is strongly condemned by Mr Badami. Pedestrians cross the road wherever they want because safe crossings are few and far in between. There is clearly an apartheid on Indian roads which works against pedestrians. (EPW 15-8-09).

Providing for high speed for motorists comes at high infrastructure costs and limits access to other road users. As Ivan Illich, the renowned scholar points out, motor cars create long distances and only a few, that is motorists, can shrink this distance. For them it is all right, for others it means more hardships. In other words motor vehicles rob the poor of their time and even money.

For example, a man who could formerly walk a distance of one km to the railway station, now cannot do so as roads are very crowded. So he has to take a bus, wait a long time for it, travel in overcrowded conditions, or take an auto rickshaw and see the bill go up in the traffic jam.

Provide better facilities for pedestrians, even motorists will start walking at least for short distances.

To talk of a signal-free drive for motorists while denying facilities to pedestrians is like denying the right to life, said the traffic additional police commissioner. Praveen Sood.

A signal-free ride for motorists between Bangalore city and the airport kills one person every two days and many are injured daily. Manjula, a fruit seller, 58, finds the road so unsafe that she has to take an auto-rickshaw just to cross it.

The traffic police put front page advertisements in daily newspapers appealing to motorists to stick to the limit of 80 km per hour. This itself is very high and deadly for pedestrians. But they go much faster. (Deepa Kurup and Divya Gandhi in Hindu 12-7-08). It is strange that public money is being spent on issuing such appeals instead of checking dangerous driving.

Top priority should be given in transport planning to pedestrians and cyclists, not to cars, said Chiranjeev Singh, a former additional chief secretary of the Karnataka government. A large number of citizens are now voicing their protests under the banner of Hasiru Usiru against the anti-people form of development. Joining the protests are MLAs like Hemchandra Sagar, K.J. George, Gundu Rao and activists like Leo Saldanha of Environment Support Group.

In Kolkata the CPM union sold footpath space in the prime Park Circus area to hawkers for hefty amounts. (TOI 20-7-08).

In America, the notion that people who go around on foot are criminals until proved otherwise was actually a matter of policy until about 20 years ago, the New York Times reported. That is when the courts struck down a state law that allowed the police to stop, detain and record information on (usually nonwhite) walkers whom the police judged by some vague standard.

The sinister pedestrian who turns suddenly monstrous is an archetype in the creative imagination of Los Angeles (NYT Brent Staples. 26-7-03). The menacing character shown in films after a catastrophe like an earthquake, volcano eruption or alien invasion is usually out there on foot, looking for somebody to murder. That is how the human on the street is maligned.

In the original Terminator movie which came to the screen in 1984 a killer cyborg from the future, the Terminator, materializes in predawn Los Angeles as a naked pedestrian who seems pretty much like the rest of us, until he punches into a tough guy's chest and rips out his heart.

Some critics dismissed the movie as trash but young theatergoers made it into a culture picture, then a long-term hit.

A science fiction story 'Revolt of the Pedestrian' written in 1928 depicted an era when the pedestrian is no longer a protected species and is hunted down by motorists. So pedestrians become nearly extinct. Some are secretly born as pedestrians to parents who have never used an automobile. They live in a community hidden away from the world, they run, swim, hike, activities forgotten by other humans. A stage arises when no pedestrian is seen for hundred yeas and are forgotten. The story by David Keller is included by Asimov in his collection of best science stories.

New Yorkers tend to get surprised on the first few trips to Los Angeles. The footpaths are empty. Walk a little distance and you can sense motorists' staring as though you have suddenly grown a second head or split the seat of your pants.

The suspicion of pedestrians is a common theme in writing about Los Angeles. Ray Bradbury took it up in his short story The Pedestrian in the early 1950s about a perfectly innocent man who enjoys walking the vacant street after dark and is dragged off to a mental asylum.

In the widely reported case of civil rights in 1975 Edward Lawson, a black man, was jailed by the police 15 times between 1975-77 as he asserted his right as a pedestrian and a human being. He was jailed when he refused to give his name and identity to the police when he was walking on the road in California. He was prosecuted twice and convicted once.

A California statute requires that a person who loiters or wanders on the road is required to give his identity and account for his presence on the road. The Supreme court ruled in Lawson's favour with a 7-2 decision. Lawson, 37, a bachelor was the head of a consulting firm in San Francisco. He was fond of taking long walks, often in the dead of the night. (Time magazine. Walking Tall in California. 16-5-83).

You start walking in America and you are seen as a threat to public order, you are treated like a dog, wrote the French philosopher Jean Baudrillard in his book on the US. Another interesting observation he made was that the rich are socially retarded. A friend of Paris Hilton, the celebrity model, said she would rather go without food for 15 days than her cell phone.

All this is chilling and shows how perverted values are in some parts of America. In India some people show the same suspicion, hatred and callousness towards pedestrians. But in America at least in some regions pedestrians are respected by motorists and a big movement of pedestrianisation of streets has begun. One can take a sandwich and book in hand at sit in a lane near Times Square in New York that once belonged to cars. It sends a signal of pedestrian pride, the New York Times wrote (14-2-08). New York's traffic commissioner Janette Sadik Khan often commuters by bicycle and is called a guerilla bureaucrat.

John Kerry also introduced a bill to protect pedestrians, especially the blind, from new electric and hybrid cars which are silent and render them dangerous to the blind. The blind listen to traffic to discern the speed and direction of vehicles. But if the vehicle is noiseless, they would be rendered more handicapped.

In India it would be difficult to find even one street where this happens. No wonder facilities for pedestrians are so neglected. Worse, life is being made more and more miserable for pedestrians. Barricades are being built along footpaths and road divider are built so that crossing the road becomes more and more difficult. A Hyderabad resident Kanthimathi Kannan has set up a Right to Walk Foundation to assert the cause of pedestrians. The Hyderabad civic body favours beautification instead of providing basic amenities for walking, said Vijay Kishore, director of the school of planning and architecture.

The pattern of urban planning has harmed pedestrians in India, argues Vivek Moorthy, economics professor in the Indian Isntitute of Management, Bangalore. There is no space to walk for pedestrians around the IIM campus, he says.

But here is an incident which shows the real cruelty and anti-pedestrian nature of the traffic system. A noted urban designer of America Charles Atherton was given a traffic ticket for jaywalking by the police even when he was seriously injured by a motor car while crossing the road. He died subsequently in hospital.

Atherton was for a long time the secretary of the U.S. commission on fine arts and had supervised the work of such major projects as the Roosevelt Memorial, Vietnam veterans memorial and the world war II memorial. His family found the penalty ticket in his pocket (Washington Post 4-12-05).

Planners and engineers pay little attention to the needs of pedestrians, said Dinesh Mehta, professor emeritus at the School of Planning in Ahmedabad. Worse, police apprehend and fine pedestrians for walking on the road even though the administration denies them elementary facilities.

It can be said that pedestrians suffer from what can be called an apartheid regime. In Mumbai police look the other way when motorists merrily park on pedestrian crossings at the traffic junction of India's prime public space Marine Drive. Yet, they want to punish pedestrians and turn a blind eye to what is known as drag racing by motor cyclists in the dead of the night on Marine Drive (stop the speed devils. HT 22-9-09).

Loitering, one of the most innocent, simple activities is considered by the establishment as particularly dangerous. Keep Moving. That is the motto of the paranoid security forces after the attack of September 11 Bernard Henry Levy, a French philosopher, had this experience in America when he was loitering as part of an assignment for Atlantic Monthly. His task was to retrace the steps of Alexis de Tocqville, the renowned French traveler, who has left such a fine account of America, as a tribute to 200 years of his birth. He got away lightly because of his work.

Pedestrian bridges are so narrow and congested at railway stations that a stampede could occur any time. Many times policemen have to control the walkers. Such is the criminal neglect of pedestrians at every level. A pedestrian bridge nearing completion collapsed killing two workers and injuring 11 others at Dombivli station on the outskirts of Mumbai in January, 2004 on a local train during the morning peak hour of 10 a.m. and it is a miracle casualties were not heavier. The casualties would have been far bigger had the bridge been in use. Dombivli, 49 km from Chhatrapati Shivaji Terminus (CST), is one of the busiest railway stations catering to a predominantly middle-class population and the distance shows how far ordinary people were flung from the city since the 1950s.

Worse, the collapsed part of the bridge was kept in a nearby garden for several months robbing children of their only source of open space.

Another pedeststrian bridge fell a year later, at Charni Road station, a prime area in South Mumbai, 3 km from Churchgate terminus as if another reminder of callousness was needed.

People are literally treated like cattle. At some railways stations railway bridges are so narrow that one has to wait for a long time merely to come out of the station or to reach it. The humiliation begins at the stage of ticket-buying itself as people are made to wait in long queues. It gets worse in Chennai's or Mumbai's stifling sultriness, heat and heavy rain. It is not that the railways are short of space or number of employees. The railways have so much space that railway minister Laloo Prasad Yadav spoke of using railway land for shopping malls.Yet, there is no land available for the most essential activities.

In contrast facilities are getting better and better for pedestrians in many parts of Europe. The Queen of England inaugurated a bridge exclusively for pedestrians on the river Thames in the year 2000. The 18 million pound bridge, called Millenium bridge, is designed by the leading architect Sir Norman Foster. Connecting St Paul's to the Tate modern art gallery. At the inauguration there were colourful banners, fanfare, fireworks and barges on the river. In India one cannot imagine so much attention being paid to the needs of pedestrians. Built of steel with stainless steel balustrades at night it forms a blaze of light across the river.

Corporates donated handsomely for the pedestrian bridge, HSBC gave three million pounds. The initiative for the bridge was taken by David Bell, a former managing director of the Financial Times. One can't imagine our elite taking so much interest in a pedestrian bridge which would be considered as something very downmarket in India.

A foot bridge on the river Seine in Paris opened in 2006 is named after Simone de Beauvoir, the celebrated feminist and novelist. It is modern, graceful and wide and connects the national library Bibliotheque Francois Mitterand and the entertainment complex at Bercy. The history of Paris is said to be the history of river crossings. There are 37 such bridges, more than in any other city, and this has helped even development of the on both the sides of the river.

The beauty of the Latin Quarter lies in its sheer contrast to the other parts of car-clogged Paris. This student area is inaccessible to cars. It is so lovely, recalls Neha Bhayana who visited Paris while studying in London. Our cities and towns desperately need car-free roads where people can move about freely, democratically without fear of being knocked down. (HT 25-11-06).

Even in automobile dominated US, much more cognizance of pedestrians and biyclists is taken than in India. The Bureau of Transportation and Statistics, headed by Dr Ashish Sen, collects information on facilities for pedestrians and bicyclists as required by the Transportation Equity Act for the 21st century.

But by European standards US is a hell for pedestrians because cities are designed for motor cars, not pedestrians. Not many places are accessible by foot and there are so many barriers that it could take half an hour to reach a distance which should normally take five minutes.

Even reputed architects are not friendly towards pedestrians. The Walt Disney building in Los Angeles, designed by top architect Frank Gehry, reflects so much sunlight as to cause sunburn to pedestrians and even melt plastic.

Brasilia, the new capital of Brazil, which was opened in 1960, was built for cars with numerous flyovers, not for pedestrians. A journalist of the Telegraph reported that her car from the airport to the hotel in the town did not stop even once. (Telegraph 17-6-06). The city has spectacular architecture created by the top architect and staunch Communist Oscar Niemeyer, but it is not designed on the human scale. Car is king here with high fatality rate of pedestrian deaths. The situation is so bad that in 1996 nearly 25,000 marched to the office of the Congress demanding protection to pedestrians from street violence. Efforts to check the speed of cars with use of electronic cameras was brazenly contested by opposition leader and businessman Estevao. Following an uproar, several pedestrian crossings have been provided on roads and these are scrupulously respected by cars. But the city planning itself is against pedestrians. The city looks very posh and modern but it is a sterile, cultural void, an anomaly in a vibrant, colourful, multiracial Brazil and its construction nearly bankrupted the country's economy.

Even the cathedral has a drive-in and the palatial building of the foreign ministry has an exclusive internal ramp that allows the top brass to motor right up to the offices on the first floor.

Simone de Beauvoir, the distinguished feminist author and wife of Jean Paul Sartre, was disappointed by her visit to Brasilia soon after it came up. 'What possible interest could there be in wandering about here ? the street, that meeting ground of passersby, stores and houses, vehicles and pedestrians, does not exist in Brasilia and never will. There are few places to sit and little shelter from the blinding Sun. Brazil was subsequently taken over by the military and architect Zaha Hadid said 'all those broad streets proved useful for the army to drive through. (Atlantic July-August 2008).

Mr S.M. Sarin, former director of the Central Road Research Institute, is very critical of the neglect of the pedestrian who should get priority as the pedestrian is the main road user of roads.

Some of his points are : Road planning often ignores the pedestrians. After making provision mainly for cars, whatever is left is allocated for pedestrian needs. It is rare that provision for pleasant or even efficient pedestrian movement has been made. Pedestrian space has commonly been thought of as merely the strip of concrete between the roadway and adjoining buildings. There is no effort to make pdestrian's journey safe, convenient and enjoyable.

And cars get away by splashing water on pedestrians, honking at them, terrifying them, humiliating them at every step. In England cars splashing water on pedestrians will be fined 2500 pounds.

But some others have unusual ideas. Mr T.S. Reddy, a former head and Purnima Parida, scientist, at the traffic division of CRRI suggest that pedestrians going along highways should wear 'reflective' jackets so that they are visible to drivers in the night. Most planners, police and engineers blame the victim. The pedestrian is supposed to take all the precautions, not the motorist Traffic signals clearly discriminate against pedestrians and give them little time to cross safely. The point is substantiated by two teachers of urban engineering of Chennai, K.P. Subramanian and M Kangaraj. Across the Anna Salai road in Chennai the cycle timing for pedestrian crossing at traffic junctions is only 10 to 15 seconds. But the minimum width of the main carriage way is 20 metres.

A Mayor of Chennai is on record saying that he will remove footpaths. He has given the completely false excuse that they are not being used by pedestrians. It is a pity that while every world city is giving more facilities for pedestrians, such facilities are either being denied or withdrawn, said Prof T Ananthraj, retired professor emeritus at Anna university. (Hindu 13-11-2000).

A top police official called pedestrians a nuisance at a seminar at IIT in Chennai, recalls Karen Coelho, associate professor in the Madras Institute of Development Studies. Pedestrians in Chennai havee now formed an organization Walking Classes Unite to assert their right to walk and to protest against the outrageous conditions. The IT road, far from being modern, is most hazardous to pedestrians, especially children.

In Chennai the pedestrian movement is not biased against hawkers as in other cities. So a pedestrian walk in 2009 on the Marine Beach was flagged off not only by film actor Charuhasan but also a hawker leader M. Sangath. Sheelu, president of Women's Collective, also demanded more space for hawkers in the city's landscape. Traffic signals should have push buttons to enable pedestrians to cross comfortably, suggested K Gunasekran, professor of traffic engineer in Anna university.

The sadder thing is that at the planning stage itself there is no concern at all for the pedestrian, the important but vulnerable section. The most damning evidence against the Indian Roads Congress comes from three experts, Dr S.M. Sarin, Dr Nishi Mittal and Mr R.K. Bajpai who have been connected with the Central Road Research Institute in Delhi in senior positions.

Several documents and guidelines prepared by the Indian Roads Congress pay very inadequate attention to pedestrians. The first document dealing with pedestrians was published by the IRC as late as 1988 which shows the neglect over the years. This document itself fails on different counts. For example, the document does not provide design norms for maximum height of footpaths, widths according to different land use parameters and pedestrian flows, surface types, pedestrian amenities. Even more callous is the neglect of pedestrians in rural areas. Similarly guidelines regarding traffic signals take little cognizance of pedestrians. The Institute of Road Traffic Education (IRTE) is a unique private sector initiative in research and training led by entreprereur Rohit Baluja in Delhi.

Indifference of authorities towards the needs of pedestrians is common in most of the developing world including our neighbour Pakistan. Everywhere in Pakistan pedestrians are at serious risk because of lack of footpaths or encroachments on them by cars, says columnist Irfan Husain, in Daily Times of Pakistan (27-12-05).

Railways in Pakistan have been allowed to deteriorate because the elite now prefers to fly, state schools and hospitals are crumbling too. It is exactly the same scenario in India. If the elite is forced to use public utilities, facilities would improve considerably.

If a rich person on the road has to attend to the call of Nature he or she simply goes by car to the nearest hotel. So they are not bothered about filthy public toilets. The car indirectly promotes callousness towards public amenities. Toilets can be clean, well maintained and beautiful as is seen in several countries. Temples of Convenience and Chambers of Delight is the title of a fascinating book by Lucinda Lambton on British toilets. She drove 40.000 miles in the country to study the toilets and write on them. The British are pioneers in the public toilet culture and have some marvelous toilets. The Royal Institute of British Architects recently asked celebrated architects to design public conveniences. Public toilets are a barometer of a country's health. If we built clean, well-designed toiles, people will not object to their construction in their localities. So a major issue of public health and public realm can be handled with a little more investment.

Even brand new roads in Pakistan do not have footpaths. So the next time you curse a poor pedestrian, who slows your car down, or someone squatting in the fields, spare a thought for the person's plight, Irfan Husain rightly observes.

No place to walk in Karachi is the heading of a report in the Dawn of Pakistan which neatly conveys the plight of pedestrians in the country's most modern, populous city. In blistering heat a girl of eight and her brother of 12 years were the target of a foul-mouthed Honda City driver as they crossed the road. reported Maheen Rashdi (Dawn 10-4-06).

Old footpaths in Mumbai are much better designed, though they are now badly maintained. The newly constructed footpaths, far from being more pedestrian-friendly, are far too steep. It is a task to climb and get down even for the able-bodied and the footpaths can cause the foot to sprain or fracture and give you a backache. There is not even a graded slope for climbing and getting down. It is almost as if the new footpaths are intended to harass and torture pedestrians. As if to drive home the point that you are not wanted and we do not care for you. It is perhaps not surprising in a deeply unequal society in which the establishment favours the car lobby.

The New York municipal corporation has paid compensation for millions of dollars to citizens for injuries caused by defective footpaths. If that is to be done in Indian cities, the entire civic budget would not suffice to pay compensation.

Buses and suburban trains too are not friendly to the disabled, points out Sudhir Badami, a structural engineer trained in the Indian Institute of Technology. The crush load in Mumbai suburban trains is as high as 16 persons per sq. metre. But the railways have taken the trouble to accommodate the handicapped in a small cabin which is at the most a make-shift arrangement. The entrance to the cabin is just about half a metre wide, just enough for one ; person to board at a time. While the width is just all right for a handicapped to board, it is not possible to have another handicapped person climbing down at the same time. The signage shows a wheel chair but no wheelchaired person can board such a cabin due to the door width restrictions and the platform is much lower than the cabin entry. The seating too is inadequate. There are also severe problems for the old, pregnant women and other disadvantaged sections. The railways appear to have provided the cabin for the handicapped just to fulfil the obligation of the Disability Act (people with disabilities, equal opportunities, protection of rights and full participation act, which came into effect from 1996, Mr Badami says.

The BEST (Bombay Electric Supply and Transport) Undertaking has provided some relief to women and old persons with reserved seats. But for years the best undertaking in the country has not run low floor buses (LBS) which could make life much easier for all. It reqires the agility of an athlete and the strength of a wrester to get into a bus.

It is surprising that a scientific and political leadership boasts of our advances in Space technology cannot introduce basic people-friendly facilities or designs. Most designs at public spaces are bad because of the callousness of authorities. In the year 2004 coaches on new trains on the Mumbai-: Pune section were so uncomfortable, that they were withdrawn after public protests. Benches and chairs at railway stations, if at all provided, are so badly designed to an unbelievable degree that one cannot sit for more than a minute without a feeling of acute discomfort. Designing a bench requires no special knowledge of engineering. Just a sense of design, physiology, plain common sense and a little interest in providing some basic amenities to people are required.

The worst thing about the underpasses or subways is that they get heavily flooded in the monsoon and become hazardous, especially for school children. Yet, the traffic authorities have the gumption to order pedestrians to use these, claim they are for their safety and blame them if they do not use them. So the system is actually endangering the lives of ordinary people. A flooded underpass near the Bandra (east) flyover means thousands of school children have to battle for their lives while crossing the Western Express highway. Various agencies blame one another for the mess. The underpass on the Eastern Eastern Expressway near Evarard Nagar in Sion is completely unusable because it is always wet and slippery and sometimes flooded and dark. Because of admittedly defective work by the state government's public works department (PWD). (Mumbai Mirror 11-2-06).

This is the condition after only three years of construction. Drainage water seeps into the subway because of callous construction work. The Expressway accounts for some of the heaviest and most reckless traffic. When the subway fails, pedestrians have no option but to risk their life and limb to cross the road. The authorities have worsened the problem by removing traffic signal at the spot. So, they have converted this into an accident and death spot. Yet, policepersons, bureaucrats and ministers have the gall to blame pedestrians for carelessness.

Crores of rupees literally went down the drain in 2006 due to defective design of a subway at Kurla, the heavily populated working class suburb with a large number of pedestrians.

There is a telling photograph in the Times of India showing huts of very light, cheap material on the footpath with workers wearing lungis standing while a motor cyclist passes by on Maharshi Karve Marg (Queen's Road) in Mumbai. The immediate reaction to such a sight is one of blaming slum dwellers for grabbing a footpath and ultimately getting entitled to a free, pucca house free.

The caption for the photograph tells a remarkable story. The reality is vastly different from popular prejudice. The workers from 150 families are not encroachers and lazy bums as they are normally seen through the prejudiced eye. They have been given accommodation on the footpath because they have to do the work of converting the road into a concrete road in the next few months. The contractor was officially granted permission by the municipal corporation to set up the huts.

It clearly means that the system is directly responsible for the growth of slums because it wants to hire workers but does not want to give the workers a proper housing or even a proper shelter. These people are not encroachers on public space. It is the administration, the upper class which is clearly responsible for the situation.

In an important judgement a Los Angeles court has held that the police must not punish involuntary sleeping, sleeping, lying on public footpaths. It is an unavoidable consequence of being human and homeless in the city that people lie on the footpath, the ninth circuit court ruled in April 2006.

Human beings are biologically compelled to sit, lie down or sleep and rest. It would be wrong to criminalise such behaviour, the court ruled.

But even resting one's head on the footpath requires money, influence and contacts. Several prime pavements and their occupancy are controlled by different powers that be, ranging from the local corporators' followers to the beat policeman to the local restaurant owner, according to activist Simpreet Singh. A pavement dweller usually shells out a one-time payment of upto Rs 500 so that the space can be booked for him. If it is a family, the charges are more. If a person chooses to put a tarpaulin sheet above the head, the charges run upto Rs 2000. The nearer the railway station, the higher the charges, said Shakeel Ahmed, a lawyer and activist. Rising up the ladder, getting shelter in a slum is more expensive.

Impoverishment, neglect of rural areas and growing investment in cities has intensified migration and homelessness in urban areas, said R.N. Sharma, dean of social sciences in the Tata Institute of Social Sciences.

If the relentless drive against the poor continues in India in the regime of globalisation, even loitering on the road can be treated as an offence as in the United States. The anti-loitering law allowed the arrest of more than 42,000 people between 1992-95 in Chicago until it was declared unconstitutional by the Supreme court. The law made it a crime to remain in a place for no apparent reason.

For ordinary people life is worse. The poor, particularly blacks and Spanish-speaking people from Latin America are routinely searched, arrested by the police for no apparent reason. Woodie Guthrie, the fine folk poet and singer, spoke in his songs of the numerous homeless people. I ain't got no home, I am just a roaming around, just a wandering worker, I go from town to town and the police make it hard for me wherever I go, he wrote.

He also wrote 'Take off your shoes and pray. The ground you walk is holy ground. Every spot on earth I traipse around, every spot I walk is holy ground. Every grain of dirt is holy ground.'

Historian Felipe Fernandes Arnesto of Tufts Univesity was arrested, handcuffed and thrown into a filthy cell for eight hours because he crossed the street in Atlanta to attend a convention of the American Historical Association in 2005. He is the author of a number of books including Pathfinders – a global history of exploration.

Anti-human architecture can also create feeling of alienation among pedestrians. The twin towers of the World Trade Centre, destroyed by terrorist attack, darkened life for pedestrian down below. Such buildings have a dehumanizing effect, the noted architecture critic Paul Goldberger noted. The best urban spaces invite passersby asking them gently to come and rest, contemplate in their vicinity. No one felt that about the WTC, said Bob Fox, renowned New York architect.

Even the Freedom Tower coming up in place of the World Trade Center is conceived as a barricaded fortress, its base a two-story high windowless concrete bunker. It is a building armoured against an outside world that the American establishment no longer trusts. It speaks of a paranoia. (NYT 19-2-07).

In contrast the lobby of the Phare Tower in Paris is conceived as an extension of the public realm drawing in the surrounding streetscape and tunneling deep into the ground to connect to underground trains.

Good architecture connects with people and the streets. Mantralaya, the state government headquarter in Mumbai, is on the same level as the street and is much more friendly than Council Hall or Vidhan Bhavan, across the road, which is heavily barricades and aloof from people which is odd for a building meant to represent the people.

A large number of new buildings in India appear in a hostile relationship with the pedestrians and streets with their forbidding exterior, heavy gates, security and unpleasant architecture. Instead of merging with the street, they create an alienating effect with their driveway extending on the street, creating a very unpleasant environment for pedestrians.

In Latin America life is worse for pedestrians. There are two kinds of pedestrians, the quick and the dead, according to Eduardo Galeano, the top left-wing intellectual It is as if pedestrians have no right to walk, their very breathing is stifled by the traffic system.

A graphic description of the plight of pedestrians is conveyed in a report in Business Week (19-3-07). They are left stranded like ship-wrecked sailors in median strips just outside the electronic city in Bangalore. Motorists jump the red light and pay no heed to pedestrians.

Europe is far more friendly to pedestrians. A pedestrian does not have to wait for more than 60 seconds at a signal to cross the road in England and Germany.

A nation boasting of technological advance has still not found a proper way of building roads and footpaths. Interlocking tiles or paver blocks, which were advertised by the municipal corporation in Mumbai as the panacea, have proved to be a disaster as the tiles have come off and mess is visible all over the financial capital city.

Wide footpaths create a marvelous environment not only eliminating conflict between pedestrians and hawkers but in fact promoting a bond between them. This is evident on Lady Jamshedji Road between Shivaji Park and Mahim in Mumbai where one can see a lively, picturesque interaction between fruit, vegetable and flower sellers and people. Besides, these sellers lend so much colour, so much greenery.

Curiously, in India the initiative for creating a pedestrianised street has come from a small town Fazilka on the India Pakistan border, not from any major metropolitan centre in India. In the rice growing, cotton rich area, the town has created a lively pedestrian street with art, food and culture. A city is a social structure, not just a physical structure and should cater to the basic needs of citizens, points out Asija Nardeep, a highway engineer with rare sensitivity, who has studied the street.

Some walkers are particularly careful not to harm the environment even a bit. One of the best memories of Laurie Baker, the eminent architect who died in 2007, is that when he met Mahatma Gandhi as a young man he wore shoes made of waste cloth. Today this may see odd but it is even more relevant now.

When you walk you are massaging and honouring the earth. The earth is trying to help you to balance your organism and mind, says Paulo Coelho in his discourse on meditation walking.

Officials do not think so. Former municipal commissioner of Mumbai, K.C. Srivastava, dismissed a demand for footpaths in the city telling citizens 'I will construct footpaths if you tell me how to remove hawkers from them.' This is a completely false logic and an alibi for municipal callousness. Not all footpahs are encroached upon by hawkers but this is used as an excuse to deny basic rights to pedestrians. (TOI 28-6-01).

Sadly, the talk of world class infrastructure often means improved facilities for motorists and robbing pedestrians of the most basic amenities, points out Jayati Ghosh, the noted economist.

Nothing shows the apathy if not antipathy of engineers and officials to pedestrians than the suggestion of RITES to do away with separate footpath for pedestrians in the highly engineered Bus Rapid Transit (BRT) project introduced on a five km road in in Delhi in 2008. It sought to give the space to motorists. Mr V.K. Agarwal, the managing director of RITES, the prominent transport engineering consultancy organization in the public sector, made the suggestion following an outcry from motorists that the just-introduced BRT system left little space for them, though in fact for decades motorists have been hogging road space. (Express India 6-5-08).

BRT is good but should have been preceded by a lot of public education. BRT has succeeded in Bogota partly because there were not many motorists competing for the road, said Dr Adhiraj Joglekar, who has studied the traffic pattern in Mumbai, London and other cities. Besides, even if successful, can take care of only main roads. There are thousands of other streets which will continue to suffer from congestion caused mainly by motor cars.

Gautam Bhatia, noted architect, while strongly supporting BRT, said with a road system free of private cars the city will not just breathe easier but will once again become a place for all its citizens.

Car owners are afraid of loss of status, he says. How can a bank clerk in a bus reach ahead as they are left behind in the BRT which gives priority to public transport. Even in the best of conditions some motorists behave abominably. Bhatia, who lives near the upmarket Asiad village in Delhi, says very often he sees cars driven at full speed toss a plastic bag full of garbage on to the road spreading the dirt around.

It makes no sense to drive a car to bring a loaf of bread and a BMW, which properly belongs to the German autobahn, makes little sense on crowded roads in India, Mr Bhatia says.

Road congestion tax on cars too will be effective in curbing traffic only if we dramatically improve our poor public transport system, point out Prakash Apte, a consultant to the World Bank on transport, and Aneeruddha Paul, director of the Kamla Raheja Institute of Architecure and Environmental Studies in Mumbai.

The first skywalk in India is the 1.3 km bridge connecting Bandra suburban railway station in Mumbai with the Bandra Kurla complex, a fast growing business district with swanky corporate buildings. It is ugly and shoddy and garish yellow and in three weeks its surface began to crack. Clearly we need better taste, more sophistication in our public projects, as architect Chandrashekhar Prabhu pointed out. They should have invited designs from architecture students, these would have been far more imaginative, useful. In a way, the bridge gives us a raw view of Mumbai as it straddles slums, a dirty Mithi river, a forest of mangroves in the Bandra creek and the roar of vehicles on the Eastern Express highway.

The sinister part is that the civic body wanted to make money even while treating pedestrians sadistically. It forces them to go underground and or on skywalks and at the same time exploit their space commercially for profit. The proposal to allow shops on some 40 skyways planned in Mumbai in 2009 was shot down following strong protests by pedestrians' organizations led by activists like Krishnaraj Rao and Vidya Vaidya and the federation of retail traders led by Viren Shah. The congestion would turn the skyways into death traps.

The proposal for some skywalks seem dubious. Naresh Fernandes, editor of Time Out magazine, says the area outside his office near the Racecourse at Mahalaxmi has the widest uncluttered expanse of footpaths and yet the authorities want to impose a skywalk there. Equally ridiculous is the proposal to construct a skywalk between CST and Churuchgate railway stations since the area is well served by wide footpaths. Pedestrian mobility can be further increased by removing the fence across Azaad Maidan and giving access to pedestrians. Rahul Mehrotra, associate professor of architecture design at MIT, said pedestrianisation of streets was a much cheaper and walker friendly solution, rather than skyways. Pedestrian streets also preserve the visual integrity of historic places. The world over they are removing freeways and skywalks that have sliced the city and visually destroyed cities. It is time we give up ill-conceived projects, wake up and not repeat the mistakes made in the West. It is also felt that skywalks will destroy the social life of streets as also rob shops of their customers. In the CST area the skywalk will also spoil the ambience of heritage buildings, poined out Sharda Dwivedi, a scholar of the history of Mumbai, and architect Pankaj Joshi of the Urban Development Research Institute. The skyway will be an eyesore, said Nayana Kathpalia, an activist for defence of public spaces in Mumbai. There are solutions to increase people's access and mobility without spending a penny. A little walkway through the Kalina campus of Mumbai university will vastly reduce the distance between Santa Cruz and the Bandra Kurla complex and provide a wonderful healthy walking experience. Saving on money and time in vehicular, congested journey will be another advantage. This can be replicated all over the country with a little imagination.

A study has shown that the expensively built skywalks in Bandra and Kanjur Marg are used by much fewer people than was expected. Another study by Ashok Datar, transport consultant, has shown that much fewer people used the Bandra Worli sealink than was expected and the revenue from toll is far below expectations. A roundtrip on the sea link is 3.6 km longer than the road link. Obviously, the sea link has not proved as beneficial as was expected.

A study of skywalks in Mumbai by Vinit Nikumb, architect, shows that this vertical urbanism destroys the social life of the street and some skywalks obstruct sunlight on the road below.

A car-free, environment-friendly city is being built in Abu Dhabi by leading British architect Foster for communities with reduced need for energy, water, land and other resources. Can't we have even a few car-free streets ?

4

Road Deaths

Nowhere is the plight of the common people more visible than on roads. Increased motorisation of our society it not accompanied by a safety net for the poor. Cars occupy most of the road space, terrorise pedestrians, humiliate them. And often, they maim, cripple, kill poor people and literally get away with murder. A new phenomenon in the last few years is that completely innocent people waiting at bus stops or on the footpath are getting killed as drivers are becoming more arrogant.

The killers on the road now are young, well-educated, rich men, often under the influence of liquor or talking on a mobile phone while driving.

And the police are indifferent if not hostile to the poor. This comes from none other than Mr R.K. Raghavan, a former director of the Central Bureau of Investigation. He says the police view the pedestrian as a subhuman species.

Accidents are common at traffic junctions. Even here drivers flout rules and run over a pedestrian after he or she gets a green signal and walks. Mr Raghavan says when he stops at the traffic junction in Chennai's famous Anna Salai road, he becomes a comical figure. Few others respect the signal.

At the same time there is an increasing tendency to blame the poor. They are accused of coming in the way of the motor car. The truth is there are few facilities for the safety of pedestrians.

Growing income inequalities are causing more crashes elsewhere too. There is a telling study by David Krus, a professor at Arizona state university in the US, makes this amply clear. It is about the situation in capitalist, post-Communist eastern Europe. There is the same scenario everywhere.

He found that as some people became very rich after the collapse of Communist rule they became owners of luxurious imported cars, became very arrogant drivers and killed a large number of people on roads. This arrogant new class has no compassion for the poor or the needy. They are only concerned with display of ostentation. (Psychology Today July-August 1998).

In post-Communist Russia pedestrians are terrorisedto such an extent that walkers huddle together seeking safety in numbers while trying to cross the road. The Walk sign at traffic signals means nothing to motorists. They do not know the meaning of culture. (ABC TV 6-11-05).

In a drive to humanize the traffic system the police have started giving incentives to polite motorists. They are given free entry in lotteries and given appreciation souvenirs. Polite motorists carry stickers on their windshields 'I let pedestrians pass.'

The terrorist attack on the World Trade Centre caused a horrific loss of life. But the death toll on roads is equivalent to a 9/11 tragedy every day. One reason this does not trouble the world's conscience to that extent is that a vast majority of victims are poor and from the poorest countries. Every time there is a plane or rail crash there is a big furore. But the automobile's killing thousands of people every day makes little news.

Suppose 245,000 Americans had died in terrorist attacks since September 11, 2001. That is the number of Americans killed in road accidents since that date till 2007. But the September 11 attack has been used for justifying the war in Iraq and has caused death of hundreds of American soldiers.

Road crash is the fastest rising cause of death in the world. But one hears more about avian influenza than over a million being killed by the motor car each year. In 2006 1.2 million people were killed in road crashes against an estimated 100,000 in combat. It is for the first time in history that the last decade showed that roads are more dangerous than wars.

One reason deaths caused by vehicles are downplayed is that cars are big advertisers on television and in newspapers and fetch so much revenue to the media.

The most visible evidence of the lack of democracy in our public life is the absence of footpaths. While motor vehicles, belonging to the privileged sections arrogantly rule the roads, pedestrians are treated like third class citizens without a rightful space to walk, constantly facing the risk of being knocked down and injured.

A very large number of accident victims are pedestrians. The fault lies mainly with rash driving and authorities who fail to provide safety to pedestrians. But usually the pedestrian is blamed. That is the real sinister part. It is as if people want to die on roads at the hands of motorists.

The extent of cars hitting pedestrians is now so widespread that a question asked by a management expert all over the world to other managers pertains to this phenomenon. In fact, his management book is titled 'Did the Pedestrian Die?.

The author Fons Trompenaars tells the managers about a man driving with his friend, exceeds the speed limit and hits a pedestrian on the road. The question posed to the managers is that if you were the motorist's friend would you testify against him ?.

The question, the author says, was asked in 65 countries to nearly 65,000 managers. The general answer in the US and Europe was that they would testify against the friend while many in Venezuela and China said No. The author attributes this to a higher level of ethical behaviour among managers in the West.

There is much greater chance of being killed by an automobile in America than by a stranger with a gun, a study by FBI (federal bureau of investigation) has shown. But while there is a justifiable uproar on gun shooting, there is little on the killing of pedestrians. Similarly, in India a mentally challenged person, who is normally perfectly harmless, is seen as a much bigger threat than a rash motorist. This happens mainly because of a widespread prejudice against the poor and a tendency to take lightly crimes committed by the wealthy.

For motorists life is now much safer. There is the mandatory crash testing of cars, seat belt laws, drunk driving programmes and road construction and redesign efforts. Pedestrian safety on the other hand has focused largely on telling pedestrians to get out of the way, as if they are pests.

In New Bombay or Navi Mumbai the fanciful sounding Palm Beach road has become a death trap for the poor as the rich use it as a racing track.

A lobby of motorists in the U.K. want to drive like zombies, oppose speed limits and say they are such good drivers they can never make a mistake and cause an accident. There is a similar anti-social class in India. But there are many dissenters. John Rentoul, the political commentator of the Independent on Sunday, does not own a car, does not like driving in a metal box and demands a severe limit on speed.

The much touted Mumbai-Pune expressway has proved to be graveyard for motorists and has the highest rate of accidents per km of highway (Hindustan Times 26-8-05). It keeps the large Lokmanya hospital at Nigdi near Pune busy with constant arrivals of accident victims. Dr Parag Modak, a specialist in trauma cases, said in six years there was not a single day when he did not come across accident cases. Dr Kumar Rakshe, in charge of medical services on the expressway said a large number of accidents were related to drunken, speedy driving and lack of sleep and rest. Speed was the main culprit, said S.R. Tambe, a senior road engineer and former secretary of the public works department of Maharashtra. Most people died due to tyre burst and it was found that the quality of tyres and road surface is not suitable for fast driving. The accident figures have doubled on the expressway as compared to the old Mumbai Pune highway.

One of the few voluntary bodies working for accident prevention and medical help is the Rajashri Parmar memorial foundation set up by her father Chandmal following her death in a road accident.

In Chennai road crash deaths have nearly doubled since 2004. The CT scan equipment in a leading hospital does not function after 5 p.m. and often there is no neurologist on duty in hospital at night. Patients are sent from one hospital to another and there is an increase in the number of people using the wheel chair and crutches. (TOI 16-1-09).

There is a clear-cut relation between poverty and road deaths. The more poor a person is the chances of his or her dying in a road accident are higher. Besides, there are far more deaths in poor countries as against advanced countries. Within richer countries though the accident death rate is declining, the poorer people are victims in much larger numbers than the rich. This is amply demonstrated in a study conducted by Vinand Nantulya and Michael Reich of the Harvard Center for Population and Development Studies, U.S.

Even among motorists there is a big difference of class, the higher ones dominate the ones below. There are only a few like Prof Shreekant Gupta of the Delhi school of Economics who fight back against discrimination.

Prof Gupta was driving in Delhi when the motorcade of the Lt Governor of Delhi came menacingly from behind. The police threatened him with dire consequences for not yielding way to the VIP.

Mr Gupta said there is hardly a driver in Delhi who has not been rudely and abruptly elbowed aside by a VIP's car or motorcade which appears out of nowhere, sirens blaring, lights flashing and menacing security flunkies in tow. These high speed convoys are like mini tornadoes which bulldoze their way through traffic and signals leving a trail of chaos in their wake.

Mr Gupta says the VIP motorcades are a metaphor for a deeper malaise which is the predatory nature of the Indian state. It is no longer, perhaps never was, a welfare state. Like its motorcades, it is a state that elbows aside the political and economic emancipation of its citizens to make way for its own kleptocracy. Several leaders whether it is Mulayam Singh of Samajwadi party or Bal Thackeray, Shiv Sena chief, are known to travel in large motorcades. Motor cars are also used in the exercise of one-upmanship by politicians. It was this display of motor cars by Shiv Sena leader Raj Thackeray that led to a major confrontation with rebel Sena leader, later Maharashtra revenue minister, Narayan Rane, in the Konkan region in 2005.

Udhav Thackeray is known for breaching security by driving his Mercedes without taking with him the police security officer who is trained like a commando.

Former deputy chief minister and home minister R.R. Patil is known for sitting in front rolling down the pane of his bullet-proof car. (HT 23-6-06).

Formerly criminals used dark glass for their cars, now the rich and policemen use this in breach of norms, to gain privacy.

The vulgar rich flout all democratic norms on roads. There are very few exceptions like the late Mr J.R.D. Tata, industrialist, who made it a point to give a lift to anyone in his car and made sure his car followed rules. Mr Darbari Seth, former director of Tata Chemicals, encouraged bicycling and walking in the company's plant at Mithapur.

People lose their life and limb because of the arrogance of the rich on roads and the sadder part is that it is difficult to get compensation from courts. It takes years to get relief for various reasons. Posts of judges remain vacant and thousands of cases pile up. Some years ago the motor accident tribunal courts were located on the fourth floor of a building in the Fountain area in Mumbai. One can imagine the difficulty faced by crippled accident victims to reach the court, leave alone get justice.

While the poor are the main victims of road accidents and are often left to die on the roadside, VIPs get all the attention. When external affairs minister Pranab Mukherjee was injured in a road accident in West Bengal in 2007, he was immediately airlifted to Delhi and got the best treatment in a military hospital. From the accident site he had to be taken to a nearby hospital in an auto-rickshaw like an ordinary man.

Mr H.Y. Sharada Prasad, a former adviser to the Prime Minister, wonders what is gained by covering the two km distance between South Block and the Prime Minister's residence in two minutes instead of four minutes. Mr Sharada Prasad, who travelled in the Prime Minister's convoy for several years, says he used to be in constant dread that some arrogant driver would lose control and plough through a crowd or ram into a tree.

Delhi is full of civil servants who are very conscious of their status, they are the most uncivil of people, Mr Sharada Prasad says.

Our rich want to drive fast but the highways are not well designed and not safe, especially for pedestrians who have few safe crossings.

Many stretches of the new highways have deep stormwater drains running along them in the middle or on the side. Others are on high embankments without wide enough shoulders or protective guard rails. Such elements of road space function like booby traps killing and maiming motorists if they stray off the road for any reason.

The corporate sector is a big killer on roads, though, the lorry driver is normally the target of attack of mob frenzy and the media. Nearly three million trucks ply on Indian roads daily and of these nearly 90 per cent carry overloads of between between 50 and 80 per cent, says reputed, no-nonsense journalist Sucheta Dalal, quoting a nationwide study. (Indian Express 16-10-05).

All overloaded trucks are insured and insurance companies would be within rights to deny payment. But palm-greasing goes on at all levels. So when an accident takes place, the police suppress the overload factor. Everyone makes money while the victim loses life or limb. Can anything be more cold blooded ?

The greed of a few factory owners is responsible for the mess, said Baljit Singh Bal, convenor of the action committee of truck owners.

Mr R.K. Raghavan, a former director of CBI (central bureau of investigation) and writer, says it is not uncommon to find that if a driver is found to be under the influence of liquor in an accident, this fact is often suppressed. Not only that efforts are made to show that the victim himself was drunk.

Accident investigation is a serious science but this is not taken seriously in India. More than any other area of police work it is here that there is a definite scope for the use of science and technology if only to make investigation more acceptable.

Mr Raghavan said he came across a professor at a leading engineering school in Austria who had developed an expertise in accident investigations and was being consulted by both the police and insurance companies in coming to conclusions on how exactly an accident occurred. The tyre marks of a vehicle after the accident and the nature and extent of damage suffered by different parts of an automobile are all significant indicators which are unfortunately ignored by most of our investigators.

There is little road accident research done in India though India accounts for the highest number of accidents in the world.

China, which was on top of the ugly chart, has considerably reduced its rate of accidents while India's accident rate continues to increase.

In a way the Indian State is responsible at least partly for the massacre of the innocents on the road. A high level committee appointed by the Central government concluded in 2007 that existing institutions are not fully equipped to deal with the rising road traffic and road safety is not taken seriously in the country.

The committee was headed by Mr S. Sundar, senior fellow, Tata Energy Research Institute and a former secretary of the ministry of surface transport. Other members included Dr P.S. Pasricha, former director general of police, Maharashtra, Prof Dinesh Mohan and Prof Geetam Tiwari of IIT, Delhi, Dr Verghese Matthew, a medical expert, Mr D.P.Gupta, former director general, road development in the transport ministry in Delhi, Mr Rohit Baluja of the Institute of Road and Traffic Education, Mr P.C. Chaturvedi, Mr G Gururaj, Mr A.P. Bahadur, Mr Ramnath Jakhu, Mr Jagdish Khattar, managing director, Maruti Udyog, and S.K. Dash, joint secretary, union transport ministry.

The committee noted that though road accidents killed many more people than epidemics the amount spent on prevention of road deaths was much less. For example tuberculosis accounted for 37,000 deaths in the year 2004 and road accidents killed 92,000 in the same year. But the government plan allocation for TB for 2002-2007 was Rs 680 crore and for road accidents it was just Rs 187 crore.

In India in many cases the police are a problem, not the solution. People have come to accept corruption but insensitivity in the killing of innocents by motorist is clearly unacceptable.

Aggressive behaviour is central to the mindset of motorists in an anti-social environment. 'Have you ever experienced your mind engaging in murderous thoughts towards other drivers on highways during rush hours ? If you have, you are not alone, says a researcher Linda Luizzi.

This is a direct result of an environment in which the interests of the automobile are allowed to prevail over those of the people, according to Kenneth Schneider, author of the book Autokind vs Mankind, one of the earliest critiques of the motor car which he sees as anti-human, anti-social.

Several fancy hospitals in the country are notorious for flouting government regulations. In Maharashtra private hospitals have to earmark about ten per cent of beds for free treatment of the poor but the provision is invariably flouted. The hospitals claim to be run as charitable hospitals and secure a number of concessions from the government. But they fail to show basic humanity towards other human beings.

Many are permanently maimed due to accidents and this is a fate worse than death. There are only a few like Arun Sondhi who do well in life after being maimed and reduced to the wheel chair. Sondhi, a St Stephen's college student was badly injured while riding a motor cycle in Delhi in 1983. He was lucky to have been taken to the state of the art rehabiltation centre in Sweden. Later he became an instructor in the same institute and represented Sweden in weightlifting for paraplegic Olympics in Atlanta and won a gold medal, setting a record. He also set up a successful software company. He now makes frequent trips to India, works with institutions to improve the quality of wheel chairs and helps the disabled rediscover their inner strength, to learn to be completely independent again. (Pankaj Butalia IE 20-10-07).

Mr Dinesh Mohan, transport expert, says recording of road deaths is reasonably all right in India but injuries are very much under-reported. That means the poor, who get injured, have no chance of getting any compensation as their cases are not registered at all by the police.

A farmer injured by a jeep carrying former Prime Minister Rajiv Gandhi and Sonia Gandhi in 1999 had not received compensation from the Congress party even after a court verdict. Rajiv Gandhi was on his way to file his nomination when his vehicle ran over the farmer Dharmaraj Mishra. A

Congress MLA, driving the vehicle, allegedly destroyed the medical records of the farmer. (IE 1-6-08).

In many hit and run accidents a case is not even filed because the vehicle may have sped away without anyone noting down the number of the vehicle. The police rarely follow up properly unless the victim is high profile (Swati Deshpande. Times of India. 18-4- 2005).

The standard practice is to book the accused for rash and negligent driving, a bailable offence punishable by a maximum of two years in jail And few people ever get convicted. The more serious charge of culpable homicide is not registered even when the culprit caused death after being drunk and reckless. The signal sent out to anti-social elements is you can kill someone and get away with a token fine or a few months in jail.

Sometimes there are no witnesses, sometimes witnesses are simply bought. In the case of Sanjeev Nanda, grandson of former Indian Navy chief Admiral S.M. Nanda, the witnesses turned hostile. Six persons were killed in a gruesome incident under the expensive BMW car driven by Sanjeev Nanda, a U.S. educated young man in January, 1999 near Lodhi hotel in New Delhi.

Nanda and his friends including Siddharth Gupta were returning after a late night party at Sainik Farms and were reported to be drunk. The car was reportedly driven at a speed of 140 km per hour. Two of the victims were policemen. After the incident the young men went to the house of Siddharth Gupta at Golf Links and the blood stains on the car were washed. All youths belong to high society.

The BMW was not even registered and Nanda did not have a driving licence. The car was traced as an alert policeman noticed that an oil leak from the vehicle led to the Golf Links house.

The case took a dramatic turn in 2007 when NDTV television news channel telecast scenes in which the defence lawyer was seen to be discussing bribe of nearly Rs 2.5 crore to a key witness Sunil Kulkarni so that he does not depose in the case. The hidden camera showed the prosecution lawyer I.U. Khan and defence lawyer and former Rajya Sabha member R.K. Anand working in tandem to save the accused.

Even school students have now started celebrating their secondary school examination results by drunken driving. The incidence was found to be higher than on new year eve, the police said. (TOI 11-6-07).

It was only after media focus on drunken driving deaths that the Mumbai police launched a drive and for the first time the culprits were sent to jail in 2007. The big number of cases of drunken driving detected during a drive surprised even the traffic police. Most people caught drinking think they are in control of the vehicle, said joint traffic police commissioner Vijay Kamble.

Manish Khatau from a rich industrialist family in Mumbai allegedly drove so fast that he slammed into barricades near Police Gymkhana at Marine Drive. One of these went flying at a traffic constable, Jitendra Rokde, 40, who was seriously injured and lost much of his forehead. Khatau, 20, reportedly tried to speed away but was arrested after a chase. When the police opened the car door, the entire vehicle was reeking of liquor, said deputy police commissioner Naval Bajaj.

Manish was not put in police lock-up and was shown special consideration after his arrest. One officer told journalists 'He is only a Bachha (lad), he did not do it intentionally.'

Sometimes the parents and relatives of rich kids do not accept that the kids have committed a serious crime and instead of being apologetic, they choose to shout at the police insultingly. Rich, young rash drivers also threaten police when questioned.

Khatau was acquitted by a fast-track court and it was widely felt the police had acted rather leniently. Shockingly, immediately after the acquittal Manish and his parents met

Maharashtra's home minister R.R. Patil in his official bungalow. The minister had a word of advice to the young man 'do not drive rashly.' (Mumbai Mirror 28-4-06).

We are afraid of stepping out of the house at night for fear of being run over by some manic driver, complained Anil Bhatia, secretary of the Marine Drive Residents Association. He said the association sometimes rushed victims of hit- and – run accidents to hospital. Police are often helpless as the arrogant kids flaunt their connections.

Pune is an ideal city for potential citizens' activism. Once it was the bicycle city. In the thirties Shakuntala Paranjpye, Marathi writer and mother of film maker Sai Paranjpye, used to attract a lot of attention by riding a bicycle on the streets of the city. Now, the city is overtaken by big money and its middle class, once famous for its social activism, has now become too placid, complacent and has lost the zest for a fight. Traffic is now as bad as in Mumbai, there are few footpaths and public transport is weak. City buses are uncomfortable, crowded and it is not rare to find breakdowns on the road or even smoke coming out of the engine.

The car of Salman Khan, film star, ran over four people killing one of them in 2002 when they were sleeping on Hill Road in Bandra, after a hard day's work in the popular local bakery A 1. It was very rashly driven allegedly under the influence of liquor. Salman Khan, was returning home from a luxury hotel late in the night on September 28, 2002. Initially denied that he was at the wheel.

Police bodyguard Ravindra Patil, a key witness, failed to appear in the court in several hearings in 2005 despite arrest warrants. He died as a destitute in 2007 of tuberculosis, reduced to a skeleton.

Unfortunately, even after committing serious crimes film stars go scot-free because many politicians, bureaucrats and businesspersons with a pitifully low cultural level, hanker after them because of their glamour. There is an apt cartoon by Mario

Miranda showing a drunk film star knocking down a pedestrian. And then comes a traffic constable running to the film star saying 'Aaah, may I have your autograph, Sar.'

In the notorious Alistair Pereira case of drunken driving a Toyoto Corolla car crashed into the huts of of municipal construction workers killing seven of them in their sleep on the pavement on the posh seaside Carter Road in Bandra in 2006. The incident also showed how badly housed are workers engaged in the project of converting Mumbai into a world class city.

Two years after the crash, one of the survivors Ramlo Harijan had spent thousands of rupees on treatment but got no compensation from the motor accident claims tribunal. He was among 20,000 people waiting for their compensation from the understaffed tribunal.

The youths had consumed liquor in a five-star hotel Taj Land's End at Bandra Band Stand at a party hosted by a liquor company. The alleged culprit Alistair Pereira, declared that it was just an accident and he felt no remorse for it. He was also later charged with committing forgery to obtain a driver's licence when he was only 15 years of age.

Worse, after the incident the authorities began a drive to evict people sleeping on footpaths as they were seen as a nuisance, not the victims. And a section of the upper class too blamed the poor for sleeping on the pavement, saying that it was their fault. But if people were walking on the footpath at the time, they would certainly have been killed.

Severe strictures were passed against the Mumbai police by the sessions and high court for poor investigation into the case. Though this was a highly publicized case the police failed to produce basic documents like medical reports of the victims or to examine key witnesses resulting in Pereira getting only six months' jail in the sessions court.

Parents can be charged with an offence in case of serious accident caused by someone driving with a fake licence, according to Mumbai's joint traffic police commissioner Satish

Mathur. If parents give a car to their child of 15, how can we blame the child, asks Sunil Merchant, president of the Western India Automobile Association. Mr Julio Riberiro, former Mumbai police commissioner, also felt parents needed to be punished.

About 1000 Parsis rode on their motorcycles from Dadar Parsi Gymkhana to Andheri and back in January, 2008 to focus on the tiny community's dwindling numbers and its love for the vehicle. I think Parsis were born with motorbikes between their legs, said Neville Choksi, vintage bike collector.

Delhi is the graveyard of the underprivileged as many more die in road accidents. Children, especially those belonging to the lower and lower middle class have to ferry over long distances in the absence of good state-run schools in their neighbourhood. But with public space in Delhi being usurped by the affluent few and private transport businessmen, who drive recklessly to make a quick buck, accidents increase, points out Mr Amar Farooqui.

The worst such accident took place on November 18, 1997 when an overcrowded school bus plunged into the Yamuna river at Delhi killing 30 school children.

Two years later 41 school children were drowned in the Narmada when the State Transport bus crashed from a bridge near Vadodara in Gujarat. The bus was in a rickety condition and it is common to find such buses on rural roads where the poor have little chance to complain.

With the state completely abdicating responsibility for good quality education, the middle class sends its children to private schools which are far away from homes. A most irrational and inefficient transport system is visible on the streets and main roads of Delhi every working morning and afternoon. Enormous resources are used to transport children. The sheer scale of this activity is mind-boggling, school buses, private buses, public buses, taxies, autorickshaws, cycle rickshaws, vans, jeeps, cars, mini buses and all types of two-wheelers are engaged.

In Mumbai school buses were found to be keeping emergency exits closed or locked, their drivers were without licence, there were no attendants and the vehicles lacked a fitness certificate following raids ordered by transport commissioner Deepak Kapoor in 2009.

Not only school buses but other private city transport buses have earned notoriety for terror on roads. The system of giving incentives to conductors and drivers for faster trips adds to speeding and danger. In both the cities the conductors and drivers under tremendous pressure to make fast trips often lose their cool and have started attacking passengers, event pushing them out.

Responding to pedestrian deaths cased by buses and trucks West Bengal's transport minister Subas Chakravarty chose to blame the victims, displaying enormous insensitivity. (Telegraph 7-9-07).

In Kolkata riding to school in the so-called pool cars is extremely hazardous for students, many of them are huddled into these vehicles. A drunk driver of one car, carrying eight students, rammed into a stationary bus as he was talking on the mobile phone. When seven such cars were impounded, all the drivers went on strike leaving 25,000 students stranded. (Telegraph 20-12-07).

Hospitals routinely turn away road accident victims as they cannot produce the hefty amcunts as deposits in Kolkata resulting in several deaths. (Telegraph 8-12-07).

In Shanghai the government has a new class enemy, the pedestrian as Time magazine put it (17-07-06). Nearly 112,000 pedestrians were slapped with a fine of six dollars each in 2006 in a drive to discipline common people for the World Expo event for 2010. Pictures of some of the alleged culprits were printed in the papers and their increments withheld by their employers. A woman who contested the fine was jailed for six days.

In Delhi several of the private 'killer Blue Line buses are owned by politicians, their henchmen and policemen. They ensure that private buses get more passengers at the cost of the state-owned DTC (Delhi Transport Corporation) buses. (Powerful Patrons of Killer Buses.Tehelka weekly. 22-9-07). So that is how privatization works through unfair, corrupt, inefficient means.

Vijay Goel, a leader of the BJP (Bharatiya Janata party) and former union minister, drove a Blueline bus from the party office to the chief minister's house a couple of km away without a proper licence to draw attention to the menace on the road. He was arrested but only for protesting on the road not for licence infringement. (TOI 11-10-07)

Following the controversy men of the Air Force and the Navy were deployed on the streets of Delhi to help the police in checking traffic offences. Delhi's Lt Governor Tejendra Khanna said if the police officers think they can control traffic sitting inside their offices they are living in a fool's paradise. (TOI 11-10-07).

In some of the Western countries equal attention is paid to pedestrian safety while designing cars. The front part of the car is designed in such a way that in case of an accident, the pedestrian suffers minimum impact and injury. Such concerns are unheard of in India.

Usually, large number of residents come out in protest after accidents. But otherwise citizens are quite apathetic towards the menace of arrogant motorists. All that they do is to demand constructing of speed breakers or humps on the road to check vehicular speeds. Mr Baba Siddiqui, Maharashtra's former minister of state for housing, has been consistently campaigning for retaining of speed breakers.

Marshall McLuhan, the distinguished media critic, points out that emotionally the violence of millions of cars in our streets was incomparably more serious than anything else. All the rhinos and hippos and elephants in the world if gathered in one city could not begin to create the menace and explosive intensity of the menacing internal combustion engine.

Transport expert Dinesh Mohan says it is very crucial to limit vehicle speeds for traffic safety. It is not enough to improve the design of vehicles. However, in India the top priority for the system seems to help vehicles go as fast as possible without hindrance.

He says we can reduce road accidents only if our society and politicians understand the ethical and moral responsibility of the state and civil society to ensure the right to life of all its citizens. The right to life includes living in good health. Maharashtra accounts for the highest road accidents and deaths in the country but is completely callous on the issue. The Central government offered financial assistance to state governments in 2007 for trauma care centers for road accident victims but the Maharashtra government failed to take advantage of the scheme. (TOI 4-1-08).

Worse, it is yielding to superstition by seeking to ward off evil by installing pyramids of the so-called Vastu Shastra in accident-prone zones. And the admission has come from none other than the police commissioner of Nagpur (rural), Yashasvi Yadav, while releasing a booklet on traffic rules. He claimed that no accidents had taken at spots where these devices were installed. (TOI 10-5-08).

Road safety research in the advanced countries has involved a large number of very gifted professionals from a variety of disciplines over the past four decades. Some very innovative work has resulted in a theoretical understanding of accidents as part of a complex interaction of sociological, psychological, physical and technological phenomenon.

But clearly, the mindset of the political elite too will have to change. It is surprising that Kerala's former chief minister K Karunakaran should be so crazy about speed. He has frequently met with accidents and attributed his survival to the deity of Guruvayoor.

Once he drew a lot of flak for his public statement that he liked to travel at the maximum speed. 'I did get involved in a number of accidents in which many were injured. But so far nothing has happened to me.

India accounts for the highest number of road deaths in the world and the number must be actually much higher because accidents are severely under-reported because of lack of education, corruprion and callousness.

Fatalities have been increasing at about five per cent a year over the past two decades. (Road Safety Digest. 2004 of Loss Prevention Association of India) shockingly, the government has allowed the disbanding of the association which was doing useful work. Lack of money is cited as the reason which shows the callousness over a major issue.

In developed countries there are roads parallel to limited access expressways and these are used by vehicles not allowed on expressways. In India highways pass through rural areas with high density populations where most of the people do not have access to motor vehicles. Four lane divided highways in India do not have parallel road links for slow and non-motorised traffic. This forces slow and non-motorised vehicles to use these highways and to cross them under very hazardous conditions for all concerned.

It is not surprising that a majority of victims of road crashes on inter city highways are the vulnerable road users.

Dinesh Mohan warns that teaching traffic sense to children is by no means enough or helpful. On the contrary, such education can make them very confident without necessary cognitive and mobility skills. This in turn may increase the chance of being involved in a crash. This fact seems extremely important and is little-known.

Mr Mohan's observation is also extremely important considering that traffic authorities indirectly pass on the blame for traffic accidents on children. They think they have done their bit and if an accident has taken place, the child must be responsible. This is absolutely irresponsible thinking. Moreover, the authorities shirk their most basic duty of providing footpaths which are crucial for child safety. Actually, they deserve to be charged with child slaughter. This may seem a harsh judgement but if one just goes around and observes the utter lack of basic facilities on roads, this would seem far from harsh.

Studies in the UK show that safety education literature does not actually reduce the incident of road traffic crashes. This may increase knowledge of children and others but this does not translate into greater safety. What are known as accidents are crashes or collisions, someone is always responsible for the incident. The word accident makes it out as if it was something unavoidable, beyond the control of the driver etc.

The word accident has been banished from the highway code in the UK in an attempt to persuade motorists and police that someone is always to blame for injury and death on roads. One cannot evade responsibility. (Times 12-5-07). The word accident encourages police that no action need be taken. UK has brought down road deaths from 9000 in 1931 to 3100 in 2006.

Use of seatbelts and airbags can increase safety for motorists but this can also make drivers more confident and aggressive. Their chances of driving recklessly and hurting, killing others increase.

Traffic calming, that is reducing the number of vehicles on the road, is a very effective technique and has shown significant safety benefits. Narrower an urban road is, there are fewer chances of accidents. This is confirmed through studies.

There has been a long standing under investment in infrastructure for vulnerable road users and in the design and construction of our cities and intermodal points (bus stops, tram and train stations), Dinesh Mohan points out. He is absolutely right. Look at the investment on flyovers and expressways which benefit mainly the motor car lobby. In a hot country they do not even have the decency to provide bus shelters at many places. See how well equipped airports are. If bus depots and train stations are allocated more funds, provided more facilities, made cleaner, there will be a great increase in civic sense and pride among the people. Also, there must be separate lanes for bicycles and compulsory provision of footpaths.

States run by the Left and democratic forces in India are by no means models of good traffic norms.Kerala is a wonderful, green state. But travel here can be scary as vehicles drive really fast on narrow, winding roads without protection of footpaths to people walking on the road. A pity that this happens in such a green, beautiful state with a high literacy rate, harmonious community relations and generally a high level of political consciousness.

One can never be safe in a car-dominated environment even in countries with a high civic awareness and driving manners. In England nearly 15 per cent drivers have admitted to be close to falling asleep at the wheel, according to a survey conducted by the Royal Automobile Club (RAC). And many said this happened more than once.

The RAC recommends that one should not drive for more than two hours at a stretch. If you are driving on a busy motorway, remember there could be as many as 20 drivers within a mile or two of you whose eyelids are dropping. That is really scary.

In India if you hire a vehicle, just see the driver's face, his eyes. It would be clear he needs rest badly. Usually the driver gets the blame when an accident occurs but often the real culprit is the owner who in pursuit of increased profit makes him overwork.

The biggest story of road rage in India involves. Navjot Singh Sidhu, former Test cricketer, jolly, joke-cracking high profile TV cricket commentator and judge at mimicry contests.

Psychological studies show that the motor car tends to create in-built feelings of hostility, superiority and alienation in the motorist on crowded roads. Aggressiveness and a macho feeling are promoted by car manufacturers. Look at the names of some of the cars Jaguar, Mustang and Speedster. Our own Maruti derives its name from the flying Hanuman of the Ramayana.

Indian drivers are so bad that Prime Minister Manmohan Singh posed a question to motorists 'where are your manners ?' while inaugurating a ten-lane road project at electronics city in Bangalore (TOI 24-6-06). He said wind-swept roads and fancy cars did not denote progress, good manners and discipline do. Motorists should learn to respect pedestrians, how to park, not to blow the horn unnecessarily and not to flout rules while overtaking.

The car can be a private bubble that allows Mr Hyde in the motorist to emerge when he is aroused. This explains the wave of murders related to traffic tensions.

The sad part is that the more safe a motorist becomes because of the seatbelt and other facilities, he or she becomes more confident and arrogant and life becomes more insecure for the pedestrian or the cyclist. That is because now the motorist knows that when he is rash, he does not get hurt, the other person suffers.

This is confirmed by tests carried out in England, according to the British Medical Journal. An indication is that seatbelt enforcement has resulted in reduced accidents and injuries for motorists and increase in injuries for pedestrians and cyclists.

The steering wheel of a motor car has the same effect on a modern, civilized man as the smell of blood as on the average tiger. The Japanese are normally very polite. But once they get behind the steering wheel, they can be deadly, says the humorist George Mikes in his book The Land of the Rising Yen.

The real reason people buy these monstrous vehicles is to intimidate people in smaller cars, according to Car-free Times, an anti-car journal. They know that passengers in an SUV will be safe in case of a collision and those in cars will be killed.

Another reason why people buy SUVs is that many Americans are growing up in isolation, in suburban fortresses. They are afraid of their fellowmen and want to protect themselves. And SUVs are considered safer. The number of SUVs on the road suggests a social breakdown in the US. When people care so little about the consequences of their acts so as to buy dangerous vehicles, what does it say about the health of social ties that once bound American society together, experts wonder.

The monster vehicles should carry a warning that they are dangerous on the road, wrote the British Medical Journal editorial. Desmond O'neil, professor of medical gerontology at Trinity college in Dublin and co-author of the editorial said 'if you hit a pedestrian with an SUV you increase the chances of the victim's dying two to four times. The SUV hits the head and abdomen, more vulnerable areas while other cars hit legs and are less deadly.

In Mumbai motorists park on pedestrian crossings at signals even in front of the state government headquarters Mantralaya. Mr V.W. Pradhan, a retired inspector general of police, who lives near Mantralaya, has complained to the police and the home secretary many times with little effect.

The offending vehicles include those of ministers, bureaucrats and police officers, he says and this is absolutely true.

The cult of the car also means that the car is valued above human beings. This is best illustrated in a cartoon by veteran R.K. Laxman which shows a heavily bandaged man sitting in his bed in hospital. His wife exclaims 'Good heavens. What happened to our car ?' (Times of India 20-7-2000).

Sadism is closely associated with the car cult. Many enjoy computer games in which you drag out someone from the car, beat him or her and steal money. One of the most violent video games in America is Grand Theft Auto 3 which shows wantonly antisocial carjacking escapades in which players are rewarded for having sex with a prostitute, killing her and stealing her money.

It is no problem in the computer game to grab a rifle and shoot innocent pedestrians (blood spurts from their heads when they are hit) or to toss a grenade in a busy city intersection or to simply whale passersby with a baseball bat until they collapse in writhing heaps (New York Times. 12-5-02).

The role of transnational companies and trade in killing innocent people on roads is brought out well in a study by Ian Roberts, professor of public health in the school of social hygiene and tropical medicine in London.

He says economic globalisation generates huge goods traffic and longer journeys. Big companies are not visible at the scene of accidents but they are responsible for the deaths as they force drivers to drive fast. Much of the international trade is not between countries but between big transnational companies. It is these vested interests who want cheap transport, cheap oil and good roads, preferably paid for by the public.

Road accidents are the single most neglected aspect of public health in the world though these account for more deaths than malaria and tuberculosis (TB). Yet, expenditure on treating victims is far less than in treating malaria and TB patients. Nearly 50 million people are injured in crashes each year, mostly in poorer countries. We have wrongly come to accept road accident deaths as inevitable, as part of a car-dominated society.

The issue of road deaths is neglected because rich countries are responsible for causing most accidents through increased transport in poor countries and this is seen as the unavoidable price for doing business. As global transport industry expands so will the death toll. (Guardian 16-5-07).

WHO (World Health Organisation) has shown much more awareness of injuries to pedestrians and cyclists in its report while a study by private automobile companies and other interests has played down the fact that pedestrians and cyclists are the main victims.

Poor countries in a bid to reduce road accidents may now drive away pedestrians and cyclists from the road and this will be a classic case of enclosures through which the rich are able to secure the resources of the poor, says Monbiot.

The World Bank and other donor agencies countries are blamed for road accidents and injuries in developing countries for building unsafe roads. They have failed to earmark funds to ensure that a significant portion is earmarked for safety measures, according to David Ward, director general of FIA Foundation set up by automobile associations. The organizations are making life worse for common people. (Guardian 23-4-07).

A World Bank team, which came to India to assess highways in 2006, has criticsed the highway upgradation plan of the National highway authority of India terming road safety as a serious problem on the highways.

Talking even on hands-free cell phone and driving is dangerous because talking distracts attention. However, regulation against cell use while driving is not strict because of pressure from the phone companies. The New York High Traffic Safety administration quashed a proposal of a large scale study of cell phone risks and withheld hundreds of pages of research that warned about the dangers of cell phone use. The fact that 955 people were killed and 240,000 accidents were caused in 2002 due to cell phone use was withheld from the public. (New York Times 22-7-09). It is more dangerous than drunken driving.

People talk on phone while driving because of intense social pressure to stay in touch and be always available to friends and collegues. There is also the neurological question of addiction to gadgets. When people use digital devices, they get a burst of adrenalin dopamine squirt without which people get bored. The modern brain is being rewired to crave stimulation. It is an acquired attention deficit disorder, psychologists point out. There are too many attention distracting devices in cars nowadays. So despite all the safety measures in cars and safe roads, accidents soar partly because of the devices.

Auto companies are busy creating new crack hits for our self-destructive cravings. Ford is developing a system that would let drivers use phones and music players and surf the internet with voice commands and audible responses. Sounds like a computerized death machine, says Maureen Dowd, columnist.

While genuine accident victims find it tough to get compensation, unscrupulous elements have cooked up bogus accident cases to make crores of rupees in league with corrupt elements in the insurance, police and motor vehicles department.

Stunts performed by John Abraham in the film Dhoom and more recently by Hrithik Roshan in the film Dhoom II have misled several youngsters. Some have even committed thefts to buy motor cycles.

Worse, television advertisements glamorize stunts and reckless driving. This forced Mumbai's joint commission for traffic Vijay Kamble to appeal to the Advertising Council of India to crack down on advertisements encouraging youths to perform dangerous stunts.

Buses for children of elite schools are these days fitted with special safety devices. Dhirubhai Ambani interanational school, named after the prominent industrialist, has buses with seat belts for every child and padded grab bars in front to soften the impact in case of sudden use of brakes. Each bus has a woman conductor.

The incidence of chauffeur driven car trips to school for children was reduced only because of huge traffic jams. For non-elite children conditions are bad. Usually the worst buses are used for carrying school children, said top rung traffic police official P.S. Pasricha.

Children lower down in the social ladder are huddled together in auto-rickshaws and cycle rickshaws in extremely unsafe conditions.

Walking to school campaigns as in Britain are unheard of in India and walking to school in India is highly hazardous. This is nothing but cruelty to children. Surely, the future generations deserve a better deal.

Besides, heavy vehicular traffic on highways and other roads severely disrupts the lives of rural communities. Many people have no option but to cross the highway or other roads to reach facilities like hospitals and schools. And the state takes little care for their safety.

Very often officials are not worried so much about loss of life and limb of ordinary people but about traffic disruption caused by accidents.

The authorities are only interested in ensuring speedy movement of private cars. That is why they have sought curbs on movement of buses because they halt often on roads to take in and off load passengers.

The bus stand of the State Transport corporation in Dadar in the heart of Mumbai was sought to be shifted by the traffic police in 2005 although this would cause great inconvenience to thousands of people. This was done cynically to give priority to car traffic. Private bus operators were ironically allowed to do business at the busy spot, possibly because they can bribe the cops while the ST cannot do that.

The increased availability of tuning kits that transform an ordinary two-stroke engine into a beast for Rs 1200 to Rs 7,000 emitting menacing noise has welled the ranks of bikers. Rich youngsters spend over Rs 100,000 on renovating, ugrading their bikes, increasing their speed and noise level. Of course, the silencers are removed to create maximum sound. Thre is a big craze to modify the bikes, said Bonito, son of car stylist Dilip Chhabria, who is known for re-designing cars. People are willing to spend lakhs of rupees on these things.

Concrete roads are dangerous and not conducive at all for racing. Tar roads are much safer because of the grip, says Praveen Sathe, a founder of Yedzi club. What is more dangerous is that 90 per cent of these bikers do not wear helmets.

The Yezdi club organized races in Chennai and Bangalore due to dearth of racing strips in Mumbai. The Juhu aerodrome used to be a popular spot before permission was revoked a few years ago.

A new threat emerging on roads comes from the rich and famous and corporate executives who drive drunk and recklessly at night scaring, maiming, killing innocent people. Mr Neel Chaterjee, vice-president and head of the corporate divison for Asia of Standard Chartered Bank was arrested by the police in Mumbai on 2006, for drunken driving and causing the death of a pedestrian in the night. He was driving a Mercedes sports car whose speed can go upto 250 km per hour.

The fatal accident shook even the fun-loving upper class circles normally indifferent to human suffering. In a city where party-hopping, pub crawling and downing tequila shots is common, there is considerable soul searching, said Malavika Sanggvi, a party-loving journalist with a social conscience.

However, a section of the upper class at the same time was opposing government action against early closure of pubs and the drive against illegal, fashionable liquor bars in Mumbai. At the same time luxurious lifestyles were being glorified.

The car has become an instrument of oppression as national budgets are hijacked to cope with the demands of car users, John Whitlegg, a noted analyst of car culture observed in the Guardian (27-3-06).

How children's freedom on the roads is restricted by vehicles is brilliantly shown in the massively influential book One False Move written by Mayer Hillman in 1991.

He also points out that if the number of accidents goes down, it does not mean that the roads are safer. It only means we measure accidents, not the extent of danger on roads. Even when the number of children's deaths on roads fell in England, this did not mean children felt more safe. They did feel afraid of roads and the fear was and is genuine. Roads are now more fearful places.

The danger should be removed from children's path. It is not that children should be removed from roads. (Guardian 3-11-02).

Hillman compared the life of children with that of criminals in jail. Both categories have roof over their heads, get regular meals and entertainment. But they are not free to go out. The point is children are not criminals and it is criminal to create conditions that make it dangerous for children to go out on the roads.

Hillman holds that cycling is the panacea for our transport and traffic ills. People are afraid of riding bicycles. But the situation can be changed. Hillman cites the experience of Denmark which had the highest child mortality in accidents in western Europe. Then a new road traffic Act in 1976 made it the responsibility of the police and the traffic authorities to protect children from traffic, especially on way to school and back home. A big network of traffic-free foot and cycle paths was created. Low-speed areas were created, roads were narrowed, traffic islands were formed. Accidents fell by 85 per cent.

He helped change the official attitude to cycling. Before 1992 the government was reluctant to promote cycling because of safety concerns. He wrote the seminal report Cycling Towards Health and Safety published by the British Medical Association. Based on actuarial figures and comparisons he showed that the benefits of health and other factors far outweighed the losses incurred by cycling. If one cyclist died in an accident, many others who take to cycling prolong their life and a healthy life they lead. Besides cycling improves mental health, boosts self-esteem.

Hillman also suggested that exhausts of cars should be designed to turn them away from pedestrian. At an international conference on cycling in Scotland he said globe-trotting cannot be justified as air travel was a big contributor to global warming.

The statement was met by silence and watching of shoe laces.

There is total inequality on roads. On the one hand is the driver with a massive motor vehicle moving at great speed which can cause great harm to a pedestrian. The motorist enjoys the protection of the car while the pedestrian not only lacks protection he or she can cause no damage to the car. This inequality should be corrected by law, argues Leonard Evans in his book Traffic Safety.

It should be specified that a driver must not crash into a pedestrian whatever the pedestrian does, just as a vehicle is not expected to crash into another vehicle it is following.

A breakgthrough in traffic safety can be achieved only by adopting the same principles as in air safety. The primary goal must be to prevent crashes, not to make it safer to crash.

Some people want to excuse speeding motorists on the ground that otherwise they are law-abiding citizens. But then by the same logic people would get away with child molestation and wife beating. The point is there is a lunatic fringe which opposes any restriction on speed, it can go to the extent of damaging speed cameras with hammers and airguns. (New Statesman, 9-9-06).

Motorists must be forced to acknowledge that the possession of a dangerous weapon, that the car is, requires extreme caution and diligence. There is a menace on our streets, one that threatens the lives of our children on a daily basis, ten times more dangerous than paedophiles. The threat of cars on roads and in residential colonies, buildings imprison children in homes. Motorists are the only people who are allowed to kill with impunity. They are a much bigger threat to children than danger from strangers.

People's right to life must take precedence to motorists' right to drive. Those who kill must lose their licence for life. (Mark Lynas New Statesman 23-4-07)

Though pedestrians are the main victims of road deaths, India's former President A.P.J. Abdul Kalam, known for his expertise in missile and space technology, did not have a single word for pedestrians when speaking at a seminar on automotive safety at the Automotive Research Association of India in Pune in 2007. At the same time he spoke at length on the need to increase the safety of motor vehicles and about the impact vehicles suffered from crashes in front, at the back and sideways.

India has one of the world's worst records of road deaths per 10,000 vehicles. India has far fewer vehicles than the US has.One can imagine what will happen when the vehicle ownership goes up. More vehicles would mean far more number of people are killed, crippled, intimidated and many will simply not venture out due to fear.

More accidents occur in Western countries but the rate of deaths is not so high as India because there the medical facilities are far superior. (TOI editorial 28-8-07).

Special investigative agencies inquire into every major railway, aircraft or shipping mishap but there is no special agency to investigate road crashes though these kill a far higher number of people. One of the reasons could be the extremely influential car industry, one of the biggest capitalist enterprises in the world.

The State contributes substantially to the massacre of innocents on the roads with inefficiency and corruption of its machinery. There are lakhs of bogus driving licences in operation. This means you commit a crime as a driver and literally get away with it. You can get a fresh licence any number of times even if one is confiscated.

Deaths caused by cars, instead of arousing anger, are now being accepted as something natural, to be expected in our motorized society. In the 1920s in the West the car was seen as a death dealing monster in the media. Later on the car lobby became successful in convincing the public that it is not the car but the driver, bad roads and careless pedestrians to blame, points out Peter Norton author of Fighting Traffic. Jaywalkers were portrayed as the new villains by the car lobby. Others may be at fault to some extent but the car culture is mainly to blame.

The car lobby promoted the idea of fool-proof streets which are safe for motorists, not to other road users. It promoted arrogant, fast driving.

Some people play internet games in which you get points for killing pedestrians with your car. In reality some people have a similarly contemptuous attitude towards the pedestrians though it may not be so brazen as the that of the French aristocrat in Charles Dickens's famous novel A Tale of Two Cities whose horse carriage kills a child on the road. He says he will crush all who come in his way and hopes his horse has not suffered any injury. The same attitude persists today among many. The difference is only of detail. The basic attitude remains the same.

This attitude is heightened by the spread of the culture of highways expressways, flyovers and fast cars, the glorification of speed and contempt for the poor in general and people who move slowly as pedestrians or cyclists in particular.

A cartoon by Sudhir Tailang in Hindustan Times showed two men with a car. One of them says 'smart car – this new impact-proof model. Even if you hit ten people, it won't have a single dent.

It is against this background that one needs to see the incident in which the car of Shiv Sena chief Bal Thackeray's then personal assistant Ravindra Mhatre killed two innocent women, a mother and daughter, and injured two others at Vile Parle in Mumbai in 2005. It was the day of revelry and Holi and drinking. Mhatre, who was at the wheel, was found to be under the influence of liquor. The police obviously did everything to save him and did not carry out the breath test immediately but public pressure prevailed.

The police, whose credibility is extremely low, normally pass the blame on pedestrians whenever such incidents occur. Fortunately, the women, Neelam Mashelkar 77, and Swati Pawaskar, 47, were standing at a bus stop and there were many witnesses as the incident happened in broad day light so there was no way the authorities could manipulate things and say that the women were at fault.

It was only because of the tenacity of the old lady's grandson Manish that the police acted on other complaints. It took a directive from the Mumbai high court to make the police lodge an FIR (first information report) against Thackeray's assistant regarding irregularities about his car papers.

The public works department of the Maharashtra government contributed to the accident as it has been preventing the BEST bus undertaking from constructing bus shelters on the highways in Mumbai on the ground that these will hinder the flow of traffic, according to Ashish Chemburkar, former chairpeson of the BEST committee. (Maharashtra Times 14-5-04). Apart from blatant flouting of all norms, this shows criminal negligence.It is always a pathetic sight to see people standing precariously on the highway in the hot sun without a shelter, shade while waiting for a bus.

The punishment for traffic violations by motorists is far more severe in the Netherlands and Germany than in India. In the two countries motorists are presumed to be at fault in such accidents and get severe punishment. The researchers Rajeev Kamboj and Jhansi Rani say that in Germany and Netherlands it is a serious offence if a motorist does not stop for pedestrians at zebra crossings. Guilty motorists receive tickets by mail together with photos of themselves while committing a traffic violation.

A crucial aspect of driver training in Germany and Netherlands is the need to pay special attention to avoiding collisions with pedestrians. It is assumed that pedestrians will make unsafe moves in traffic. Motor vehicle drivers are required to anticipate such unsafe moves by carefully noting the presence of pedestrians anywhere along their route so that they can react quickly.

Though France has far fewer road accidents than India and its accident rate is declining, French president Jacques Chirac declared in 2002 that the violence on our roads is unworthy of a great modern country. This was after the number of road deaths had come down from 16617 in 1972 to 7242 in 2002.

At a recent seminar on automobile technology at the Automotive Research Association of India in Pune I was surprised to hear representatives of the motor car lobby refer to the industry as the mobility industry. In reality the growing number of automobiles results in hampering mobility in numerous ways like traffic jams which have the worst impact on the less privileged road users.

5

Social Life of Streets

Streets have been an integral part of India's social life for centuries. They were never mere corridors for traffic as at present. It is understandable that cars cannot be kept out totally though they kill life on streets. But through a more humane planning it is possible to retain the social life of streets. Streets can be and should be places where people can linger, meet friends, gossip, and watch the world go by – in a word, places to enjoy. This is not something fanciful.

In several parts of Europe and other countries street life is being vitalized through greater facilities for pedestrians and promoting social interaction.

Organisations like Living Streets in England are implementing these ideas and making a big success of them.

Streets and public spaces are ours. It is our public realm, says Andrew Purkis, chairperson of Living Streets.

The bazaar, that most colourful feature of towns in Asia, is a mix of street use both for transport and meeting, buying and selling with all its sounds and colours and smells. This is something the Westerners die for.

The street is where one has interesting and sometimes marvelous encounters, the place is pregnant with the possibility of interesting happenings, poins out Dipesh Chakrabarty, an eminent analyst of public spaces. The famous Urdu poet Ghalib asserts his right to sit in the street. This is a public space, who can dislodge us ? he asks.

Tasneem Mehta, convenor of the Mumbai chapter of the Indian National trust for Art and Cultural Heritage (INTACH), who has lived on Mumbai's elite Carmichael Road for many years, laments the loss of life on the road.

'Children used to play cricket on the road, now the road is taken over by cars. We used to go for long walks in the leafy, quiet neighbourhood,' she says. This is what Mumbai misses, areas where one can just walk through.

The rich have now begun planning to make their streets livelier. Altamount Road at Malabar Hill in Mumbai, considered one of the ten most expensive residential streets in the world, is to undergo a major renovation with places for children to play and an art and history corner and beautification. The initiative is taken by affluent residents who include Mukesh Ambani and Kumar Mangalam Birla. A proposal has been submitted to the municipal corporation, according to Gautam Vatsa, secretary of the residents' committee. The problem is that roads in less privileged areas are becoming more and more unlivable and a pain to walk along in the absence of public spaces and footpaths.

Well managed streets are good for health because people will walk more and drive less. They are good for communities because more people will meet, stop and talk. They are good for security because in busy streets crime drops.

So an effort has to be made to get people out on the streets – the one area where everyone meets. It is accessible, egalitarian and just the place for markets, parties, poets, pavement artistes, gymnasts and jugglers. These voices are increasingly winning recognition from authorities in England. And such voices need to be raised with a much bigger impact in poorer countries where there is much more need for public space and sharing it in a more democratic way.

Be subtle, be street-shrewd and you can make a dangerous road safer without having to ban cars or infuriate drivers. Local people should be recruited in the project. We will know we have succeeded when road deaths and injuries are down, vehicle speeds are lower and broken footpaths are speedily repaired.

And when people feel safer on the streets, there are more local walking journeys, there is a more accessible street environment, people enjoy the streets, so they use them more, people linger on the streets. Then we can be proud of our public spaces.

Social life on streets is being systematically killed to serve the interests of the car lobby.

Actually, India has a long tradition of the street as a public space to be used for many other purposes than merely as corridors for vehicle. Processions are an integral part of our cultural life for centuries, points out historian Narayani Gupta.

People want and like open spaces and want to use them. In Lahore the exuberance for kite flying during the Basant festival cannot be curbed by Mullas or law courts. Hundreds of people protested on the streets in Lahore in December, 2005, against the Supreme court's banning kite flying. There is massive following for Basant celebrations in Lahore, says Murtaza Razvi, Lahore editor of Dawn. The mullahs gave up on trying to stop Basant. Zia-ul-Haq did not even try, reported Mini Kapoor in a report from Lahore. (Indian Express 23-1-06). President Musharraf had been winning popularity among Lahoris by supporting Basant, the spring festival which marks the end of winter. The celebration is also important from the point of view of secularism. Fundamentalists have already banned Hindustani classical music and classical dance in Pakistan on the ground that these are Hindu in origin. Fortunately, at the popular level, people have resisted such compartmentalization.

As for art and artisans festivals and processions play a big part in their domain. Gulammohammed Sheikh reputed Gujarat poet and painter, makes some very interesting observations. He says that in the urban sector a vast number of unorganised labour is involved in making cultural objects, a toy or a kite sold in the bazaar, the massive effigies of Ravana for Dusshra of Tazias for Muharram.

Pupul Jayakar once remarked that the number of practitioners of the visual arts in rural India was equal to the entire population of Australia. To extend the assumption further one could saw that every home in India harbours a potential artist, Sheikh says. Scores of women in South India and elsewhere make animated patterns of various designs rangolis etc. at their doorstep every day.

The streets have for a long time been the battleground for Left wing groups and political parties. Street fighting years is the apt title of a book by celebrated left-wing writer Tariq Ali. However, the right-wing too has been using the streets for its own agenda.The Rath yatra, led by Mr L.K. Advani in 1990 from Somnath to Ayodhya was politically motivated and it shows how the streets can be used for dividing people rather than uniting them, promoting social interaction and friendship as has happened over centuries. Hitler also used the streets for his demoniac rallies.

The Congress party's annual sessions indicated a weakness for being mounted and not pedestrian. Subhas Bose led a procession in 1928 mounted on a horse, J.B. Kripalani was accompanied with bands and camels at the Jaipur session of 1948 after Gandhi's death, P Sitaramayya saw fit to use a silver chariot drawn by two bullocks. This prompted Blitz weekly to remind its readers that Christ had entered Jerusalem riding on an ass, says Narayani Gupta.

Kolkata's long tradition of processions has currently taken a beating with the Marxists remaining in power for more than 30 years. And there is a general dilution of radicalism. However, the tradition is recounted with feeling by Dr Ashok Mitra, a noted economist and former finance minister of West Bengal having a long association with the Communist party of India (Marxist). Mr Mitra says that in respect of processions the superiority of Kolkata over other cities is beyond dispute.

Writing in 1982 in the Illustrated Weekly of India, Mr Mitra says there were miles and miles of people, morning noon and aternoon on the march, four-deep, even ten-deep. Processions which perhaps start at a dozen different points of entry to the city planned to converge into one gigantic mass in the Maidan, a huge ground, Processions with flags, festoons and banners, processions exclusively dependent on lung power.

Now, another aspect of streets. Narrow streets, lanes and paths also serve a far more useful purpose for the common people than some people would concede. Paths exist in nature. Wild animals make them as well as humans. Walkers who leave the normal trails in forests often find those made by animals. Even in deserts there are routes in the sands, between water sources. Road and way are two of the richest sources of metaphor in the English language.

The superhighway concept had its origin in the Austrada begun in Italy soon after dictator Mussolini's coming to power.

The explosion of highway culture did not come about as a result of the fair operation of the free market. It came about after destroying public transport and in this the lead was taken by General Motors, Standard Oil and Firestone Tire who systematically destroyed trams and buses to pave the way for motor cars. If you build 48 lane highways around the earth at the equator and put all the world's 350 million cars on the road, there will still be traffic jams bumper to bumper. We would require at least four times more space for all the cars and 192-lane highways would be needed. And them imagine the hassles in building the 193rd lane and so on.

Our street life is so dull, unfriendly. Not only do we not have proper footpaths on which people can walk and chat with each other, there is so little street furtniture. The streets cry out for benches and chairs, more trees, more shade All this can be created and the cities and towns can be made much more friendly, humane and social spaces at very little cost. And there is so little public art on the streets. What a rich tradition of artistic paintings on house walls and doors we have had as is clear from the Warli tribals' paintings in Thane district, not far from Mumbai, which are now such a rage in Mumbai. And then we have the rich living tradition of Gujarat and Rajasthan which one can see if one wanders the streets and lanes.

In Bhopal the walls on either side of an arterial road have been covered with tribal paintings which give the area a wonderful look.

Artiste Tushar Joag says we should not wait for the government to allot us spaces for art. We have to go out and reclaim spaces. Public art need not be concrete and metals, we can carry out momentary interventions.

David Harvey, the eminent Marxist geographer, says in the sixties spectacle was equated with public protests, demonstrations. Now, spectacle is characterized by consumption in privately-controlled settings like waterfronts, markets and shopping malls.

Advertisers and the corporate sector are the biggest enemies of trees in cities. Visibility for billboards is far more important to them than trees which come in the way. Advertising professionals would be shocked to know what their doyen David Ogilvy had to say about billboards in his autobiography Confessions of an Advertising Man.

He said he had a passion for the landscape and had never seen the landscape improved by billboards. Man is at his vilest when he erects a billboard. The advertisement guru said after retirement he wanted to form a secret society of masked vigilantes who would travel round the world on silent motor-bikes chopping posters at the dark of the moon. How many juries will convict us when we are caught in the act of beneficent citizenship ?. (quoted by Naomi Klein, author of No Logo) The poet Ogden Nash put it neatly when he wrote 'Unless billboards fall, I shall never see a tree.'

Throughout India hoardings have damaged road safety and aesthetics, says a study by N Mittal, S.M. Sarin, R.K. Bajpai and K.V. Ganesh Babu, experts of the Central Road Research Institute has shown.

Curiously, Detroit, the former car capital now in distress, is seen to have high potential to become a new bicycle utopia. Bicycle shops are thriving near the General Motors headquarters in the city. (Bike Among the Ruins. New York Times 5-7-09).

It is not enough for a city to have green spaces, a sea front or a river front. It has to have a central area where people can assemble and there has to be a lot of social life, space for mingling, talking, discussing.

Reputed architect Charles Correa has made a very good suggestion. If a street is narrow, there should be no high rise buildings on it. This will help avoid traffic chaos and avoid streets being converted into nightmares.

Streets have nurtured so much social interaction, solidarity. One of the finest theatre groups in the country Prithvi Theatre, founded by Prithviraj Kapoor of Mughal- e-Azam fame, was essentially a touring theatre in the fifties and sixties. The actors put up with a lot of inconveniences on the way. But it was great fun. The young Shashi Kapoor was a part of this theatre. Another fine touring theatre was led by Kendals, Jeffrey, Jennifer and Felicity, immortalized in the film Shakespearewalla made by Ismail Merchant. Prithvi Theatre, now a landmark theatre in Juhu, Mumbai, is lovingly run by: Prithvi's grand-daughter Sanjana.

The Bazaar, such a typical Asian phenomenon, is perhaps the most lively feature of street life. The Bazaar is seen as one of the great achievements of Islamic civilization. It is remarkable for its smells, sounds and colours. There is the delicious smell of spices, cries of sellers and the sounds of artistes. The word is derived from the Persian word Wazar. The Bazaar spread in Europe from Constantinople.

Kabir, the lovable medieval poet of equality and religious harmony, uses the Bazaar as the symbol of the most public space.

It is cleanliness that we really need on our streets, water fronts and other public spaces. That would make jogging, cycling, walking, skating, kite-flying become more enjoyable. Instead, the authorities come up with fake, expensive beautification schemes which are a total failure. But our upper class spends much more on interior decoration than on the house itself. Ask it to pay even a little for up-keep of its housing society or the street outside, it will not.

During colonial rule the rulers wanted to control everyday uses of space on the road as an indispensable part of establishment of their sovereignty. The same ideas have now been imbibed by the middle class, points out Sudip Kaviraj, a noted scholar.

The rulers saw the cities as orderly, hygienic, technologically superior and more civilized than rural areas and so increasingly order is being imposed on urban streets. The ruling class insists on controlling these vital public spaces. Since the state machinery like the police and the municipal staff are not enough to control these spaces, the middle class has been roped in in the exercise. It is now becoming increasingly intolerant of hawkers and others who belong to a different class. For the middle class the fixity of regular shops is more reassuring than the alleged chaos presented by street vendors.

The street space and the air space above, spaces in the open and in residential buildings are blatantly used by corporate houses, commercial film producers and others with giant hoardings which require huge steel structures dug deep into the ground for support. Superstar Amitabh Bachhan came under severe criticism in early 2006 for appearing on the hoardings for a film with a cigar in his mouth.

But Bachhan deserves some credit for not abandoning the sociability of the street. He and another film star Salman Khan live in houses which face the street. They also have some interaction with their fans, Amitabh is known for waving from the balcony of his bungalow at Juhu to his admirers. The newer breed of film stars have completely islanded themselves, away from the gaze of public.

Increasingly, types of spaces that were traditionally part of the public realm like markets, streets, squares, places of congregation and worship are becoming private territories ruled arbitrarily by private corporations with their own rules. These erode individual freedom and enforce rule of mediocrity, points out architecture critic Peter Davey. (Architecture Review, January 05). This also holds true for Indian cities like Mumbai which are seeing increasing presence of big corporations, shopping malls and luxury residential buildings.

London is invaded by cars. The car is king here. London's public places must be given dignity and pedestrians given high priority, said John Gehl, urban designer and a great champion of public spaces, in his report to the organization Transport in London.

Gehl, who is now being consulted by various cities including New York and Melbourne, stresses the importance of creating spaces in cities, on streets an squares where people can talk and mingle.

People are drawn to crowded, bustling spaces, people make detours to pass through busy streets. The bench, which is most used in a park, is the one that faces a crowd. There is a Scandanavian proverb People go where People are. Widen the footpaths, have cafes, put attractive benches, street pavings, encourage students to live in the city, reduce car parks and so on. Do it slowly to encounter less resistance and you have a recipe for a lively, vibrant city, Gehl points out.

Cities are not just physical spaces, they have to be made for human beings. The idea came to Gehl sharply when he married a psychologist Ingrid Mundt and psychologists asked him 'are not architects interested in people, are they interested only in buildings ?'

Gehl says there are four kinds of cities, (1) the dense and traditional ones, (2) cities invaded by cars like London and Bangkok, (3) cities where people drive everywhere, shopping etc takes place at higher levels via skywalks in cities like Atlanta and Houston and (4) reconqured, redesigned cities made friendly to people like Copenhegen and Barcelona.

Our lives are becoming privatized, confined to the house, the car, the office and the shopping mall. We have to live life in the open, in public spaces and these spaces have to be created and they can be.

Architects like Le Courbusie saw the city as a machine, clean, functional, divided into zones for residence, recreation, work. The highway linked the zones and the car was the king. This concept has to change. The city can and have a soul, it should be friendly, inviting, a city should not be designed just for people to be made to work and live like robots so that some people can make huge profits.

Cordoba town in Spain has marvelous zig zag streets which create an intimate setting not seen anywhere else in the world. Under Moorish rule Cordoba became the greatest city in Europe boasting of paved streets, public hospitals, street lights, mosques and libraries. There were nearly 900 public bath houses.

In the last 20 years there is growing awareness of the concept of sharing the steeets, sharing for various uses like social contact, striking convesation, street art, hawking goods and not just for vehicular traffic. This is a highly innovative concept, Architecture Week noted in an article Streets for People (5-1-04). The concept has been outlined by such outstanding architectural experts in the past including Kevyn Lynch, Donald Appleyard and William Whyte.

Such streets with social life have disappeared from suburbs in big cities in America but they are very much there in the inner cities and countries like Japan and Netherlands have implemented the concept of shared streets substantially.

The emphasis in this concept is on community, children at play, bicycles, social contact. It is not so much anti-car but it stands for integrating vehicular traffic with other road users. The philosophical roots of this innovation lie in the Colin Buchanan report of 1963 Traffic in Towns in England.

Buchanan is seen as the father of traffic calming, the concept of reducing the number of vehicles on the road through various devices. Car driver should drive at walking pace in some areas, he argued.

A novel approach to make roads safer is to remove traffic signals and allowing pedestrians to cross anywhere they like. The idea is working extremely well in several towns in the Netherlands and there is no reason why it cannot work elsewhere. Once motorists realize that they cannot afford to drive anyway they like, they will be more careful, more respectful towards pedestrians. Drivers will look at people, not at signs.

The idea, propounded by a Dutch transport engineer Hans Mondermann, has caught on and it makes streets more democratic. It will not appeal to the car lobby and speed fanatics. Mondermann created a gentler streetscape. He achieved this by resisting a world that lets the needs of car drivers to spoil city life for everyone. In a traditionally conservative profession he succeeded in challenging many assumptions about safety and relationship between motorists and pedestrians, public space. His approach has helped create more civilized streets and his influence is spreading to several cities in Europe and has won approval from the European Union. It can be best seen in Kensington street in London. (Guardian 8-2-08)

The rich can have sex without disturbance in their moving 34-ft long Limo which requires no less than 68 ft of move to turn. But such people who monopolise so much of road space are not called a menace while, innocent pedestrians are. The New Yorker had no hesitation in calling such motorists SOBs (sons of bitches) (Revenge of the limos. Pedestrians beware 1-1-98).

Another radical and humanist uban planner is Danish John Gehl who is being consulted by several prominent cities like New York, Sydney, London and Stockholm. Like a Scandaniavan ice-breaker he cuts through nonsense and comes up with innovative solutions as in Sydney where he has created environment-friendly, livable streetscape. (Sydney Morning Herald 20-1-08). Gehl, 71, the traffic-curbing guru took New York city's planning chief Amanda Burden and traffic czar Janette Sadik Khan on a bicycle trip around Copehegen to show them what could be done to make biking and walking safe. (Copenhegen's sage of post-car culture pedals into New York - New York magazine 5-11-07).

Many Germans had their first kiss on the pedestrian zone, ate their first ice-cream and bought the first shoe here. Kassel city, heavily destroyed in the second world war, was the first city in the country to have a pedestrian plaza and redesigning of the city in 1953.

Streets free from cars are excellent for social life. But this is seen as a threat by the car lobby and motorists. The French sociologist Jean Baudrillard observed that if you get out of your car and start walking you are seen as a delinquent or a threat to public order in the same way a dog is viewed while wandering on the road. He also sees the most frequent burning of cars in France as a very understandable sign of protest against the establishment and car is one of the most glamorous symbols of the establishment and so is a regular target. (New Left Review, Jan-Feb 2006).

But then streets, like everything in life, are being privatized for the use of the motor car excluding the common people. We speak of privatization of education, health care and natural resources. But the process is much vaster, our communal spaces, town squares, streets, schools are being displaced by market forces, points out Naomi Klein, one of the foremost fighters against globalisation, still in her thirties.

It is an irony of our age that when the street has become the hottest commodity in advertising culture, street culture is itself under siege. Hawking on streets, street art, street protest, street theatre is criminalized without police permission.

But things are changing. People are asserting their right to streets. In Europe parties are being held at road intersections to drive home the point that roads are not merely for cars.

The life of Bismillah Khan, the famous Shehnai player, and other musicians of Banaras is unimaginable without the role played by lanes and bylanes in their lives. Bismillah Khan made it a point to play the Shahnai walking on the road one day in a year.

The street where you live early in life is very dear to you and forms an inseparable part of your mental life. Mr Vijay Kumar Malhotra, a senior leader of the Bharatiya Janata party, was thrilled during his visit to Pakistan to see the streets of his childhood like Guru Nanak and Shraddhanand streets. He was glad their names had not changed. There is also a Bano bazaar in Lahore which is for women only.

But elsewhere in Lahore there is a move to Islamise Hindu names of 38 streets drawing criticism from scholar Saleema Hashmi who said we are erasing history. The Lahore conservation society president Dr Ajaz Anwar and architect Nayar Ali Dada too have expressed similar sentiment. (Yahoo India News 2-6-05).

In China old streets and historic building were demolished as if by bombing. All to prepare for the Olympic Games of 2008. The historic areas include the spaces around the Tiannamen Square and the Great Hall of People. Streets, courtyards, homes were destroyed and the land given to profit-hungry developers. (IHT 12-7-06).

Elsewhere entire urban treasures are being lost and a desperate effort is being made in some places to preserve the old culture. Old casbahs with their winding streets are wonderful spaces in north Africa and parts of Asia. The casbahs of Algiers and the colourful Medina, the old part of Marrakesh city in Morocco have been declared UNESCO world heritage sites.

The casbah is entirely different from the French quarter and the winding streets, impenetrable to motor cars, served as the main sites of resistance to the French and captured so picturesquely in the classic film Battle of Algiers.

The central square in Medina is full of colour, noise and smell with barbeques and vendors selling herbs, lotions, candles, oil, spices and meat. One of the most enjoyable spaces in Lahore in Pakistan, not far from Amritsar, which I enjoyed is the food street. The street truly becomes a social space here at night.

The casbah with its secret passageways, labyrinthine streets and connected rooftops is celebrated in the film Pepe le Moko.

The 1937 French film is a timeless romantic thriller directed by Julien Duvivier. The atmosphere of the casbah is so thick and rich you can almost smell it, said one reviewer. Come with me to the casbah has become a standard romantic line for all French lovers, thanks to the film.

The film creates an exotic layered North African atmosphere in the casbah with its sun-drenched, baked clay buildings and honeycomb of winding streets.

Nothing shows the character of a nation so quickly to anybody than the way the streets are treated. Nothing says how a nation feels about itself than the way it dresses it streets, points out Bill Brysson of the English heritage movement.

Vincent Scully, a scholar, compared the onslaught of the car to the holocaust. The automobile was and remains the agent of chaos and breaker of cities, Scully points out. In his book

Modern Architecture.He wonders if the automobile and the civilization as we know it can co-exist.

Public squalor and private luxury, the expression used by economist John Galbraith former US ambassador in India, applies very much to India. Our street life is extremely drab, unimaginative, shoddy with broken footpaths and rubble while excessive care is taken by the rich to decorate the interiors of their houses with enormous amounts of money. Even big builders do not repair footpaths outside their house. Nothing makes a street more inelegant and ugly than car ramps which block a good portion of the road and the footpath. These eyesores also are a major obstruction and an insult to pedestrians.

However, there is a greater awareness of surroundings in large housing complexes with several buildings spread over several acres. There is now a realization that many of the high rise buildings are essentially ugly and even hostile. So to soften the impact, landscaping is now seen as a major solution.

No discussion on street life can be completed without reference to the foremost experts on the subject, the two Jacobs, the great Jane Jacobs, author of the path-breaking book Death and Life of Great American Cities, and Allan Jacobs, author of Great Streets.

Jane Jacobs, the most influential writer on urban planning in the last 50 years, was a great enthusiast for creating an environment in which streets are very friendly to pedestrians, conducive to social life, and mixed land use. A street should not be purely commercial or residential. Shops and hawkers, she says, are essential. They fulfil a major need and also provide safety. Streets should not be purely residential.

Prime Minister Manmohan Singh has strongly supported hawkers in a letter written to chief ministers of various states in 2009. He said the states should implement the national policy on urban street vendors and allow them to do business without harassment from anyone, they need space and facilities for their needs. The point is that streets belong to all. Not that there should be anarchy on streets. But the automobile should not drive out other road users.

When a neighbourhood is oriented towards the street, when pavements are used for socializing and play and commerce there is a stimulating effect. Relationships are formed and casual contacts are made which would have never been possible otherwise.

Some would say that this was all right for the bygone era and not relevant now. Actually, this can very much be done and is being done as Jane Jacobs's thinking has been extremely influential. Even corporate offices have adopted her ideas providing more space for social interaction among employees who would otherwise be confined to their desks.

Allan Jacobs, another progressive architect, argues that streets are places of social and commercial encounters and exchange. Best streets are comfortable to walk along with leisure and safety. Here both pedestrians and motorists can get along without conflict. For almost 60 years engineers have been anti-pedestrian and against mixed land use. When there is greater awareness among motorists about the importance of pedestrians, their integration into the street structure, then both cars and pedestrians are safe.

Allan Jacobs was the director of city planning commission for San Francisco and his work has created some of the best spaces in the city. Sir Norman Foster, a leading architect in the world, says buildings as well as streets have to be sustainable, people friendly. Architects can design buildings which will use a fraction of the current energy levels and with better urban planning can reduce dependence on the motor car.

In England the government's Manual for Streets gives guidelines that streets should be social spaces, not just places where traffic whizzes by. The country's commission for architecture and built environment says better-designed streets can slow down vehicle speeds.

In our elite's queer ideas of progress, we want to ban hawkers, cycle-rickshaws, bicycles, street food, small shops. But livable cities in the West are better precisely because they have a varied, rich street life precisely with these entities. Our city making completely lacks imagination. We can easily improve cities, make them more friendly with street cafes which provide so much charm. We need more public spaces. People like to see each other, talk to each other. But all this is actually being banished by making streets available almost exclusively to the mechanical, life-destroying motor car.

Los Angeles has a less vital political culture than my city San Francisco, says Rebecca Solnit, the radical writer on walking. L.A. has little pedestrian life, no boulevards which are ideal for political marches and no plazas for speeches. It has nothing of the old civic landscape that has made Paris and Prague ideal for revolution.

In most cities in India cars are the measure of all things, human bodies feel hapless, obsolete certainly inadequate for navigating spaces. There is a continuum between promenades, parades, festivals and uprisings, continuum of active bodies and public boldness. Walking is seen as a rural, pleasant activity. We do not take enough stock of urban walking, the life of crowds, of vitality of streets and the potential for revolt that always hovers over us.

Cities are now built in such a way that the human body and ordinary people cannot traverse the vast scale which can only be covered by the motor car. That, Solnit feels, is the real ecological and political catastrophe.

The rich and the powerful enjoy center stage in conventional histories or in drama theatres. Ordinary people are reduced to just subjects or audiences with no role to play in the drama of life. The same with cars. These dominate our streets, these are at the center stage. Pedestrians are pushed to the margins.

Barbara Ehrenreich, a brilliant writer on working class and women's issues, has celebrated life on the street in her book Dancing in the Streets. Carnivals and ecstatic rituals on streets have been part of social life for long and she wonders why we do not come together more often. Carnivals are the best public expression of giving vent to their bodies, unrestricted by command and authority. That is why rulers are afraid of carnivals and suppressed them for a long time since the 16th century.

The carnival against capitalism was a big event in different parts of the world during the anti-globalisation protests. The FBI was so worried it warned against carnivals. Clowns, jesters, people with masks, fire eaters, jugglers, stilt walkers, streakers, those who dance in streets were all seen as a threat to the establishment because they defy hierearchy, authority. The carnival is the very opposite of Fascist spectacles like the Nuremberg rally which are orchestrated, scripted. At fascist rallies people do not voluntarily assemble, they are rounded up, brought in. At the carnival people assemble spontaneously. One of the biggest assemblies in the world is the Kumbh Mela where millions take a ritual bath in the river Ganga or Godavari in India. All these people come on their own which is amazing, says Marky Tully, the ex-BBC veteran.

Bakhtin, the eminent political thinker, observed that the carnival renewed the social body through laughter, celebration and liberation from etiquette. It is a world turned upside down. In time carnivals became inseparable from rebellion.

Life can be so much more fun if streets are used more imaginatively. In England, jumping stunts, somersaults, back flips, landing gracefully on the floor are proving a great attraction. People are fed of traditional sports. They can be given alternative, more lively forms of recreation in the public spaces, streets around their homes. (Guardian 5-8-08). Streets ought to be freed from the regimentation imposed by the motor car lobby and the police.

But in India public spaces and streets, far from becoming democratic spaces, are becoming inaccessible for various reasons to women. The nation's capital Delhi has the dubious distinction of being one of the most unsafe cities in the world for women. Women here face more violence than in any other city in the country. Delhi tops the list of all crimes against women including molestation, rape, dowry harassment, domestic violence. (Kalpana Viswanath and Surabhi Tandon Malhotra EPW 28-4-07).

Everything works against women. The street lighting is such that the light caters mainly to vehicle traffic not on pavements or the roadside. Bus stops have no lighting of their own. The presence of vendors makes women feel much safer. Outlying areas in Delhi are so unsafe that some parents do not even send their daughters to school.

Cars and pet dogs enjoy precedence over ordinary human beings on roads. Even on Mumbai's most elite Carmichael Road residents refuse to clear the mess left by their dogs. Anita Lawyer, an activist, has been fighting on the issue for 15 yeas. It became a big public issue when Indian Express columnist and dog owner Tavleen Singh got into a big controversy with the then Mumbai municipal commissioner Johny Joseph after she refused to clean her dog poop on Marine Drive.

Street life has been killed by car traffic and other forms of development in India. In Bangalore, India's IT capital, dominated by cars and flyoves, life is miserable for pedestrians. Participants in a marathon race in Bangalore in December, 2007, found dogs snapping at their heels and traffic coming to a halt for ten minutes at some spots due to vehicular congestion. (TOI 17-12-07). The marginalization of the poor in Bangalore is best described by sociologist and author Ramchandra Guha. He was struck by the sight of a Muslim cart puller, was completely sidelined by impatient motorists. (Telegraph 25-10-08). That marginalization exists every where.

Curiously, the initiative for Mumbai's first car-free street came from jewellers, driven by business interests. They demanded that Zaveri Bazar, the old street of jewellers near the Chhatrapati Shivaji railway terminus in the Fort area, be banned for cars as the area has become a soft target for terrorists. The jewllers will have their own security and closed circuit television sets. Pedestrianising the street will also attract tourists, said Ramesh Paheljan, a member of the Bullion Association. But building high rise car parks in the area may not be such a pleasant idea.

One of the brightest ideas to enliven the streets has come come from an unlikely source, Maharashtra's labour minister Nawab Malik who comes from a poor slum area. He has suggested that the long stretch of the road from Crawford Market to the Gateway of India in Mumbai, dotted by heritage buildings, can be converted into a bazaar in the evening for pedestrians and closed to cars. Tourists can ride on horse carriages and such measures can make Mumbai a live and pulsating city.

6

Traffic Calming

Traffic calming was born in Delft town in the Netherlands in the sixties. A group of neighbours, frustrated by the roar of cars zooming past their houses, placed furniture and other large objects at strategic points on the road forcing motorists to slow down. City officials, called out to clear the obstructions, knew a good thing when they saw one and began installing their own more sophisticated traffic calming devices. The idea spread across Europe and Australia and has now come to North America.

Traffic calming encompasses a whole set of street designs that increase safety and aesthetic satisfaction for pedestrians. The aim is twofold, to slow down the speed of traffic and to give drivers a visual reminder that they must share the street with people.

People are rising in protest against the unpleasantness created by the car culture and the road lobby. Even in the automobile-dominated auto-happy southern California, the cities of San Bernandino, Riverside and Beverly Hills have narrowed major commercial streets.

Streets represent the single most important factor in shaping urban form. Streets set at regular intervals and with sufficient width to accommodate both pedestrian and vehicles establish the grid and help to ensure that building heights, bulk and scale will not overwhelm the users below. Most cities have developed over time and feature street grids that vary in length and visibility.

Reputed architect Charles Correa is among the few to have thought in terms of town planning and streetscape. He has some interesting observations on Tulsi Pipe road in Mumbai which was once a nondescript road. Its importance has suddenly gone up as textile mills along the road have suddenly been converted into shopping malls and spaces for advertising and banking offices and television companies.

That in the process the lives of thousands of textile workers and other ordinary people in the heart of Mumbai have been wrecked is a different matter. A visitor from Delhi compared the street with Madison Avenue of Mumbai. Correa says the British played a different role in Mumbai than they did in Kolkata. They did not build Mumbai. Indians did. But the British gave the city its civic structure, its DNA which allowed Indian energy and initiative to find fruitful expression.

That is the tragedy of Tulsi Pipe road, Correa says, all that energy is there but no sub-structure of supporting roads, engineering services or of a rational decision-making system.

Mumbai has been often compared to Manhattan. But Mumbai does not have the east-west arteries that Manhattan has. A Manhattan without any of such arteries 23rd, 42nd, 57th etc. is unimaginable.

Mumbai's road structure is developed only on the north-south avenues. What we are doing today is absolutely myopic, bordering on the criminal, Correa says. We have allowed huge chunks of textile mill lands to be sold without any concern for creating cross-island, east-west arteries. This is going to make it impossible for everyday city services like sewage system, water supply, electricity to be installed, not to mention ambulances, police security services and so on.

The mill lands area totals as much as 600 acres compared to 18 acres of Ballard Estate, the office-district in south Mumbai or 65 acres of Nariman Point. Providing civic amenities and infrastructure does not lose money. It makes real estate more valuable. That is why people pay more for flats along Oval Maidan. Good planning makes for good real estate values. Some developers understand this but it seems most mill owners do not, Mr Correa feels.

Similarly, Nariman Point is badly planned, there are no east-west arteries, with the result one has to take a long detour to reach a place which is actually so close as the crow flies. With a little imagination these facilities could have been easily provided as this was a virgin area. But it is designed for motorists, not walking. Walking could have been far more pleasant in this area than the ugly experience it is as the basic needs of people have been ignored, this could not happen without contempt for the citizens in general.

So arrogant and short-sighted are private mill owners that they did not even provide access to the mill areas to the Charles Correa committee appointed by the state government in 1996 to make recommendations on the use of mill lands. The government timidly refrained from insisting on access and the committee could only visit mills belonging to the public sector National Textile Corporation (NTC).

7

Craze for Speed

A movement challenging the craze for speed of modern life, speed of motor cars is emerging. It is called the Slow Movement which argues that life is lived much more meaningfully at a slow pace.

Carl Honore, a young journalist, has written a widely praised book In Praise of Slowness published in 2005. It shows how one can live a rich, meaningful life by slowing down the speed of our lives. A big worldwide movement is building up for slow food, slow cities. Even slow sex. And it works.

Grassroots groups are now emerging worldwide including Japan' Sloth Club, Europe's society for deceleration of time and U.S.'s Take Back Your Time coalition.

Walking is slowness at its most effective. It is the most democratic means of transport, it promotes physical and mental health, reduces depression, increases virility, helps fight erective dysfunction.

People walking together in a march are a powerful symbol, like Mahatma Gandhi's padayatras or the civil rights movement.

Martin Luther King was profoundly influenced by the writing and actions of Mahatma Gandhi, and he adapted from Gandhi both the general principle of non-violence and the specifics of marches and boycotts that had hastened India's liberation from British rule. Perhaps Gandhi was the founder of the political pilgrimage with his famous Salt March of 1930.

Rebecca Solnit, author of the book Wanderlust, a history of walking, points out the power of walking. Images of protests during the walk aroused worldwide interest. King and hundreds of others were arrested for marching to Birmingham and after the supply of willing adults began to run out, high school students were recruited and their younger siblings volunteered. That year 900 children were arrested. To go out onto the streets knowing they risked attack, injury, arrest and even death took an extraordinary resolve and the religious ardour of southern Baptists as well as the Christian iconography of martyrdom seems to have strengthened them.

One of the famous spirituals of the blacks is I want Jesus to walk with me.

Poet Wordsowrth defied restrictions imposed by landowners and trespassed on the land asserting people's right to walk there. The lords have no right to seal off land, he said. Not surprising for a man who was deeply committed to people's struggles for justice.

Charles Dickens, the great humanist novelist of 19th century England, loved walking and portrayed outdoor life, the life and problems of the underclass as few others did. 'If I could not walk fast and far, I should explode and perish, he once told a friend and he walked so fast and far that few ever managed to accompany him.

Marx and Engels talked with each other often while pacing up and down in Marx's house in London.

It is generally believed that history is made either by politicians talking in closed spaces carrying out negotiations or through wars. But history is also made in a big way by people marching in the streets, either through violent or non-violent means.

That is people making history with their feet. The Berlin wall fell after half a million people took to the streets, singing and chanting, with lit candles and carrying flowers.

Reclaim the Streets was founded in London in May 1995 with the understanding that if the twin forces of privatized space and globalized economies were alienating us from each other and from local culture, the reclaiming of public space for public life and public festival is one way to resist both.

Sensitive politicians have used walking as a symbol of being close to the people. President Carter broke with tradition after his inauguration and walked down from Capitol to White House along with family members.

In India currently we do not have much of a walking culture, at least not at the popular level unlike in England where people have been desperately wanting to walk out into the countryside as an escape from the narrow confines of urban life. There almost a thousand year class war has been going on between the rich and the poor over the right to roam the countryside. Landowners have been closing more and more space, setting aside huge chunks for their selfish pastime of hunting, closing down lands which once belonged to the community.

Hiking was in England a component of the socialist lifestyle. Solnit says one has only to read Frederich Engels's book on the English working class about the deformed working conditions to understand why striding across open space under clean skies was a liberation many were willing to fight for.

Subsequently the working class began to assert its right to walk and a big movement for walking, rambling in the countryside grew in the teeth of opposition from big landowners.

Solnit writes fascinatingly about the street life of Paris. Parisians inhabit their public gardens and streets as though they were salons and corridors and their cafes face the street and overflow into it as though the theater of passerby were too interesting to neglect even for the duration of a drink.

Street life in many cities is now very mechanical and drab because of the onslaught of the automobiles which monopolises road space. There is little social space for pedestrians in this landscape. The elite has therefore internalized walking by walking on the treadmill rather than on streets. This is ridiculous, doing exercise indoors instead of outdoors in a much more natural environment.

The tread mill was invented in 1818 by William Cubitt of Ispwich and was used for punishing prisoners.

It is quite strange that the boring treadmill has become a matter of fashion and it is being used instead of walking in the open. For a long time people will remember the image of Mr Pramod Mahajan on television doing the exercise on the treadmill even while results had started coming for the Lok Sabha elections of 2004. The leader of the right-wing Bharatiya Janata party was so confident of the BJP's retaining power that he dismissed queries from journalists and kept walking on the treadmill. And within minutes it was all over for the party.

Walking helps you see life around, you get in tune with nature and nature in turn inspires you, says Prasoon Joshi, a prominent figure in the advertising world. I find gym equipments boring. It was while walking on the promenade in Bandra that Joshi got an idea for a lyric for the hit film Rang De Basanti on revolutionary Bhagat Singh.

Speedy travel by trains or cars has not made travel more interesting, it has made it duller because you cannot enjoy and savour nature while going fast.

Modern political leaders have often held crucial conversations on walks in order to avoid being bugged.

Sunil Dutt, former film star and Congress politician, narrates an interesting story of his young days in western

Punjab now in Pakistan. There was a holy Muslim shrine in the village. People riding horses invariably dismounted when they came to the shrine, walked the distance for some time and then mounted the horse. This not only showed respect to the shrine but also showed that walking is associated with humility in comparison to horse riding.

The grand film Mughal-e-Azam opens with an interesting scene showing Akbar walking to a shrine seeking the birth of a son, an heir to the empire. He is not riding an elephant or a horse. That again shows how walking is associated with humility as against the arrogance of the power-driven vehicle.

The Dhammapada, the ancient Buddhist text, makes a critical reference to the vanity associated with the vehicle used by the big wigs of the time, the chariot. The uneducated, fools sit in chariots, the discerning have no glamour for it.

Since the middle ages some pilgrims have walked barefoot or with stones in their shoes or fasting or in special garments.

Pilgrims, clothed in simple white cotton wraps, have walked to Mecca since the beginning of Islam 1400 years ago. But in the last few years pilgrimage to Islam's holiest site has become a torture because of the excessive reliance placed by the Saudi authorities on motor transport which creates serious traffic jams. Mecca has become a death trap and the authorities should further avoid disaster by making people walk, says Ziauddin Sardar, a regular contributor to the New Statesman (NS 26-3-99).

A web of multi-lane roads, flyovers, spaghetti junctions and suffocating tunnels make the place look like a science fiction nightmare.

Worse, pilgrims from Asia and Africa are viewed with suspicion as illegal immigrants. Asghar Ali Engineer, Bohra social reformer and scholar, also feels that it would be best to take passengers by public transport buses.than by cars.

In a technologically advanced society with total breakdown of social bonding, walking will be viewed with greater suspicion. Noted writer Ray Bradbury has brilliantly portrayed this problem, based partly on his own experience of being questioned by a policeman for walking at night.

In the story titled 'The Pedestrian' While the pedestrian was taking a walk at night a lone car suddenly flashed a fierce white cone of light upon him. He stood entranced stunned by the illumination and then drawn towards it.

A metallic voice called to him. Stand still. Stay where you are. Don't move. Put up your hands. Your hands up, or we will shoot.

The police cannot believe his explanation that he is walking for air, walking to see life around him. He is taken to the psychiatric center for research on regressive tendencies. This is an ominous story and don't think it is fanciful and exaggerated.

The philosopher Theodore Adorno says right to walk should be treated as a basic human right. It should be part of human dignity. We should have a right to walk, right to a rhythm not extorted from the body by command or terror. Walking means to be free to make choices, choice to stop and linger to communiciate, to play.

It is necessary to create a new manifesto for the 20th century to assert the right to walk, says Daniel Sauter, a pedestrian activist based in Zurich and trained in sociology and political science.

He also questions the false notions of speed and time saving promoted by the car culture. He quotes Michael Ende's novel Momo in which little grey men tell adults to stop convesation and give up time-consuming hobbies. The idea is to save time. But then people find that the more time they save, the less time they have. They remain constantly busy. That is what has come to be known as the Momo effect.

Our transport policies are a prime example of the Momo effect. The more cars we have and faster they go, people spend more and more time in traffic jams and in traveling. There is really no time saving taking place. And pedestrians are the worst hit.

Actually there is a great Time Robbery. Time is being stolen from pedestrians because of the car lobby. Higher car speeds means more waiting time for pedestrians at traffic signals, less freedom for pedestrians. Car culture also robs children of playing space and has long-term negative impact on health, causing obesity and other problems. Because other cars make walking dangerous for children, parents have to again use cars to drop children to school and ferry them home again. High speeds narrow the field of vision leading to a loss of perception and sensitivity to others.

Increased car use makes people obese and this in turn increases their dependence on car. They do not like to walk. Other problems begin like back pain, low self-esteem and even alcoholism. Increased car usage and use of fuel means less fuel for agriculture which is heavily dependent on oil in terms of fertilizers, pesticides and irrigation.

Sustainable solution the global food crisis must include measures to reduce transportation oil demand, greater investment in walking and cycling which in turn will reduce obesity, point out Ian Roberts, professor in the London School of Hygiene and Tropical Medicine, and Phil Edwards (Lancet 21-5-08).

Slower traffic speed is of immense relevance to children and young people as they are the major users of the outdoor environment, through play, school travel, leisure activities. Walking and cycling are important for long-term health and well-being and establishing a habit of physical activity in early life helps to foster an active lifestyle in adulthood. Walking and cycling can help children to learn about their local environment, acquire and develop road sense, assess risk and learn to rely more upon themselves, the UK department of transport has noted in several studies.

Speed management initiatives such as as speed limits can significantly reduce parental fears about traffic danger. The heavier the motor traffic volume, the less streets are used by people. Communities are stripped of their social capital and there is a decline in the quality of life. Cyclists and pedestrians find it harder to get around. Older people and families with young children report that high road traffic volumes result in insecurity.

Lower speed can reduce noise, reduce damage to roads, reduce road maintenance and repair costs and most importantly reduce accidents and the huge costs involved in hospital treatment and insurance. Controlling speed lies at the heart of road safety strategy, declared the UK Prime Minister Tony Blair in 2000 and there is all the more reason why this strategy should be adopted in India with its high death rate on roads.

Mahatma Gandhi's favourite disciple Vinoba Bhave was known as a walking university because he talked on various subjects during his walks which gave a wealth of information to others.

Bhave used to wake up at 2.30 a.m., do his chores and begin walking at 5 a.m. He walked across most of India as part of the Bhoodan yatra in which people donated him land for public use.

Even industrialist G.D. Birla was a good walker and there is a documentary film on his trekking to Jamunotri in the Himalayas, according to his biographer R.N. Jaju.

In the car culture walking and playing on the street is considered undesirable. Children should be able to walk to school. They are major users of streets. But their needs are never taken into account. They should be involved in designing of neighbourhood streets, experts point out.

The American Academy of Paediatrics in a policy statement in July 2007 declared that children who do not walk are likely to develop serious health problems in later life including diabetes, heart disesase and hypertension. Riding to school is far better than being driven by car. The Congress in America allocated 612 million dollars in 2005 for five years to help communities to create safe routes to school.

Children with vigorous physical activity show a remarkable improvement in concentration, memory, problem solving and creativity. (Jane Brody NYT 1-9-07).

How can we fight the car culture and promote walking ? One of the ways is to create a longing among people for livable streets, for the pleasure of walking and public space. In the Tibetan language to be human means to be on foot.

When you walk you have the freedom and the self-determination. But advertisers create the impression that only cars can give you freedom. Car advertisements celebrate freedom to drive but complain about inadequacy of the road system. Similarly, we can celebrate the joys of walking and denounce the deficiency of infrastructure for pedestrians.

Actually, experts point out slow tempo of life should be made into a positive value. Slow pace enhances the quality of life. This can be popularized through some ways. There can be a slogan like this. Looking for inspiration ? Walk. And indeed walking is excellent for stimulating the mind and fighting depression.

We have to create a parallel view point. Actually, it is walking that is really liberating.

We have to seduce people to walking and reverse the hierarchies in transport policies. Christopher Alexander, a radical architect, points out that pedestrian space must always come first and vehicular space afterwards in conception, layout and construction. Serve cars and trucks but this must be done in the context of the pedestrian.

Another dimension to walking pertains to women whose right to use of public spaces is severely restricted by curbs on women's movements, says researcher Shilpa Phadke.

With more women working now in offices and other places, they are much more visible in public spaces. But there is what Phadke calls the tyranny of purpose. In group discussions and interviews she found that women have the highest degree of comfort in public places where they have some specific task to accomplish or are commuting from point A to point B. Women cannot just wander on streets for relaxation. They are immediately suspected of being street walkers.

Most women prefer to wait at a bus stop or in shops for friends rather than at street corners as these have greater legitimacy. The greatest fear is that of being perceived as soliciting men for sex.

The most exhaustive study on pedestrians was done by William Whyte for 16 long years in the automobile-dominated US. He did it quite unobtrusively, he watched people and used photographs to chart the meandering of pedestrians. What has emerged through his analysis is an extremely human, often amusing view of what is staggeringly obvious about people's behaviour in public spaces, but seeming invisible to the unaware. One of his acute and very relevant observations is that pedestrians are so considerate and sociable. Have you ever seen a clash, a collision between pedestrians coming from opposite directions ? On the other hand look at the behaviour of motorists towards other motorists coming from the front or going in the same lane as them. Pedestrians always make room for the other.

Pedestrians in India, are particularly considerate to one another. Betsy Karel, a Washington-based photographer, has observed about Mumbai that at Churchgate station she faced a Tsunami wave of people heading in her direction. People would part just enough so that I could get through, she says. I don't think that anybody in New York would do that. (Aseem Chhabra, Mumbai Mirror.

Whyte was the editor of Fortune magazine and author of the the book Organisation Man in which he took a hard and critical look at business practices.

Whyte wrote that the street is among the greatest of our cultural legacies. It is the river of city life. It gives the city continuity and coherence. It defines its scale. But it is under attack.

He set up the Street Life Project to learn how city spaces are used. One of the first findings was that the overcrowded city is a myth. Most of the spaces observed were not overused. They were underused. This is true of urban spaces in India as well. One will find that where footpaths are provided, they are so badly built that few people use them. It is a massive waste of space where space is scarce. If only footpaths are made more people-friendly, they will be happily used. But most footpaths are shoddily built. Instead of giving grace to the street, they give ugliness. Where footpaths are not there, the street becomes even more chaotic.

People tend to sit where there are places to sit. But what is just as important as a good place to sit is what you see from. The prime places are those with full views of the main show, the street. Sitting spaces, benches and chairs on streets, in gardens, railway stations are desperately needed in a poor and hot country like India. But this aspect is totally ignored in our planning. Such spaces will also give some character to streets, make them more humane and will act as a check to speeding traffic in residential areas.

Where the civic corporation and other authorities have failed miserably, an entrepreneur in Mumbai Mahavir Prasad Saraf has donated 14,000 benches at various spaces in Mumbai. He has come to be known as Benchwalas. His benches are also well-designed and comfortable to use.

Successful spaces are not cut off from the street, they are not elevated high above it nor are they sunk beneath it. Sunken plazas are usually empty.

The elements of a good city space, then are basics and it is interesting to note how many of them are natural – people to watch, sun to bask in, trees to sit under, water to splash in and listen to. Nowhere does nature seem so important to people as in the city And enjoyment of the city outdoors is increasing.

Open spaces are important not only because they make good postcards, but also because they make the city attractive to the bright and the young from elsewhere. Without that infusion of energy the city will have lost its meaning because it is the verve, the buzz that powers the engine.

Not one Indian city made it to a list of most livable cities worldwide in 2005. It is not just poor infrastructure, as shown by the Mumbai floods of the same year, but the apathy towards promoting an ethos.

The survey of 127 cities ranked cities worldwide on the basis of stability, healthcare, culture and environment, education and infrastructure. Most of the top ranking cities are located in Western European hemisphere or in North America and Australia.

Most of our cities have lost their identity because we have not cared for our core values, our tradition, our old city centres, public spaces, architecture. Sydney appears as one of the most livable cities in the world. And it has retained and used its basic identity. The Sydney harbour is the central point of cultural confluence with the Opera on one side and traditional market on the other. People of all ages and walks of life gather here and exchange ideas, points out Piyush Tiwari, of the University of Abdrdeen Business School, Scotland. (IE 22-10-05).

Melbourne's historic landmark the Queen Victoria market, a 125-year-old open air market, is still very much the soul of the city. And we are rushing to build and patronize shopping malls.

A livable city requires a public realm that exists in multi-functional public spaces, squares and markets places for meetings, encounters, dialogues among young and old with a diversity of backgrounds, acquaintances, friends and strangers. For this the planning system should incorporate human-scale architecture, mixed shops/houses, compact urban design with outdoor cafes and space for local fairs, says Piyush Tiwari.

If you look at cities around the world such as Vienna, Paris, Madrid and Lisbon all have a functioning public realm right in the heart of the city. Our city centres, whether in Delhi or Mumbai, turn dead during the night or during week-ends because the planning system has kept commercial areas separate from the residential. They are too far away from our homes to visit during off-hours. What a wasteful use of urban space.

Portland , which is very friendly to pedestrians and mass transport, is one of the most livable cities in the US. An interesting lesson from Portland is that restricting road traffic has attracted smart businesses to the city, according to transport expert Ben Plowden (New Statesman 8-1-01). Walking in the city one forgets that one is in the most car-dominated country in the world. A big board in the city asks motorists 'for kids' sake slow down.' What prevents our traffic police and transport establishment from implementing such people-friendly schemes ?

The street as a marvelous social space is best seen in the first scene of George Bernard Shaw's ebullient, ever green play Pygmalion written in 1913 and made into the famous film My Fair Lady featuring Audrey Hepburn and Rex Harrison.

It is only in the public space that Henry Higgins, the phonetics expert, could have recorded so many accents and where so much action could take place, so many social contradictions, so much mingling of different classes could take place.

Unfortunately, we have failed to create public spaces where people could gather, exchange ideas. Noted architecture author Gautam Bhatia laments that we have not created any prominent landmarks either. All the famous landmarks of our cities, the Gateway of India in Mumbai, the Howrah Bridge in Kolkata, India Gate and Connaught Place in Delhi are all created by the British. (Hindustan Times 18-12-05).

But then what we need urgently are not such imposing architectural structures but small social spaces dotting our cities and villages. Our towns and cities are so drab. Bhatia mentions that he once overheard a friend giving directions to a wedding venue in south Bangalore. He described a right turn at a Pepsi hoarding, a left turn near a pubic urninal, a right turn at a garbage dump and so on.

The foremost principle of a lively urban system is to create a city of short distances where balanced transportation planning makes possible commuting via pedestrian networks, bicycle networks, traffic-less streets and public transportation. Planning in Indian cities has covertly or overtly promoted urban sprawl and private transportation systems while completely disregarding all that you need to maintain the cultural identity of cities.

The tragedy of Mumbai and several other cities is that the rich and the powerful who run the cities have stopped walking on the streets years ago. Of course they do not use buses and train. They rush around in air-conditioned cars with the windows rolled up talking to their peers on cell phones. So they have no idea about where Mumbai is going wrong. They have lost touch with people, says Pritish Nandy, poet. (Bombay Times 16-11-05).

Look at how we treat our children on roads. Most drivers drive on roads without any concern for the safety of children. This obviously has an indirect impact on children's psyche, they grow up with latent fears, anxieties, stress. If we want a bright future for us and for our children, we must create a proper atmosphere for them on roads and through centres where there will be plenty of scope for them to grow in a more humane, civilized way.

Whyte advocated narrower streets for cars and wider sidewalks for people. Cram as many stores as possible along the streets to bring them alive, he said. Do away with skywalks, abolish sunken plazas and tear down walls in front of parks and playgrounds because they all increase isolation from the city experience. How very right Whyte is. If one walks along Azad Maidan, one of the biggest grounds in Mumbai and one of the earliest laid during the forming of the Esplanade in the 19th century, one will find much of it is fenced and the view is blocked by walls, constructions along the periphery. If these impediments are removed, one would get a lovely view as one walks from Metro Cinema to Chhatrapati Shivaji Terminus or on another side from Metro Cinema to Bombay Gymkhana.

Similarly, much of the view of the Maharashtra legislature building at Nariman Point is blocked by a more recently constructed compound wall.

The city is no longer suited to manufacturing and is losing that function. But the city can reaffirm its great and most basic function as a place for people to come together. This the street: busy, noisy, crowded, tacky but full of life and vitality. And full of continuity – the sense of where we are and where we have come from. There is our future.

Whyte noticed remarkably similar behaviour of pedestrians in different cities. People liked to meet on the street, converse with each other and not in a corner but where the crowds were highest.

Food stalls make a place highly attractive. People who come to eat attract other people. Water fountains and waterfalls in urban public spaces are a great draw. Whyte insists that people should be allowed to touch water. The safety record is excellent. I am aware that water falls in the Sahyadri hills which are a great draw in the rainy season on the Mumbai-Pune route are not so safe. But here we are talking about urban water places. Even those in the countryside can be made safe with a little designing and education.

Plazas, open spaces should not be walled or cut off from the street. They should provide a direct access from the street. It is best when you cannot tell where the street leaves off and the plaza begins. Plazas should not be elevated or sunk. Public spaces can be enlivened with a little imagination at at very little expense. One of my favourites is the tree in the center of the Swargate bus depot in the heart of Pune city. A lot of people sit on the circular cement platform built around the tree. It is far more interesting than the covered waiting hall space fitted with seats transplanted from state transport (ST) buses.

There is need to create more democratic spaces, spaces for the poor for their basic needs, like studying for children.. . Behind :Podar Ayurvedic hospital at Worli in Mumbai a street is used by hundreds of students for studying. This is marvelous. Of course, the best solution is to; provide sheltered and large spaces for studying. But otherwise, this is a lovely use of the street. It is certainly better than allowing the car to dominate the street. All these facilities are mainly in the old city, not in the suburbs which are newly developed and ought have; provided for these basic amenities.

Closing parts of the road to cars does not create jams for others. Traffic adjusts quickly to what is available. As space for it diminishes, so does the traffic.

Cities should take a closer look at what they already have. Most of them are sitting on a huge reservoir of space yet untapped by imagination. This is true. Near the SNDT university in Juhu there is a big vacant plot belonging to the police as a big board prominently shows. But the big space is simply wasted. It is full of rubble and is occupied with old, decrepit dust-laden vehicles apparently seized by the police. Cities do not need to spend millions creating space. In their inefficiently used rights of way ,their vast acreage of parking lots there is more than enough space for broad walkways and small parks and pedestrian places – and at premium locations, at ground level.

How wide should footpaths be? Studies by transportation planners have provided useful guidelines Whyte points out that the footpath alongside the Exxon building in New York was 45 ft wide. Our planners and politicians, activists and bureaucrats, please note. I doubt if anywhere in India there are such wide footpaths. We desperately need such wide and even wider footpaths because we have a much larger volume of pedestrian traffic.

Whyte's studies also show that pedestrians do not like to use skyways or footover bridges anywhere. These are too cumbersome. But the real point is that they show the utter dishonesty of the authorities who seek to penalize pedestrians for the convenience of motorists.

Art also thrives on the street. This is best seen outside Mumbai's best-known and oldest art gallery, Jehangir art gallery. The scene outside is much livelier than the gallery. Painters display their works, artistes draw portraits of visitors which attract big crowds. Perhaps for the same reason books sold on the streets make a much livelier scene than in book shops.

Public space is the space upon which the drama of community life unfolds. Streets, squares, parks are dynamic spaces if properly used. There is a close connection between public spaces and a democratic way of life. The first thing totalitarianism does is to prohibit gatherings in public spaces and curb free speech there. This happens in different ways.

In Mumbai the Tree Authority, far from protecting trees, is brazenly giving permissions to cut thousands of trees including old and rare ones. It has a big annual budget of Rs 21 crore, much of it remains unspent thanks to the apathy of the organization. Mr Ram Maheshwary, geenery-loving media executive in Mumbai, has drawn attention to the failure of the Authority to conduct a mandatory tree census in the city. His letter to chief justice Dalveer Bhandari on the issue was converted into a public interest litigation by the court.

Street life also needs to be made more friendly to the physically handicapped or to use the more humne expression, physically challenged. Design for the handicapped. That will solve more than one problem. It will help the handicapped and others as well. Drinking fountains which are low enough for wheelchair users are good for children. Oddly, children are thoroughly ignored in most public utilities in India.

Street performances, street artistes, musicians too should be encouraged, experts point out.

Is it not more fun and is it not more democratic to have performances in the open than in formal, enclosed spaces where everything is so meticulously planned, pre-ordained. There is also much more flexibility in street performances. Vested interests have opposed street performances because they are afraid of people's power, afraid of people who are not under their control. Poet Allen Ginsberg and folk singers legally challenged the ban on street music.

We need to heed the warnings given by Whyte who felt that ultimately, pedestrians may be pushed off the street altogether, putting them in underground passages, shopping malls, in skyways.

The idea is to totally separate pedestrians from vehicles. They say this is for the benefit of the pedestrian. That is not true. The separation is for the benefit of vehicles. Who gets the prime space ? Not the pedestrian. He or she had it, once at the ground level. Now, the pedestrian is being pushed upstairs on skyways or footover bridges or downstairs into underground passages.

It is because of this callousness of the authorities that our streets are extremely unsafe for pedestrians. Walking in Mumbai is more dangerous than climbing the Everest, declared Jamling Norgay, son of the famous Everest climber Tenzing.

But in some cases hierarchy prevails even in so humble an activity as walking. A remarkable picture on the front page of the Indian Express showed the joint police commissioner of Vadodara K Kumaraswamy being carried on the shoulder by a police constable through knee-deep water during floods. It seems the officer chose to sit on the back of the constable after his vehicle failed. It is a telling, cruel picture (1-7-2005).

Subsequently, Kumaraswamy apologized to the director general of police A.K. Bhargava for his action but said the constable had volunteered to carry him on his shoulders. The high-ranking officer was transferred in two weeks. The director general described the officer's behaviour as 'un-officer like'.

Mr K.P.S. Gill, a top police officer, said the graphic image of the police officer riding on a constable's shoulder reflects the collapse of administrative machinery.

One mentions this in some detail because the car culture is certainly responsible for this state of affairs. Officers have become so lazy because of the growing comforts of car travel that they do not like to walk, leave alone wade through flood waters.

The most successful projects integrate a variety of techniques that make the street more attractive and inviting for people on foot and bicycle. The Institute of Traffic Engineers has published a manual on traffic calming. A lot of work has been done and is being done in several Western cities. It is regrettable to say the least that our engineers and planners are either ignorant about this or they do not care. Worse, there is no political awareness and will.

We should create in people a longing for livable cities, a longing for the pleasure of walking. Walking is a human right and we should assert it. Advertisers create the impression that cars bring people together, bridge distances, bring freedom. We have to show that it is walking which really liberates, when you walk you see so much of life around you, you understand life much better, you meet poor people whom you would never meet while going by car. This enhances your understanding of life. In Tibetan language to be human means to go on foot, to walk.

Walking lets your brain do something else while your body is moving, talk, think, connive, dream, plan, negotiate, work through the budget numbers, recite epic poetry. After millions of years of walking we are programmed to think while we walk, says Ellen Vanderslice of America Walks organization.

Once you have developed the ability to walk a couple of miles, you will be surprised by the walking spaces available around your area. The main thing is to get out of the car and start walking. (Washington Post 1-10-2002).

Pedestrians are the agents of community development. Children, who walk to school, make friends with other children en route. Those who walk their dogs, quickly bond with other dog owners. The residents who walk to the local shops meet their neighbours on the journey and get to know the shopkeepers and their staff. Mothers who walk their children to the nursery become familiar with other mothers. Retired people going to collect their pension link with other pensioners and in so doing they all take note of each other's welfare. The community is enriched by the sum of all this social interaction and exchange of information, says Philip Connoly of Living Streets, London.

Pedestrians Are Second Class Citizens is the title of a German book by Ralf Risler and Doris Wunsch which looks at discrimination against pedestrians in Europe. If that is the condition in Europe, which is the most pedestrian-friendly region in the world, one can say about pedestrians in India that they are some sixth or seventh class citizens or rather not citizens at all. In fact, some elites in Mumbai want ordinary people to be denied voting rights and by corollary denying them citizenship itself.

In India it is impossible to find a signage system providing directions to pedestrians about landmarks. But every effort is made to give information to privileged motorists. There are big signsboards for them giving directions. Now, motorists will also be given information on electronic boards on roads about which roads be avoided for congestion and which one to be taken. The whole system is geared to serve only one class of road users - the motorists. It is as if the others do not exist or do not matter.

For much of Mumbai's elite the Mumbai marathon has become an occasion for showing off and publicity-seeking. In

January 2005 film star participants and industrialist Anil Ambani got much more coverage than the black champion Julius Sugat. To the credit of Ambani it must be said that he is a fitness freak and actually covers the marathon distance on Mumbai's streets. He has an obsession with fitness which began a few years ago when a foreign investor said he would think twice about investing in a company whose management was not in good health.

'I have been running long distance for many years now, at least one hundred km a week,' Anil Ambani wrote on the front page of Times of India (16-2-04). On most days he runs alone, before even dawn breaks. It is an experience akin to meditation, he says. Running has helped him reduce weight from 105 kg to 68, going from a speed of one km an hour to running more than 21 km in less than one hour and 30 minutes.

Experts sound a note of caution about marathons on city roads. Our concrete and tar roads are just not the surface to practise on, says Dr Ashish Contractor, cardiac rehab specialist and the official medicine man at the 2004 marathon in Mumbai. It is far healthier to walk on grass with bare feet but people are now leading such artificial lives, they are so removed from nature, they are confined to their automobiles.

Running causes impact on the joints and cartilages of the body and a hard surface is not appropriate, said Dr Kaushal Malhan, a specialist in sports medicine. Unfortunately, many residential buildings and other complexes have lined their jogging tracks with tiles and concrete, he says. Rijuta Divekar, health trainer of many Bollywood personalities, says overweight people should not take to running or jogging without medical advice. They should reduce their weight first.

Road and highway lobby

The showpiece of Mumbai, the Bandra Worli sea link, hid a harsh reality. Life was far from glamorous for the workers who built the bridge. Sometimes they were not paid for months.

(Working for Peanuts on the Great Bridge. Indian Express 31-3-05).

But the sea link has become an icon, a show piece for the elite as a symbol of progress, a shining India. So the film world's supestar Amitabh Bachhan, six foot plus, was striding along like an an overlord on the bridge in a video film on a Resurgent India. He talked how India was on the rise. And characteristically, he blamed the poor for holding back India's progress.

But the ruling class has always blamed the poor, in a typical case of Blaming the Victim Maharashtra's public works minister Anil Deshmukh blamed fishermen for forcing relignment of the bridge and accused them of doubling the cost. The point for some people is that no one should come in the way of the automobile and highway lobby.

Many high-profile road projects, which are launched by rulers to boost their egos and win public recognition, are built on the misery of the poor. There are two notorious names, Haussmann of Paris of the 19th century and Robert Moses of New York in the middle of the 20th century.

But rural roads are sadly neglected, points out Ratnakar Mahajan, deputy chairperson of the state planning board.

Haussmann's unhealthy influence prevailed in other countries in his time and later. In Kuwait the old city was virtually destroyed and wide streets introduced. Beirut was equally ruthless, there too a relatively significant though extremely old historic center was ruthlessly converted and modernized.

Reza Shah attempted to modernize major cities by driving a network of straight roads through the heart of the urban fabric and he set up his own statues. Similar destructive took place in Iraq, Saudi Arabia and Romania of dictator Ceaucescu which reminds us that Haussmannization will always appeal to regime that have power and money or are willing to pawn the future of their nation for the obliteration of indigenous environments and the announcement of Western 'progress.' How beautifully Kostof put it in his book.

There is the case of Robert Moses, spectacular and showing intense haughtiness, hubris. But when he undertook the Cross-Bronx expressway, cutting through the borough's center, he brought about destruction at a malicious pace and scale.

After Moses's shovels and bulldozers had done their work, pounding at the old neighbourhoods and streets for ten years in the 1950s and 1960s the Expressway was installed but the Bronx was doomed. With its thousands of abandoned buildings, the borough became the symbol of all urban ills.

The new suburbs did not have to be as car-oriented as they turned out to be. For this we can at least party blame 'master builders' like Robert Moses who had an elitist attitude towards any form of transportation designed to move the masses.

On Long Island alone, Moses built eleven expressways but he fought off any attempt to incorporate mass-transit rights of way into them according to his biographer Robert Caro.

His staunchest critic was Jane Jacobs, one of the most important urban planning thinkers.

James Howard Kunstler begins his book 'The Geography of Nowhere. The rise and decline of America's man-made landscape' with this story. He says eighty per cent of everything built in America is in the last 50 years and most of it is ugly, brutal, spiritually degrading and unhealthy. This tragic landscape of highway strips, parking lots, mega malls, junked cities and ravaged countryside is not simply an expression of our economic predicament but in large maeasure a cause. It is the everyday environment where most Americans live and work and it represents a gathering calamity whose effects we have hardly begun to measure.

Urban renewal was supposed to free the cities, to enlarge the street system and to run highways into the central business district. It was the perfect vehicle through which to install the modernist city. Automobile commuting, along with vigorous lobbying by a growing highway construction industry, had put enormous pressure on city administrators to plow high-speed expressways into the heart of the metropolis. Urban renewal removed the last impediment for city centers to be tailored to the needs of automobile transit.

Urban renewal involved not only razing of slums but also many historical landmarks in different parts of the world, according to urban planners. The damage was far more extensive than caused by bombs during the second world war, says Anthony Tung in a remarkable book 'Preserving the World's Great Cities,' which chronicles the changes various cities have gone through over the years.

The trouble with building more and more roads is that this does not at all solve problems. It only creates more capacity and so more vehicles and more congestion. Some traffic engineers are now saying that 'trying to cure traffic congestion by adding more capacity is like trying to cure obesity by loosening your belt.'

The whole car and highway culture works against the interests of ordinary people. In the US it is said that 'white men's highways go through black men's bedrooms'.

That is because highways have been built by bulldozing fragile communities. Several buildings were butchered and the landscape was damaged to pave the way for roads and highways. There was a move even to shift the Washington Monument to provide space for car parking. Such is the hideous role of the car and road lobby. The same has happened in India.

Besides, the highway culture imposes a tremendous burden on truck drivers. It is not just in India that truck drives work long hours without adequate sleep or shelters on the way. In Europe a European driver Kevin Harrison once covered six countries in 24 hours, Italy, Greece, Luxembourg, Belgium, Holland and Germany, he wrote in an article in Ecologist magazine (February 2005) Mike Davis, the foremost writer on urban sociology, worked as a truck driver for years even after he had established a reputation in academics.

Environmentally-conscious people now count 'food miles' while buying fruit and vegetables. If the produce has been brought over a long distance, they would not buy it. They oppose transnational corporations which control much of food supply chain from the farm gate to our dinner table.

As incomes for some sections grow steeply in India and China there will be increased demand for breakfast foods from abroad adding to the pressure on fossil fuels and transport. Eating Irish oats and apples from Chile may sound good but it is not good for the environment and it is best to eat locally grown food as far as possible.

Increased freight traffic in the regime of economic globalisation means extremely unsafe roads for ordinary people, says Ian Roberts, professor of public health at the London school of hygiene and tropical medicine.

Much of the international trade is not between countries but transnational corporations. International trade needs cheap transport, good roads, preferably paid for by public and cheap oil. No wonder right wing and centrist political parties are so obsessed with highway and road construction. This is vital for multinationals.

During the 1973 oil embargo cargo traffic fell considerably and there was a perceptible fall in the deaths of children on roads. One may not realize this but many road deaths are indirectly caused by the callousness of multinationals or other business corporations which force drivers to drive fast and do not give them enough rest.

While goods traffic grows, truck companies seem to care little about the health of drivers. Many of them suffer from AIDS. The incidence of the disease is 20 times higher among highway drivers than in the general population, the British Medical Journal reported quoting a study carried out by Dr Kootikoopala and others in Andhra Pradesh. Sai Paranjpye, reputed film director, has made an interesting documentary on truck drivers who are victims of the disease.

Health education of drivers carried out at Transport Nagar near Nashik on the Mumbai-Agra highway has also shown the widespread extent of HIV AIDS among drivers. Many of them have little awreness about prevention of sexually transmitted diseases, according to Dr C.R. Nampurkar who runs the Manas de-addiction. Centre in the area. They think that putting soda water on the penis or applying petrol cures them of disease. Mixing chilli powder with liquor is thought to kill harmful germs.

Contrary to architect Le Corbusier's positive image in India created by his building the city of Chandigarh, the architect had an extremely negative side which is little-known. He wanted to kill life on the streets and provide priority to motor cars, construction of more and more roads and highways. This only reinforced the mindset of planners and engineers who had little sympathy for the masses.

Massive protests have been staged in America against the mindless destruction caused by highways and roads.

The result is that transit travel has increased substantially. In Sydney, Australia, graceful ferryboats come in past the famous opera house depositing hundreds of commuters on the dock right downtown. Sydney's ferry services are so extensive that a colour-coded route map looks like a guide to London's Underground. Other cities including Seattle and Vancouver have made ferries an integral part of their daily commuter and fast catamaran boats have cut travel time.

But most Americans remain car-crazy and are not even sharing the car with others so that there could be a lot of saving of fuel and road space. Sadly, the number of people traveling by car alone is rising rapidly which shows a society with very wrong priorities and approach to life.

That work on several highways is steeped in corruption and it is a driving force for much of the construction is no longer a secret. An inquiry commission studying the Rs 2500 crore Taj expressway project has observed in its report that it is the 'biggest land scam in Uttar Pradesh.'

The entire concentration of the officers involved was to ensure that more than 6000 acres of prime land adjoining the expressway is allotted to a particular developer, said the commission set up by the Mulayam Singh Yadav government The 160 km expressway linking Delhi's suburb Noida with Agra was mooted as a showpiece by the Mayawati government which even waived stamp duty of nearly Rs 50 crore on land deals. Retired high court judge Sri Rang Mishra, the one man commission, said 600 acres of land released for the project should have been valued at Rs 1000 crores but was valued at half the amount.

Another commission of retired high court judge Siddheshwar Narain, however, exonerated Mayawati of charges of corruption and the Mulayam Singh-led state government gave the contract to the same contractor J.P. Industries. (Hindu 30-10-06).

Tamil Nadu's powerful politician Mr Karunanidhi was dramatically arrested at midnight from his residence in 2001 for alleged corruption in the construction of ten flyovers during his chief ministership in 1996-2001. One still remembers the television images of the police carrying him away as he threw his legs around accusing them of pushing him and tearing his shirt. The arrest was seen as a retaliation of Jayalalitha's arrest on corruption charges in 1996. The case against Karunanidhi was dropped during his chief ministership and celebration of his golden jubilee as a legislator in 2007.

The collapse of the Panjagutta flyover under construction in the heart of Hyderabad and deaths of 10 people in 2007 sent shock waves in the highway and flyover lobby and exposed its pretensions of providing fanciful, modern technology to Indian cities.

The Hyderabad flyover was supposed to be earthquake-proof and terrorist-proof but came down with 5.7 cm of rain.

The contractors Gammon India blamed other agencies for the mishap. An inquiry into the mishap showed that engineers found to have done shoddy work in another flyover had been reinstated after their suspension.

Immediately the Communist government in West Bengal ordered the demolition of the Bagha Jatin flyover and its reconstruction. It had been built only six years earlier. We cannot take a risk, said transport minister Ashok Bhattacharya.

The Lalbaug flyover, one of the earliest in Mumbai, was demolished due to the demand of the Shiv Sena in 2009 as it was not tall enough for to allow the ultra-high Ganapati idol during the festival procession. It is to be replaced by a bigger flyover.

In Surat, the bustling diamond and textile trade city, it was found that most flyovers were defective. The design used was 30-year-old, said a professor of the Indian Institute of Technology C.V. R. Murthy (TOI 11-9-07).

The highway and automobile culture also spells the death of other modes of transport. A telling picture in Hindustan Times showed rims of handcarts seized from hawkers below the Sion flyover in Mumbai (11-12-07).

In Bangalore the Sirsi circle flyover was found to get waterlogged and the Richmond circle flyover is at hand-shaking distance from residential buildings.

Just a few days earlier in September, 2007, a bridge on the Karachi expressway collapsed killing ten people. It had been opened only a month earlier by President General Pervez Musharraf. Even before the collapse it had come under strong opposition from environmentalists and city planners on charges of corruption and infringement of environment norms.

The Karachi city government had signed an agreement for the Karachi Elevated Expressway in March, 2006 with a Malaysian company without inviting tenders. Noted architect Arif Hasan pointed out that similar expressways in Bangkok, Manila, Tehran and Cairo had failed to solve problems. In

Riyadh the expressway in the city caused so much pollution that some affected parts had to be evacuated. The archibishop of Karachi complained that a large portion of the Christian cemetery would be lost to the expressway. The project director Rauf Akhtar Farooqi, an influential Canadian national, is said to have stated that there was no need for the time consuming process of environmental impact assessment. (Ardeshir Cowasjee, Dawn 8-4-07).

A large part of the Liaqatabad underpass caved in in Karachi in 2006, a day after its opening, (Dawn 8-10-06).

But the crisis of the transport system as a whole came to the fore in 2007 when a vital bridge in Minneapolis in the US plunged into the Mississippi river during the evening peak hours killing several people. It showed that the road, highway, freeway infrastructure in the US was ageing and was unable to take the burden of increasing traffic. The freeways had got a miserable D rating from the American Society of Civil Engineers in 2005.

The country is facing an intolerable decline in the transport system's infrastructure and there is acute deterioration in the road surface, said Jeffrey Shane, US under secretary of transport.

Even the US is finding it difficult to mobilize resources for maintenance of this infrastructure. One wonders what will happen to us with our limited resource.

Says an American expert 'We had a transport system which was the envy of the world. Now we are known for our congested highways, third rate passenger train services and primitive air traffic control system. Most of the great public works in the 20th century, the dams, canal locks, bridges, tunnels, the Eisenhower highway system were built in the fifties and are now beyond their life span.' (Stephen Flynn, homeland security expert and author Edge of Disaster – Rebuilding a resilient nation. Popular Mechanics 2-8-07).

There are obvious lessons here for us in India. Even if we create an expensive highway network, we must minimize the use of motor vehicles. Otherwise, the highway infrastructure will wear out in a few years.

Road engineers in the 'developed' state of Maharashtra are among the worst enemies of trees and pedestrians. Over 12,000 trees were cut between Chembur and Mulund by the Mumbai Metropolitan Region Development Authroity in 2004 to expand and make the eastern express highway into 14 lanes.

The MMRDA authorities lied to us, they cut the trees after promising us that they would not, said Kirit Somaiya, a former member of Parliament of the Bharatiya Janata party.

But the most troubling is the hacking of a nearly 200-year-old tree at the instance of the US consulate in Paiga palace Hyderabad for widening of the road in the area. Bittu Sehgal, environmentalist and editor of Sanctuary, who studied in a public school in the area, said he felt as if his leg had been amputated. He said a condolence meeting should be held where the names of the guilty architect of the consulate project and the town planners be declared.

Besides much of the road repair, widening, construction work is done inefficiently creating severe hazards for pedestrians, motorists and construction workers themselves, according to Sudhir Badami, a civil engineer and a member of a committee appointed by the Mumbai high court to review the construction of Mumbai's roads. Much of the work is carried out amidst heavy traffic. Cars whiz past workers who are digging with hands or electric tools or heavy earth moving equipment operates at sites amidst traffic. The expert committee, headed by former Mumbai police commissioner Ronnie Mendonca, included Mr Mihir Desai, noted civil rights lawyer, Mr Gerson D'Cunha, theatre actor and activist of Bombay First, Mr Sudhir Badami, civil engineer, and Mr. Nandakumar Salvi, former chief engineer of the municipal corporation of Mumbai.

An ultra smooth and slippeyr Eastern Express highway in Mumbai led to the skidding of several vehicles, crashes and deaths in 2008. The police registered an offence against the contractor in response to a complaint filed by Kirit Somaiya. But the chief engineer of the Mumbai Metropolitan Region Development Authority (MMRDA) S Nandgirikar blamed the accidents on fast driving during the monsoon.

One of the most severe indictments of the BJP's obsession with superhighways and unconcern for the environment, comes from Vandana Shiva, environmentalist and campaigner against genetically modified foods, who was once described as the Mao of environmentalism.

The craze for highways is writing of our fate in cement and unwriting the fate of our soil, our land and our ecology. In India we have viewed our mountains and rivers as sacred, an intrinsic part of our ecology. They are precious to us. But highways are an external design like the design imposed by Hitler on Germany.

Vandana Shiva feels that former Prime Minister Vajpayee's groundbreaking for his pet highway project has parallel images of Hitler's groundbreaking for the Frankfurt Basel Hanseatic highway.

She accused the BJP of using the highway as a means and metaphor of moulding India into one monolith, displacing other road users like bicycles, pedestrians and bullock-carts.

That more freeways, highways and roads cannot tackle the problem of congestion is now proved beyond doubt. The only solution is to curb private vehicles. Look at what David Begg, the chairperson of the U.K. commission for integrated transport, says. 'The travel crisis in the U.K. is now so acute and growing demand for mobility so strong that the country cannot build its way out of trouble no matter how many motorways, bus lanes and railway lines are opened.

Private operators are in a position to increase toll charges unlike governments which are answerable to the people. The automobile and highway lobby may soon dictate terms and prevent pedestrians from using certain roads. This is quite a likely scenario unless people resist strongly.

In England 23 year old Swampy became the nation's favourite activist after burying himself underground for a week in protest against environmental destruction caused by road building. He created great awareness with his protests. Would I have had such success if I had only written a letter to the local member of Parliament ? Swampy asked (Independent 1-2-97).

The MMRDA (Mumbai metropolitan region development authority) which brutally chopped a number of old trees in Mumbai did not even take permission from the Tree Authoritity to cut the tress, according to P.A. Naringrekar, municipal superintendent of gardens. But Anahita Pundole, a medical doctor and campaigner against chopping of trees by the advertising lobby, is not impressed by the BMC's talk. The corporation simply does not take any action against anti-tree vandals. Civic guidelines make it mandatory for advertising agencies to maintain and preserve trees within 25 metres of a hoarding. But the vandalism by advertising agencies continues.

That the flyover is essentially intended to win votes was clear in 2008 when the Vilasrao Deshmukh-led Congress government permitted work on the Dadar-Sion flyover to go on in the rainy season so that it could be ready for the elections in 2009. Mr PRK Murthy, chief of transport, MMRDA, regretted the inconvenience and added it was for a better tomorrow.

There is cumulative neglect of maintenance, according to N.V. Merani, a member of a committee appointed by the Mumbai high court and veteran engineer. Only the top portion is redone during repairs knowing full well that this will last only one fair season. Roads must be certified layer by layer.

Usually potholes on roads are seen mainly from the point of view of motorists. For an engineer, pothole is the first sign that the road is falling. Scientific design is a key element. Simply adding extra bitumen to achieve the prescribed thickness does not work In case of cement roads, cars run on the road the day after the concrete work is done. This is absurd. There ought to be some discipline.

Following a public furore and a public interest litigation on the issue, the Mumbai high court appointed a roads monitoring committee headed by former city police commissioner Ronnie Mendonca in 2006.

Eighty per cent of all suburban automobile trips have nothing to do with work at all. These are short drives to places that used to be accessible on foot, such as shops, schools, parks and friends' houses. With the disappearance of that once common activity, the useful walk, the weight of the average American adult has risen eight pounds in ten years. Nearly sixty per cent Americans are overweight.

Flyovers, trumpeted by the Shiv Sena-BJP coalition, have proved to be of poor quality with big potholes injuring many and slowing down traffic which defeats the very purpose of constructing them. Several flyovers will become even more dangerous for motorists in the coming days, an expert committee has warned. Besides, the space below the flyovers, instead of becoming an interesting social, public space, is full of squalor or is used for vehicle parking or dumping of construction material. In contrast the space is used much better in Delhi with landscaping and clean maintenance.

It was only in 2007 that the government woke up to the need to ensure an aesthetic quality to the shoddy looking projects by bodies like the municipal corporation, the public works department and the Maharashtra state road development corporation (MSRDC).

Projects costing above Rs five crore must conform to certain aesthetic standards, said Sanjay Ubale, secretary, special projects, Maharashtra government. Mr Milind Mhaiskar, joint commissioner, MMRDA, admits the city certainly deserves a more attractive look.

A year later the government realized that parking of vehicles and constructing of shops under flyovers was a serious secUrity hazard. Chief minister Vilasrao Deshmukh ordered civic bodies in the state to beautify the spaces. Mr T.C. Benjamin, principal secretary, urban development department, said no new permission will be given for commercial use of the spaces.

Profligate spending on flyovers and other grandiose schemes has contributed to the Maharashtra government landing a trap with debt exceeding Rs.100,000 crore. Flyovers are spectacular and are seen as a way to hide the harsh reality of daily life. More than 1000 farmers in Maharashtra committed suicide at the end of the year 2006. So the Congress party announced construction of 16 more flyovers in Mumbai with an eye on the approaching municipal elections of early 2007.

With the flyovers we can travel non-stop along the main arteries from one end of the city to the distant suburbs, the chief minister declared triumphantly. Never mind the fact that it takes nearly an hour to reach one km in some parts of Mumbai even by car. Of course the non-existence of footpaths in most of the city and unusable condition of footpaths in other parts does not bother the politicians, officials and planners.

Maharashtra has proved to be as inefficient as Bihar and Tripura when it comes to implementation of the Prime Minister's rural roads scheme. There can be no excuse for this. Maharashtra could complete only 30 per cent of the planned roads in rural areas though the funds were provided by the Centre, according to the union rural development ministry. The executive chairman of the state planning board Ratnakar Mahajan was a lone voice in the administration to complain.

The Sena trumpeted the success of its flyovers project but the bluff was called by its own Mayor Shubha Raul who lives in the distant suburb of Dahisar. She found it much quicker to travel by the suburban train than use her Mayoral car in 2007.

Worse, roads are built deep into wildlife sanctuaries to suit business interests. These roads take a heavy toll of animals including elephants in accidents and the roar and pollution caused by traffic has its own negative impact. Such intrusion have nearly wiped out the tiger from the Sariska sanctuary in Rajasthan but business interests are opposing diversion of traffic from the areas. More sadly, the traffic is increasing each year. But it is the poor forest dweller who is treated as a threat to the tiger.

A World Bank-funded highway project connecting Mysore to Kerala will disrupt wildlife and the corridor for dispersion and migration of wildlife in the Nagarhole and Bandipur sanctuaries. Hundreds of elephants reach the backwaters of Kabini for fodder and water and later return to the forests using the corridor. Such highways also facilitate timber smuggling and poaching, points out Sanjay Gubbi, conservation activist. Noted tiger biologist K Ulhas Karanth has propoed a simple diversion outside the national park. When Wildlife First acivists K.M. Chinnappa and Praveen Bhagarv went to inspect the highway, the contractors' henchment intimidated them.

Motorists have gone ga ga over the flyovers built in Mumbai in the nineties. But many of these are shoddily built and have become death traps for the poor. The exit points for many flyovers are the most hazardous for pedestrians. Crazily driven vehicles do not slow down at the exit and run over innocent pedestrians who find themselves trapped on the road as several footpaths have been destroyed during the construction of the flyovers. This is most noticeable near the J.J. hospital-end.

The 2.4 km J.J. flyover in Mumbai has cut short the distance for the car lobby, given it a joy ride and invaded the privacy of hundreds of Muslim households on both sides of the Mohammad Ali Road and inflicting deafening noise on them. Advertisement boards have covered the sound absorbers on the flyover so residents cannot hear each other talk nor can they hear the television programmes.. Residents have to keep their windows closed all the time in Mumbai's unbearably humid and hot weather which gets worse because of the heavy traffic. (JJ flyover breaks all sound barriers. Daily 22-5-07).

To ride mindlessly over the flyover is to miss some of the most historic and lively areas of Mumbai, one of the first 'native settlements' during British rule.

The mohallas or lanes here brim with social and commercial life. Where else would you find Bishtis, water carriers cycling around areas like Pydhonie, Bori Bazar, Bhendi Bazar, Madanpura and Foras road. And then there are the calligraphers and Victoria horse carriages. The lanes and bylanes here were also home to some of the most celebrated left-wing Urdu writers and artistes including Kaifi Azmi, Ali Sardar Jafri, Sajjad Zahir, K.A. Abbas, Majrooh Sultanpuri, Ismat Chugtai. These lanes once breathed of Communist slogans and poetry. Now the area is known more for its rich and varied food. Many who sneer at the word Bhendi Bazar forget that it has given birth to a whole gharana of Hindustani classical music dating back to the 1870s. (Sameera Khan and others Time Out Mumbai 11-9\8-06).

There is something nice, even sacred, about small lanes. Here is a very interesting quote from the Bible. Enter through the narrow gate, for wide is the gate and broad is the road that leads to destruction but small is the gate and narrow the road that leads to life and only a few find it. (Matthew 7. 13-14)

Motorists are having a joy ride over the new flyovers but the flyovers have also vastly increased traveling distance for which ordinary people pay the price. They have to pay a much higher fare by auto-rickshaw or taxi than earlier because flyovers have vastly increased the distance between two points. Yet, the authorities have the gall to claim that flyovers save fuel.

The Bandra flyover was used for car racing on some days for a few years in what is clearly grabbing of public space for an exclusive group and ordinary people were barricaded.

Parents are encouraging irresponsible behaviour among young drivers by letting their children go to school on motorbikes. The Shirin Dinyar Irani school in Dahanu near Mumbai banned such students and the move was widely welcomed. It is a crime to allow such motor-bike riding to school, said Vandana Lulla, principal of the Podar international school.

Flyovers are built in the name of all but used by only a minority. In other words, these are free lunches for the better off. Sunita Narain, environmentalist and editor of Down To Earth journal, points out.

Besides the flyovers are proving to be self-defeating. 'Fly over and Crawl under' is the apt headline of a news story. Motorists may cruise and sail over the flyovers but they get stuck down below on the road beneath the flyovers. Traffic jams are still the order of the day.

Defective, badly handled traffic lights and poorly designed flyovers cause a lot of accidents involving pedestrians in several cities, a study by the Indian Institute of Technology, Delhi. Forty per cent accidents occur near traffic signals which leave little time for pedestrians to cross the junction. Flyovers promote vehicular speed and endanger pedestrians.

Besides, the flyovers completely neglect the needs of pedestrians and cyclists, says Geetam Tiwari, an IIT Delhi professor working with the Transportation and Research Injury Prevention Programme. So much money was spent on the flyover at the major public hospital the All India Institute of Medical Science (AIIMS) but no provision was made for pedestrians and cyclists.

Debabrata Sanyal, who has designed several of Delhi's flyovers, says the facilities are provided at the planning stage but eliminated during implementation. R Subramaniam, engineer-in-chief of several flyover projects, admits that in the general traffic scenario the needs of pedestrians and cyclists have been sidetracked.

While crores of rupees are lavished on flyovers, some of the oldest, heritage bridges with stone masonary remain neglected though they need urgent repairs and are an important part of Mumbai's history.

While increasing the mobility of its own people Israel is hindering the mobility of others. Sanjay Subrahmanyam, a bright young Indian historian, was present in the Israeli Supreme court when a case came up pertaining to lands of Bedouin pastoral groups which the Israeli army wanted to seize.

Nobel prize winning German writer Gunther Grass during his visit to Kolkata for the Kolkata book fair in 2005 said visiting Kolkata after 18 years he saw many changes, not all for the better. I see a lot of flyovers but they have ultimately divided the city between the haves and the have-nots, he said. Many old houses have been demolished and replaced by new commercial centres and restaurants. But the ubiquitous slums are there too. I miss the cows on the streets. They played an important role in slowing down traffic. But I am a little suspicious of this progress. If the city gets more and more developed many poor people would lose their small jobs.

Slowing down of traffic would appear to be a blasphemy to our speed-crazy culture. But in the civilized world they are indeed slowing down traffic. In Germany and elsewhere roads are being narrowed, not widened, so as to reduce traffic. But there is so much ignorance on these issues among our planners, politicians and bureaucrats that this will appear to them as fantastic nonsense.

Grass felt that culturally the British empire is still ruling India. True, but it would be more appropriate to say that the American culture is ruling India if you consider the craze in the upper class for more cars, speed, roads, flyovers, freeways. As compared to the Americans, the British look like angels especially in terms of road and transport culture.

The highway allow for fast speed but there is a hitch here. For safe driving vehicles must keep a lot of distance between them. It means that only a limited number of cars can drive both fast and safely on the highway. The highway will carry more vehicles at slower speed. But that is not what the, speed-crazy motorist wants.

Sensible people are rising in revolt against mindless flyovers. In Seoul capital of the highly advanced South Korea, a double decker highway was pulled down by Mayor Lee Myung-bak, who became chief executive of Hyundai, the leading car manufacturing company, at the age of 36. The highway in front of the City Hall caused a tangle of traffic as it used to bring 170,000 vehicles daily into the city centre. It was built in the 1970s during the scramble to build a modern city out of the ruins of the Korean war of 1950-53.

As cars took over the city, the river bed was turned into a road and then an elevated six-lane motorway was built above it in one of the worst comprehensive obliterations of the natural environment.

Tearing down the motorway was a symbolic act undertaken after extensive consultations with thousands of citizens. They were asked what was most important for the city. They all said environment and water. (Guardian Weekly 19-1-06).

The whole area is now covered with grass into a perfect, green Oval abuzz with concerts or protests. (Financial Times 17-11-05) More importantly, the Mayor has restored a stream which had remained buried beneath the road in the area. The six km Cheonggycheon stream opened in 2005. Citizens are thrilled, they are enjoying walking along the stream. Bridges have been built on the stream in styles ranging from the ancient to the modern. Since the opening of the stream surveys have put the Mayor on top among hopefuls for the post of the country' president.

The river is now acting as a natural air-conditioner. Shanghai and Tokyo are now inspired to follow the role of Seoul.

Highway engineers in the US have realized that they must give up their hubris, their arrogance and recognize the importance of environment, listen to the voices of common people.

In India the real need is not for expressways and flyovers but for little access roads and rights of passage through other properties which come up by grabbing land that once belonged to common people.

As big builders buy huge plots of land in cities and build posh housing colonies, they block lanes formerly used by common people and which lay in the properties. People do have a right to these passages under what are known as easement rights. Lawyer and consumer activist Shirish Deshpande points out that easement rights are not only about land but also light and air.

It would be criminal of a builder to block air and light to a neighbouring building. But builders are doing precisely that and blocking people's traditional routes too.

There is not much awareness among people on their right to passage and they must assert it. Why are the rich so afraid of allowing common people to pass through their properties ? Their very riches in a poor country gives them a feeling of insecurity.

The Ahmedabad-Vadodara expressway, built without concern for the surroundings, blocked the rain water and caused extensive flooding in a number of villages causing extensive damage. This expressway was earlier seen as the jewel in the crown by the government led by the right-wing Bharatiya Janata party. But when the havoc was caused the government came to its senses and wrote a strongly-worded letter to the National Highway Authroity of India regarding its defective design. The design had no space for water to pass from one side of the expressway to the other. Angry villagers protested and beat up an employee at the toll bridge at Kheda.

The flood havoc on July 26 in 2005 in Mumbai was intensified by the official work of constructing roads, flyovers, expanding the airport and strangulating the Mithi river for the Bandra Worli sea link.

The Sena chief Bal Thackeray had to be evacuated by a boat from his bungalow in Bandra (east) because of the flooding.

This had another implication. The strangulation of the river would starve the mangroves of water supply, they would die and then the builders would reap a rich bonanza of land. The river is just behind the Mumbai Metropolitan Regional Development Authrority which was supposed to deepen and clean the river. Environmentalists like Girish Raut, oceonographer A.G. Untwale and Bittu Sehgal had been repeatedly drawing attention to this problem but were ignored. Then the disaster struck. There would be an even bigger disaster if the warnings continue to be ignored.

While the state machinery completely failed to provide relief to lakhs of citizens on that day, common people displayed great spirit. As thousands waded through waist-deep water, local people guided them to avoid manholes and other pitfalls and gave them food.

Thousands were marooned and many were killed making a mockery of the government's talk of converting Mumbai into Shanghai. And the share market index rose to 7700 points, the highest ever.

It is not slums but the process of globalisation and the land grab by the rich which contributed to the flooding of waters, socially conscious architect Arvind Adarkar says.

The absence of urinals for miles together worsened the plight of thousands of commuters, especially women, stranded in buses all night. As luxuries for the rich grow in Mumbai, there is a steep decline in basic amenities for ordinary people.

It was only after the huge traffic jams caused by flooding that the government appealed to people to use cars only when they really need them and to make car pools. But then that is the appeal which should be made during normal times because even in the best of times cars create a mess on roads. Car pool are a reasonable alternative. But most motorists feel it is below their dignity to share the car.

So alarmed were car manufacturers after the floods exposed the shortcomings of the car culture, that they immediately announced a lot of incentives to motorists for repairing of the damaged vehicles. Hundreds of cars remained unrepaired for months after the floods and many were kept on open public space by car companies in the Bandra Kurla complex.

The Times of India made a special announcement that the Rs five crore Maybach car of top indutrialist Mukesh Ambani was unaffected by the floods. 'We are happy to report that the most expensive steed on the Mumbai carriageway is safe and unscathced. The thoroughbred from the Daimler Chrysler stable sat warmly sheltered at Sea Wind during the storm. (5-8-05)

That was at a time when over 600 people lost their lives in modern Mumbai, just drowned, washed away, unsung, unhonoured, unknown.

Why are builders, politicians and officials so obsessed with urban roads, highways and flyovers and not about education, healthcare and nutrition ? That is because urban road building promotes real estate interests and boosts property prices

Mr Manmohan Singh, a former general manager of Brihanmumbai Electricity and Transport Undertaking, said it is time industrialists, who have benefited so much from Mumbai, should give back something to the city. The corporate sector benefits from the public transport network which carries their workers and it should contribute to the cost of the transport.

He says the bus service in Mumbai is the best in the world, even better than the London bus service because of the sheer amount of people it carries. What he says is largely true but the BEST needs to be more people-oriented. There are no bus shelters in many areas, especially on the expressways where they are most needed as these places become extremely hot and polluted. Other areas at least provide some shade because of adjacent trees or buildings. The expressway has nothing but the roar of monotous traffic.

In America the highways served to kill mass transit alternatives. The passage of the 1956 Interstate highway Act ensured the complete triumph of the automobile over mass transit alternatives and killed off, except in a few large cities, the vestiges of the balanced public transportation systems that remained in 1950s America. Urban freeways constructed as part of the Interstate highway system bisected and destroyed a number of cohesive urban neighbourhoods and some city parks at great social cost and public expense.

Viable cost-efficient rail transportation including the Paris Metro in France and urban mass transit in Germany persists in Europe despite relatively high levels of automobile ownership and use. And in Japan, world leadership in automobile production and in automobile culture with excellent mass transit, exemplified by the bullet trains which are also subsidized. These facts unequivocally demonstrate that mature automobile cultures are compatible with excellent mass transit systems. Why then did the automobile revolution end up virtually wiping out the urban mass transit and rail passenger services in the United States ?

When America faced an imminent fuel shortage and long term energy crsis President Nixon called for decreased automobile use and imposed a national 55 miles per hour speed limit over the system's 80 mph on highways.

In a poor country, it is the pagdandi, a walkway, not the highway which should receive top priority from politicians, planners and bureaucrats Also, it is the feeder routes to the main roads which carry most of the traffic and deserve priority. But it is VIP roads which get the priority and much of this expenditure is also wasteful.

On the other hand, much of the budget earmarked for feeder routes remains unutilized. While the elite remains obsessed with highways and freeways, I found it interesting that Mr Kiran Karnik, a top figure in the information technology field, should have constantly used the imagery of the pagdandi, a walkway. He talked of information pagdandi, not information highway, in his front page article in the Indian Express (7-12-05).

An informed country means an aware citizenry, individual conscious of their rights, recourse and responsibility. Empowering India means empowering of the disadvantaged and this requires that information be available at the grass-roots level.

It is in this context that I see the Pagdandi as empowerment, he said. Literally, a footpath, it takes shape as each individual chooses a route for going from one point to another. To empower India, more power to the pagdandi, he concludes.

In a similar vein it can be argued that it is small streets, paths that provide access to the urban and rural poor which can really empower India. It is not enough to have highways and freeways which the rulers are using as showpieces and as demonstration of their power and to create a façade, a vote catching device.

From Pakistan there is this interesting story narrated by Shekhar Gupta, veteran journalist. Nawaz Sharif once insisted that the journalist travel from Islamabad to Lahore on the eight-lane motorway he had built and was so proud of. He even sent his newest Mercedes to Gupta so he could really enjoy the ride.

The motorway was wonderful but it was surprising to see how empty it was.

The driver told him that was because it is nearly a hundred km longer than the Grand Trunk Road built by Sher Shah Suri more than 500 years earlier. And the old driver explained why. He said the moment Mian saab (Nawaz Sharif) announced the plans to build his dream highway, all his key partymen from Punjab made sure it passed their villages. Meanwhile, they went and bought large parcels of land en route. These then had to be acquired at exaggerated prices fixed by themselves. So the highway has become a white elephant. (Indian Express 24-12-05).

The fraudulent exercise of building roads is at the core of a hilarious play Sadak written and directed by the renowned director Habib Tanvir. It completely exposes and ridicules the anti-social sections who build roads in the name of development when their true intentions are different.

The play received a rousing applause in Prithvi Theatre in Mumbai in 2004 though the audience was far from radical. But such is the strength and appeal of the play that the audience wanted more of the fun when the curtain came down. In the play villagers are being prosecuted in the court for breaking up a road and obstructing the so-called development. It is to Tanvir's eternal credit that he develops such a superb satirical comedy out of this situation.

The judge is turned into an intensely comic figure and the necktie-wearing executives, talking in the name of development, are throroughly exposed, mocked at.

The Jarawas, one of the most primitive communities in the world, is threatened by the Andaman Trunk Road in the Indian ocean island of Andaman in India, in the teeth of opposition from environmentalist and anthropologists. The tribal people are still in the hunter gatherer stage and extremely vulnerable to the invasion of tourists who want to turn them into a spectacle.

The road has not been closed despite the order of the Supreme court of India in 2002. It is like a public thorough fare through one's private courtyard, said Dr R.K. Bhattacharya, a former director general of the Anthropological Survey of India. (Pankaj Sekhsaria. IE 22-11-06).

Different people react in different ways when they are trampled upon by the system. A film The Tunnel made by Shireen Narayanan highlights the modern David and Goliath tale about a small group of inner city residents in Perth, Australia, who fought the construction of a road tunnel project for five years against the combined might of corporate and government interests.

What begins as a simple case of residents seeking compensation for damage to their homes turns into an epic tale of struggle for justice and exposes and machinations of a state government and its corporate masters as they collude to mislead, conceal and intimidate. Shireen was born in Kolkata in 1955 and lived in Mumbai until her migration to Australia at the age of 19, She is a psychotherapist.

In the misplaced priorities of politicians and unenlightened bureaucrats flyovers are prime show pieces. Else why should the Karnataka government have spent lakhs of rupees in publishing big advertisements in national media about a single flyover, the 650 metre Anand Rao Circle flyover in Bangalore in 2006? There were pictures all over India of chief minister H.D. Kumarswamy and other worthies. As if this was some great achievement.

The obsession with road building can take dangerous forms. It was only strong opposition from activists that forced the Punjab government to give up its plan for a multi-crore for elevated roads and skybuses around the famed Golden Temple, the most important shrine for Sikhs. The project would have also blocked the view of the 16th century temple.

The temple complex needs footpaths rather than elevated roads and the surrounding areas need to be declared a vehicle-free zone, said Dr Sukhdev Singh, convener of the Indian National Trust for Art and Cultural Heritage (INTACH). But the authorities want to increase vehicular traffic which will worsen congestion and pollution around the temple.

A similar plan for skywalks around Five Gardens in Parsi Colony, one of the greenest and quietest areas in Mumbai, has been opposed by heritage lovers.

Modern engineers full of hubris, false pride, should study how the ancient Inca civilization built fiber rope bridges as thick as a man's torso across the deep gorges of the Andes mountains in Peru hundreds of years before the arrival of the Spanish in 1532.

The Spanish had never seen in Europe anything like the bridges of Peru. They stood in awe and fear before the spans of braided fibre cables suspended across the deep gorges, narrow walkways, sagging and swaying. (NYT, May 2007.

Such is pressure for roads from the car lobby that the Pune municipal corporation constructed a road right in the bed of the river Mula in the heart of the city without any public consultation. it is like blowing a hole in your head if you are having a headache, says environmentalist Pankaj Sekhsaria. The Pune work was stopped only on the orders of the court in resonse to a public interest litigation. And this in a city known for its tradition of learning, public service, social work. It has now been overtaken by the builder lobby. Nearly 50,000 trees have been felled in Pune in the last five years by the road lobby.

Another outrageous proposal to build a road across some of the best landmarks of Pune including the Law college hill was thwarted because of opposition from activists including retired Maj Gen S.C. Jatar, academic Anita Benninger, heritage conservationist Narendra Dengle and public transport campaigner Sujit Patwardhan. Traffic police booths were built on footpaths in the city, points out Prashant Inamdar of Pedestrians First.

The highway is spectacular. But this is deceptive. Beyond it life is very harsh for a vast majority of people. Architecture critic Gautam Bhatia puts it very well. He often passes by the Moradabad bypass road where for a while you feel you are on the road connecting New York with Washington. It is so posh. Then turn off the bypass and you come across a dreary, poverty stricken scenario for miles. In the middle of the emptiness he sees an old woman sitting by the track selling a few cloves of garlic, staring into nothing. On the way back he sees her again with the same heap. Life does not change, has not changed for the common people, (TOI 28-10-06).

That is what being on the road and looking with eyes open teach you. You really understand the two worlds that

India is. It is similar in Pakistan. Drriya Kazi, Pakistani sculptor and writer, says Pakistani society too is divided between those who are grateful for flyovers and those who look beyond and feel that the problems of people are much wider and these are not being attended to.

8

Walking Culture

The motor car of course is a problem. Some years ago scientists were predicting the evolution of a race of humans without legs, thanks to the automobile. Nowadays we know they were wrong, it is not our legs we are losing, it is our minds as well, say Aaron Sussman and Ruth Goode in their readable book 'The Magic of Walking.'

Americans, who are so notoriously addicted to the evil of the motor car, woke up to the virtues of walking only during the second world war when petrol was rationed. People could not take out their cars for a Sunday drive and so they went walking instead.

They liked it and set up clubs for walking and hiking.

Walking is beneficial in many ways. Surgeons know the importance of getting a patient up and walking within hours after an operation. The purpose is to prevent a clot from forming and breaking off to cause the blockage of a blood vessel.

Walking can even reduce the risk of erectile dysfunction or even impotence, according to a study conducted by the Center for Obesity Management at Second University of Naples.

Walking briskly for about two miles can help greatly. The dysfunction results from poor circulation and good blood flow is necessary for achieving and maintaining an erection.

Some of the world's greatest thinkers have walked to do their thinking. Einstein puzzled out many secrets of the universe on his walks around Princeton. Freud, the guru of psychoanalysis, did not only his thinking but much of his discussion and teaching while walking through the streets of Vienna at breakneck speed so that his colleagues and disciples had hard work to keep with the pace of his legs as well as of his mind.

Philosopher Plato expounded his philosophy while walking up and down an olive grove in an Athens park some 2300 years ago.

Rabiandranath Tagore, the Nobel prize winning poet and nature lover, wrote 'I think that the greatest gift of god is that I can walk on a path filled with grass and my heart dances with the fragrance of flowers alongside.'

In this age of miracle drugs the gentle art of walking has been rediscovered as a best medicine for dealing with mental, emotional and physical stress that surround us.

The walk has been described as disease preventer, pound remover, tension reliever, brain stimulator, problem solver. Walking also gives you better sleep, a sense of adventure and serenity.

I saw in Italy how friendly the towns there are for walking. Since at least the seventeenth century foreigners have been moving there to bask in the light and the life. Bernard Rudofsky, author of Streets for People, spent a good time in Italy and sang its praises in his book.

Why are people so much friendlier when they are walking ? The answer may lie in Jonathan Rose's observation that there is a significant difference between running into someone while strolling down a street and running into someone when driving a car.

Why do so many people enjoy being in Disneyland? They spend comparatively little time in taking rides. People enjoy the pleasant, pedestrian friendly public space and sociability it promotes. The real reason people enjoy being there is because there are no cars inside Disneyland and this gives great freedom to people. But this fact is carefully hidden from people because it militates against the whole automobile culture. It is precisely the banning of the automobile from the premises of Disneyland that makes it so attractive.

While neglecting the construction of footpaths for daily activity for ordinary people, the upper class is building jogging tracks for its own use. It looks upon walking mainly as a leisure activity and activity for exercise.

It would make much more sense to construct nice, user friendly footpaths. This will not only make the streetscape more attractive, it will greatly facilitate walking for ordinary people. In cities like Mumbai many would love to walk the distance between their homes and railway stations provided there are decent footpaths. Now they are forced to take auto-rickshaws or buses which only add to congestion on roads.

One of the first jogging tracks to be built in Mumbai was the joggers park at Carter road in Bandra with a fine view of the sea. The initiative was taken by a school teacher and later Congress MLA Oliver Andrade in 1992 with backing from a group of builders including Lokhandwala, Rizvi and Raheja. But walking at these parks comes at a price, Rs two which is a pittance for the rich but results in keeping out the poor. So the rich can walk along with their own class, many of them wearing exclusive dress and shoes, plugged to music on their Sonys, trying to look as Westernised as possible. Anyone wearing sandals or chappals is seen as an outsider. In a sense this becomes a highly regimented place with a long list of dos and don'ts, the security people keep a close though not obtrusive eye on people inside.

Outside, a Laughter Club sees scores of well to do oldish men and women doing community exercise, laughing their hearts out, eating freshly cooked breakfast on the premises.

Jogging and running have been turned into corporate profit activities by shoe companies.

Joggers Park in Bandra became so popular even a film with the same name and using it as the main locale was made a few years ago with Perizad Zorobian and Victor Banerjee depicting the relationship that develops in the park between a retired high court judge and a go-getting, exuberant young woman and model.

Two other jogging tracks came in soon after in posh areas, in the Priyadarshani park at Napean sea Road, created by former minister of state for urban development for Maharashtra, B.A. Desai, and the park in the Hiranandani complex created by builder Hiranandani in his high-rise residential complex in Powai razing to the ground a number of green hills.

Since then numerous other jogging tracks have come up all over India. It is an irony that many rich people go to these parks in their cars and then start jogging. Vanity is one of the reasons, they do not want to be seen walking on the road like other ordinary mortals.

Shbaana Azmi, film actor and activist in the struggle for housing rights, has used government's funds allotted to her as a member of the Rajya Sabha to construct two excellent promenades in the posh suburb of Bandra in Mumbai along the seaside, at B Jeejibhoy Road and Carter Road. Nicely landscaped and designed by activist architect P.K. Das these are fine but their very location limits their access to the rich in the fashionable area with high property prices. But this and an amphitheatre at the Portugese fort at Bandra have created a fine public space used for plays, poetry readings and yoga classes.

Nowhere are class distinctions more obvious than in the upper class high-rise jungle of Cuffe Parade. There in the municipal park I saw only people working as domestic help in the buildings, not a trace of the better off. Walking a little further I found that the rich exclusively use the joggers park created out of government land by some cooperative societies of Maker Towers. It has an extremely upper class ambience and the rich get a fine view of the sea as they jog on the track close to the sea. In contrast the footpath in the vicinity including the World Trade Centre is in a shambles. So the city has no money for providing footpaths for thousands of office-goers and others for their daily needs but has plenty for the jogging of the rich.

Walk To Avoid Crutches is the telling heading of a news item on osteoporosis, a condition overtaking a large number of women at a young age while only a few years ago it affected women only after the menopause stage.

Our urban lifestyle ensures an early onset of the condition, says endoctrinologist Dr Ambarish Mittal. Weight training at fancy gyms cannot prevent it. Simply jogging in open air can help, according to orthopedic surgeon Dr Ameet Pispati Obesity and malnutrition are making Indians unhealthy. Nearly 40 per cent Indians are unhealthy, according to a survey conducted by Sulbha Parshuraman, head of the team at the Indian Institute of Population Sciences in Mumbai, as part of the third national family health survey in 2006.

While walking is seen to be democratic and mind stimulating, jogging is considered by some to be fascist, anti-democratic, an Amrican fad. The French president Nicolas Sarkozy invited widespread ridicule in the nation in 2007 for jogging and, worse, wearing an NYPD (New York police department) T shirt which was thought to be a tragic indication of slavery to American values. The French, proud of their culture and wary of frivolous American ways, were not pleased.

Liberation, the left-wing French daily, reacted by saying jogging was right-wing and the noted French philosopher Alain Finkelkraust, said walking is a sensitive spiritual act while jogging was management of the body. Western civilization was born with the promenade, with strolling and walking. Like the poet Rimbaud, who was known for his long walks, the President should walk, not jog. (More Rimbaud, Less Rambo, critics tell sweaty jogger Sarkozy. Times 4-7-07)

In France jogging is a running joke, the Washington Post said in a headline (7-7-07). Sarkozy's jogging was seen to be un-French, right wing and even a ploy to brainwash his citizens. His jogging had become the symbol of his Presidency.

Bill Clinton was known for his morning jogging and few could keep pace with him. Jogging with him was considered more prestigious than having an audience with him in the Oval office. When Clinton was in Seoul the South Korean president Kim Young insisted on jogging with him. But after delicate negotiations Clinton wore a full-length running suit as baggy shorts would have offended the Koreans. (NYT 26-7-93). Clinton used to jog for three miles on the Washington Mall with secret service agents on bicycles.

But jogging can be hazardous. The book 'Walk, don't die. How to stay fit, trim and healthy without killing yourself, authored by Fred Stuntman says it all. Jogging led to so many deaths some years ago that the Journal of the American Medical Association carried an article in an issue in 1979 studying such fatal cases. Jogging shoe companies should carry a warning about the hazards of jogging, the author says.

Mr Terence Bendixson, author of the book Instead of Cars and president of the Pedestrians Association of England for many years, had a long chat with me on the subject during his visit to Mumbai some years ago. He said the conditions of pedestrians in Mumbai were comparable to those in England in the 19th century.

Mr Bendixson said walking should be given high priority because many walking trips were for economic activity. Imagine if everyone drove a car, congestion and pollution would be intolerable.

The Pedestrians Association was formed in England in 1930 with Lord Cecil, M.P., an anti-fascist and founder of the League of Nations, as president which shows how much interest some members of the upper class took in the issue in England. The spade work was done by journalist Tom Foley.

Of course the menace of the automobiles was the main reason for the formation of the Pedestrian Association. But discontent against quality of life on the streets must have rankled sensitive minds for a long time.

It is worth reading the description of life on the street in London, the commercial capital of the world then, written in 1845 by Friedrich Engels in his superb book The Condition of the Working Class in England. The book is essential reading for anyone wanting to understand the modern city as well because the same pattern of exploitation of the masses continues.

Engels says 'after roaming the streets of London a day or two, making headway with difficulty through the human turmoil and the endless line of vehicles after visiting the slums of the metropolis one realizes for the first time that these Londoners have been forced to sacrifice the best qualities of their human nature.

Such was poverty among the Irish immigrants that they went about barefoot. In the cold English weather this must have been terrible. Going about barefoot has its advantages, but in temperate climates. Engels wrote 'The Irish have introduced, too, the custom previously unknown in England of going barefoot. In every manufacturing town there is now to be seen a multitude of people, especially women and children, going about barefoot and their example is gradually being adopted by the poorer English.

Engels gives a detailed description of the way streets and houses are built and shaped and with illustrations. This should be of great value for architects and town planners.

Quoting the journal Artisan, Engels says some streets are so narrow that a person can step from the window of one house into that of its opposite neighbour while houses are built high, one story above another so that light can scarcely reach the street.

In India as pedestrians as treated like third class citizens though they are in a vast majority in the transport system, more and more funds get allocated for the private car, its requirements of parking spaces, repair garages, petrol pumps and the like, as more money is spent on highways and as public transport is deliberately given a raw deal, the poor are the worst sufferers.

Transport and social exclusion is a very big phenomenon which is receiving considerable attention in England. Ordinary people are simply excluded in an unequal society as the transport system gets technologically advanced, as cars get faster and roads become wider. In India the poor depend mainly on state transport undertakings which run into every nook and corner of the country unlike private buses which operate mainly on profitable routes. Now, as ST undertakings are being deliberately neglected by state governments and as they run into huge losses, the poor have to shift to more uncertain and risky forms of transport like jeeps which are heavily crowded and unsafe. The department of transport in the U.K. has done a whole study on the phenomenon of transport and social exclusion.

Social exclusion takes place in various ways. For example the poor find that a school is far away from their locality. So the kids have to travel a long distance, either on foot or by bus. When even the bus is withdrawn, the social exclusion becomes worse. So, the quality of life should be determined not only by income but it should be related to quality of public amenities available to common people. Another problem is that the poor are excluded from the planning and governance of public transport.

The poor in India survive all the injustice and exploitation partly because of tremendous resilience. During the heavy floods in Mumbai in July, 2005, when hundreds were washed away, drowned, life was completely immobilized. The police were nowhere in sight. Yet, there was not a single case of looting of property. In contrast, there was large-scale looting in New Orleans two months later when the Jazz city was under several feet of water following the Katrina hurricane.

A large number of winners at the 16th Thane marathon in 2005 were under privileged children running barefoot leaving behind those wearing Nike and Reeboks. They came from the relatively backward district of Nanded and were sponsored by a Mumbai businessman. If only more people show as much social concern, life would be so much better.

How much dignity the poor show while walking against all odds. A marvelous Iranian film Children of Heaven won the hearts of all at the Mumbai international film festival in 2004 with its portrayal of a brother and sister walking to school. It is a poor family and the children are left with only one pair of shoes. They share the pair. The girl, who goes to school in the morning, runs back desperately to meet her brother on the way and give him the shoes. The film directed by Majid Majidi still brings tears to my eyes. Such is the plight of the ordinary and yet it is the highly pampered motorists who are complaining all the time.

The discrimination against the poor and walking is evident in different ways. The word sabotage which has such a negative meaning is derived from the French word Sabot which means wooden shoes used by French workers. Carlyle frequently refers to the word Sabot which originally meant working class rebellion and revolution.

For a large number of poor people, especially migrants, the street and footpath is the only refuge. Mr George Fernandes, a former union defence minister, slept on the streets of Mumbai in his young days. His name is inseparable from his association with the streets of Mumbai. Later, he also strode the streets leading numerous marches of working people He was a firebrand socialist leader then in the sixties and seventies. His image took a beating in the nineties when he suddenly switched sides and joined the bandwagon of the fascist Rashtriya Swayamsewak Sangh (RSS) and its political wing the Bharatiya Janata party to become the defence minister.

Sudhir Phadke, a well-known Marathi film music director and singer, spent quite a few days on the footpath in Mumbai and used the public toilet near Charni Road in 1939. There were no slums in Mumbai at that time but footpaths were waiting for me and welcomed me, Phadke wrote in his autobiography Jagachya Pathivar.

There is now much less tolerance of people sleeping on footpaths and they are routinely run over by speeding vehicles of arrogant , rich men. Several people choose to blame the victims for being run over and for increasing the accident statistics to the embarrassment of the police.

Maharashtra's chief minister Vilasrao Deshmukh declared in 2006 that all footpath dwellers in Mumbai (nearly 500.000) of them will be evicted as part of the road widening and city beautification scheme. And this at a time when the government's programme of housing for the poor has come to a complete halt in the regime of globalisation. And there is little provision of night shelters.

In the United States the homeless won a major victory when the court declared that arresting people for sitting or lying or sleeping on public sidewalks amounted to a cruel and unusual punishment as there are not enough beds in night shelters for a huge population without shelter in the Los Angeles area. The American Civil Liberties Union (ACLU), which filed the case in support of the homeless, has come in for criticism from right-wing media.

A walking movement called Wandervogel in Germany was destroyed by the Nazis. It was proclaimed in 1913 by the group that youths had a right to live according to their own ideas. Bored with industrial artificiality the young men took long walks amidst Nature, lived on food provided by nature and sang songs. But they refused to take a political stand. Eminent critic Walter Benjamin was involved with this movement for some time.

One result of the automobile menace on roads is that children are afraid to walk on streets. This is more so in the West where there are much better facilities for walking and yet children are not very visible on the street. A writer said that it was as if some Piped Piper has spirited away our children from our streets. In the Netherlands more efforts are being made to attract children to streets by closing them to motor vehicles and organizing parties for children.

There is a Latin dictum Solvitur ambulando which means many things are solved by walking. One wished our planners, policepersons and politicians understood these basic issues.

Walking barefoot is a sacred activity in many cultures and it is also very good for health. Indians played much better football when they played barefooted. They lost to France only by 1-2 in the 1948 Olympics. Sahu Mewalal, a member of the Indian team then, recalled that the very fact that we did not wear showed made us famous in London. For days everyone was looking at our feet. Dennis Compton, the well-known English batsman, who also played football, invited the Indians to play a friendly game against an England XI. India lost 1-2 but the Englishmen were very impressed. (TOI 16-7-04)

Prince Charles warned British people in 2006 that they were in danger of becoming obese like the Americans if they did not walk and cycle enough. He credits his trim figure to long walks and one organic meal a day. He attributes the rise in obesity partly to the design of modern towns which make the environment unfriendly to walking.

The US could save nearly five to six billions in dollars a year in costs related to heart disease if only one tenth of Americans began walking regularly, according to the Trust for America's Health, a public health advocacy group. (NYT 19-3-07)

Richard Jackson, a former health adviser to Arnold Schwazengger points to a disturbing link between the built-environment, physical inactivity and child obesity. (London Times 27-1-06). The Times carried a cartoon in 2006 portraying a scene in the year 2056, fifty years later. A man says to his wife that he is driving to the supermarket and he should be back in a couple of weeks. A British government think tank has said after extensive consultations with experts that in the year 2055 journey will become extremely difficult and unattractive We can prevent this if we oppose the car culture.

Historically Britain has been unique in embracing the walking culture. Britain swore allegiance to footpaths, not boulevards. Asserting the right to walk became closely allied with the British idea of freedom. This was in the face of the landowning classes opposed people's right to roam in the countryside. Tens of thousands of people are members of rambler organizations in Britain. Walking is the very antithesis of owning of private property.

The main charm of Sam Millar's book Delhi – Adventures in a Megacity is that it is based on his walks through the lanes and bylanes and chances upon many hidden landscapes as he stands and stares. If a movement for pedestrians is built in Delhi, Millar could be its patron-saint, says Narayani Gupta, historian.

Nothing shows the contrast between affluence and poverty in Bangalore than the little bazaar outside the fortified walls of Infosys headquarters in Bangalore. Frail old women sit bent over small heaps of vegetables. World experience shows that IT clusters are not exactly very helpful to the poor. Besides focus on a single industry can be risky. Also corporates need to be more people-friendly. Arun Maira, a management consultant, recalled his experience of working with Telco (now Tata Motors). The then managing director Sumant Moolgaonkar built a training school to train local people for jobs and planted trees. This created confidence among the people who sold their land to the company. It is not just money they wanted, but jobs. (Govindraj Ethidraj, HT 8-11-05).

Little was done in the last few years to strengthen the public transport system in Bangalore, says Janaki Nair, author of the recent book Promise of the Metropolis : Bangalore.

The elite came up with a concept of an electronic township. Jurong Consultants from Singapore were invited in 2002 to draft a glorious master plan for a 25 km corridor to cater to one million people by 2021 including all facilities to live, play, work and strike business in. This kind of vision aims to produce what the erstwhile IT secretary Sanjoy Dasgupta called 'a slice of Santa Clara' in India. It would be an independent Republic where Narayan Murthy would be the Mayor.

A good section of the elite indeed very much wants to secede from the rest of India mainly because it wants no contact with the poor, no obligation to the poor. Meanwhile, the new management elite will do its best to retain control of the city by threats of industrial withdrawal if necessary but will certainly claim autonomy in the spaces it occupies, Janaki Nair says.

So foreign investors now want to dictate the pattern of our urban development. As it is our ruling class is catering mainly to the rich. More allocation for expressways and flyovers, means less funds for facilities for ordinary people.

A call centre female employee Pratibha Srikanth Murthy, 24, was raped and murdered after being picked up from her home at two a.m. to be taken to office. There was a clear security lapse on the part of the company, said the Bangalore police commissioner Ajai Kumar Singh (Times of India 18-12-05).

The incident caused a nation-wide furore. It was soon found that similar callousness was being shown by IT companies whether in Delhi, Mumbai or Bangalore. In Hyderabad ex-convicts were found to be working as drivers for multinational corporations for transporting staff, according to assistance police commissioner Rajiv Trivedi.

After the rape and murder case, the Bangalore police conducted a check and in one single night booked 227 call centre drivers for rash and negligent driving. Twenty eight of them were found to be drunk while ferrying employees including women, said deputy police commissioner M.A. Saleem.

The IT sector's transport policy for employees got another jolt in 2007 when a female employee of a WIPRO call centre in Pune, Jyoti Chaudhari, was raped and murdered allegedly by the driver of the company's car taking her to office for work. It is found that the call centers do not take routine security precautions while employing drivers.

A bigger jolt came in 2008 when the Supreme court ruled in the Pratibha Murthy murder case that her then employer, managing director Som Mittal was liable for prosecution as the CEO of the Hewlett Packard Global company.

Every night when thousands of young Indian women leave home to work in what is known as the US or UK shift, the family members skip a heart beat and remain tense till they return safe. (Abhay Vaidya. TOI 4-11-07).

But for itself the IT sector in Bangalore has created a cosy island in the Electronic City behind six foot high walls. The loudest sounds you hear are of birds or the whirr of electric carts that whisk visitors from one steel and glass building to the next Young men and women stroll on manicured ; pathways that wend their way through the 80-acre spread or coast on bicycles (Business Week 19-3-07).

The basic needs of ordinary people's mobility are ignored in Bangalore, say U.R. Anantha Murthy, reputed Kannada writer, and Lalita Kamath, an academic.

Unlike other companies Infosys takes good care of the transport of its employees. It spends $ five million a year on buses, vans and taxis to transport 18,000 employees to and from the electronics city. In Mumbai where transport conditions are inhuman for ordinary people, the employers take no responsibility for paying the cost of workers' travel nor do most employers provide transport facilities.

9

Pleasure of Walking

The great romantic poet William Wordsworth was such a keen enthusiast for walking that a whole chapter 'The legs of William Wordsworth' has been written cn his walking by Rebecca Solnit in her excellent book Wanderlust.

In 1913 the historian G.M. Trevelyan wrote in one essay 'I have two doctors, my left leg and my right leg.' Henry David Thoreau, the great writer who inspired Mahatma Gandhi, equated walking with freedom.

Jimmy Carter walked down Pennsylvania avenue for his inauguration as president. Reagan was a pretender. He claimed to love walking but this was just to impress others.

One of the best books on walking is Alan Booth's Road to Sata : A two-thousand mile walk through Japan.

England has a long tradition of people asserting their democratic right to walk, even trespass on private property because many feel there can be no such thing as exclusive right to ownership of land. Land is necessary so that we live on it, that people may enjoy it in a variety of ways, declared a liberal member of Parliament James Boyce Hiking was a major if unofficial component of socialist lifestyle. Labourers had developed or retained from their peasant parents and grandparents a passion for the land and a whole culture of working class botanists and naturalists emerged, as did a legion of walkers. Walking in groups was partly a matter of safety as property owners had a hatred of ramblers and sometimes beat them up.

A reading of the terrible working and living conditions described by Engels in his book makes us realize why a little relaxation must have been very important to the British workers. Walking across open spaces must have been a joy to those whose bodies were so cruelly treated in factories and who suffered so badly in cramped housing in a highly unequal society.

Walking is the very lifeblood of a city. A city which encourages walking, provides good walking spaces has a much more congenial, democratic social life where citizens can interact, talk with each other, enjoy looking at each other, meeting. Italian cities are wonderful for walking and I have walked for miles in Venice, Rome, all the way from Rome to the Vatican, and then in Florence and Milan. I missed going to Bologna with its famous portico, a long covered walkway running from the central square to the countryside.

Why on earth can we not have decent footpaths, covered walkways in India where they are needed far more than in Europe because of our hot climate. And we have a far bigger and much poorer population. Bernard Rudofsky has written a wonderful book Streets for People : A primer for Americans. It is a shame it is hardly available anywhere and most of our architects are unaware of it when they should have been obsessed with it.

It is said that in Italy the street becomes a kind of theatre, girls and young men display their charm to one another with a lively sociability. The more grace they show the better the community likes them. A dance critic Edwin Denby asked dance students to watch how people of various types walk. The

Americans occupy a much larger space while walking than do Europeans. This annoys the sense of modesty of Europeans.

Charles Dickens, the great English novelist, whom I love because of his deep sympathy for the poor and for his excellent portrayal of characters, loved to walk on the streets of London and several of his novels have a lot to do with vibrant street life. The action in several plays of Shakespeare takes place on the street, there are numerous street scenes in Merchant of Venice and several other plays. Much of the early action in the play Julius Ceasar takes places on the street and other places outdoors. It is during Ceasar's procession that the dissidents realize he is becoming too powerful. And then there is the famous warning Beware of the Ides of March again issued from the street.

The play Hamlet opens with an outdoors scene on the battlements of the royal palace while the guard is being changed.

Agra Bazar, a famous play written and directed by Habib Tanvir, is very much set in a public space where people's poet Nazir Akbarabadi recites poetry in people's language as opposed to elitist poetry. He wrote in the every day language which is on people's lips. The Bazaar is a wonderful place, accessible to everyone where people can mingle. And Urdu language itself is a product of the social intercourse between people of different classes, races and regions. Can a shopping mall ever acquire the charm of the Bazaar ? In the play Agra Bazaar a cucumber seller needs to recite a song to attract customers. Someone advises him to go to the people's poet Nazir. Nazir gives him some fine lines and the Kakdiwala is very happy.

Solnit dwells at length on the connection between streets and revolution and democracy. Paris is the great city of walkers and of revolution. Historian Eric Hobsbawm once speculated on the ideal city for riot and insurrection. It should be densely populated and not too large in area. Essentially, it should still be possible to traverse it on foot.

The street has played an important role in rebellions in Czechoslovakia, Poland and Hungary and other countries. Two major dissidents Vaclav Havel, the playwright and Alexander Dubcek brought about a revolution in Czechoslovakia through street demonstrations and processions. Dubcek declared at the time 'The government is telling us that the street is not the place for things to be solved but I say the street was and is the place. The voice of the street must be heeded.

Singer and poet Patti Smith once said she roamed the streets for a few hours to prepare for her performances onstage. Walking toughens and harpens the sensibility, wrap on in an isolation out of which come songs fierce enough, words sharp enough, to break that musing silence.

Solnit has devoted a whole chapter 'walking after midnight : women, sex and the public space' to show how women walking on the street have always been discriminated against, viewed with suspicion, hostility. The English language is rife with words and phrases that sexualize women's walking. Among the terms for prostitutes are streetwalkers, women of the streets, women on the town and public women. At the same time man of the streets means something not so derogatory. But the word pedestrian does have a derogatory connotation.

In 19th century France police could arrest working class women for anything or nothing and sometimes they would round up groups of women passerby on the road to meet their quotas. Watching the women get arrested was a masculine pastime. Many innocent girls, mostly young and poor, were arrested behind the high walls of Saint Lazare prison where they lived in dire circumstances, cold malnourished, unwashed, overworked and forbidden to speak.

Pedestrians have been discriminated against in different countries at all times.

Throughout California one thousand crosswalks have been removed in recent years apparently in the spirit of the

Los Angeles planners who proclaimed in the early 1960s 'the pedestrian remains the largest single obstruction to free traffic movement.'

Several of our politicians, engineers, architects, planners government officials are far removed from the common people. And yet, they take important decisions affecting millions of people.

Footpaths have been provided on only a small percentage of road spaces and even these footpaths are so badly designed or maintained that pedestrians would rather keep off them. Far from improving the design, the municipal authorities have made it worse. Most of the newly built footpaths are so steep it becomes a pain to climb and get down.

Usually hawkers are blamed by municipal officials and some vested interests for occupying footpaths and obstructing pedestrians. The fact is the civic body has denied the elementary facility of footpaths in the first place. An utterly nefarious argument made by civic officials is that since footpaths are occupied by hawkers anyway, why provide them at all. This is a sinister argument by any standards. And in any case, hawkers do not occupy footpaths everywhere.

Barricades have been put up all over Mumbai to prevent pedestrians from crossing the road. Our minds are so conditioned by constant propaganda launched by the car lobby and other vested interests that we take it for granted that motor vehicles must get precedence on roads over pedestrians.

The very reverse is happening all over Europe and parts of the United States with high priority being given to pedestrians, creation of exclusive streets for pedestrians, more public spaces, reduction of road space for motor cars, high taxation on cars, high car parking fees etc. Yet, we are adopting the worst models from the West and rejecting the best.

The maximum facilities should be provided at busy railway and bus stations for people to come out and go in so that the least convenience is caused to them. At both

Chhatrapati Shivaji terminus and at Churchgate station terminus in Mumbai the maximum inconvenience is being caused to commuters and pedestrians because of the callous attitude of the authorities.

I remember a very good cartoon by reputed cartoonist R.K. Laxman in the Times of India some years ago which showed a policeman telling a pedestrian that he cannot cross the road at that particular place. The policeman tells him you should take a bus, travel for ten km and then cross the road.

The British showed much more civic sense and many old areas in Mumbai right from Ballard estate to Mahim and Matunga have very wide footpaths. Ironically in the post-independence period which saw rapid development of suburbs footpaths have not been built at all in many localities almost as a matter of policy. I have repeatedly asked municipal authorities for an explanation for this callousness but they have always evaded an answer. In some old areas existing footpaths have been removed. The callousness is visible every where. While driving or walking up or down Malabar hill one would be struck by the absence of footpaths in an area which has high vehicular traffic and is home to the state governor, chief minister, other ministers, and captains of industry.

We have the wonderful example of Mahatma Gandhi who walked great distances and used the medium of walking as a means of protest and awakening. Jawaharlal Nehru put it eloquently when he said of Gandhiji's Dandi march 'the picture that is most dominant and most significant of him is as I saw him marching staff in hand to Dandi in 1930. here was the pilgrim on his quest for truth, quiet, peaceful, determined and fearless who would continue that quest and pilgrimage regardless of consequences.

The march to Dandi was more than a political campaign. It was aimed at educating the people. By leading a simple life and making minimum demands on villagers on the way Gandhiji wanted to emphasise his nearness to and fellow feeling for the poor. For this reason he criticized some of his companions who ordered fresh milk and vegetables by lorry from Surat and some others who on the slightest excuse tried to climb into carts or cars passing by. He was angry when one night he found a labourer carrying a heavy kerosene lamp for the marchers.

Gandhiji told his followers that they had no right to eat food better than the food eaten by ordinary people. To live above the means befitting a poor country is to live on stolen food, he said.

Gandhi walked with about 80 male companions, chosen from the ashram and people he could trust to represent most regions of India, Muslims, Christians, untouchables as well as hindus and a wide generation span. They traveled in the early morning and cool of the evening, stopping in two villages to stay for the day and for the night, as Judith Brown has observed in the book Gandhi. Gandhi announced that the satyagrahis would sleep in the open and all he required was a clean, sheltered place to sleep, a clean washing-place and the simplest possible food, he saw this as a sacred pilgrimage in which discipline and purity were essential.

Gandhiji's famous padayatra, walking pilgrimage, has been reduced to a farce by his followers who resort to the gimmick of walking only during election campaigns. Otherwise, much of the khadi-clad political class gave up walking long ago and they now thinking walking is below dignity Some leaders are wholesale dealers of motor cars. Most others in the Congress now do not even pretend to wear khadi. Many are open votaries of capitalism.

While walking has made sense to the average person, most of the exercise experts in the United States are still promoting running, high-impact aerobics, cycling, swimming, rope jumping and use of a variety of exercise equipment such as rowing machines and exercise cycles. In a nation obsessed with youth, speed, glitz and glamour, walking was too plain and ordinary. It was the ugly duckling of exercise.

Mayers points out why running is not the best form of exercise while walking is. Physiologists specializing in exercise calculate that we land with a force of three to four times our body weight when we run. Our system does not have shock absorbers to handle such an impact. No wonder runners suffer from stress fractures, knee, hip and lower back injuries These are well-documented. Hunting animals run only for short bursts with great speed to chase their prey, they give up after a few minutes if they fail to catch the prey.

There is a misconception that one must use shoes for walking and running. Shoes are big multi-national business now and they must spread this idea to promote the sales. Meyers points out that for thousands and millions of years humans have managed perfectly well without shoes. In fact, people who do not wear shoes report fewer foot problems than those using shoes. Ill-fitting shoes can create a lot of problems. Research at the university of California at Berkeley has shown that ill-fitting shoes caused 80 per cent of all foot problems. Besides causing problems like corns and nail deformities, painful shoes can alter your gait and your outlook for the worse.

No exercise equipment is more highly promoted and oversold than stationary exercise cycles. Meyers thinks stationary bicycling is neither easy, nor fun. They are not fun unless you are a masochist. All you get is mind-numbing exercise. It would be much more fun to ride an actual bicycle on the road and enjoy the fresh air and breeze. Another absurdity is exercising on the stair climbers. It is much better to actually walk the stairs of your or some other building than spend money on the stair climbing machine and take a mindless exercise.

Amazingly, an old person doing a regular fast walking exercise can beat a young runner in a walking race. That is what Meyers, 62 of age, did when a 20-year-old runner saw him walking, made fun of him, challenged him to a walking race. The result was Meyers won comfortably because walking is a different ball game.

The transportation equity act for the 21st century (TEA 21) signed into law by president Clinton in 1998 provides for integration of bicycling and walking into the transportation mainstream. More importantly, it enhances the ability of communities to invest in projects that can improve the safety and practicality of bicycling and walking for everyday travel.

Though facilities for pedestrians are far better in England than in India, a committee of the House of Commons observed in its report in the year 2001 that pedestrians are treated with contempt in the country.

Can one imagine a committee of members of our Parliament taking up such a study for pedestrians ? successive politicians and planners obsessed with car travel are to blame, the committee on environment, transport and regional affairs noted. Walking in towns and cities is in decline because motorists have been given ; priority over pedestrians for half a century or more, the MPs found. 'in a myriad ways when we walk we are treated with less respect than when we drive'.

Walking is not only good for physical health, but also mental health and stimulating the mind. Walking lets your brain do something while your body is moving, it lets you talk, think, dream, plan, recite epic poetry work through budget numbers. After millions of years of evolution we are programmed to think while we walk.

Walking is good even for your sexual health. A brisk two-mile walk each day can reduce men's risk of impotence, according to Dr Irwin Goldstein from the Boston university school of medicine in a study published recently.

His nine-year study of six hundred men showed that those doing walking exercise reduced their risk of impotence.

Walking is the most neglected mode of personal transport. I always judge how civilized a country is by how it treats its pedestrians ; the U.K. certainly has a long way to go, according to Prof David Begg, chair of the U.K. government's commission for integrated transport. Some other experts too see a link between civilization and facilities for walking. By these yardsticks, India must be rated as a very barbarian country. No doubt about it. In fact, it would be in the pre-history age. Of course, even then, early man could not have found it so difficult to walk on earth.

The stronger walkers ruled the roost. They were more accomplished hunters and providers. Because they walked more, their strength increased. The better walkers became the first ruling class. Because the hunt was all important, it became a central theme of early religious cults and walkers were worshipped. Societies were shaped and history written by our pedestrian predecessors.

Walking is the best medicine, declared Hippocrates, the father of medicine. In hospitals many doctors and surgeons now have their patients walk up and down the corridors as part of their treatment. Post operative patients too are urged to take their first step as soon as possible to prevent blood clots and hasten convalescence through stimulation of the circulatory and digestive system. The Dutch humanist Erasmus declared 'Before supper walk a little ; after supper do the same.'

And even the most clumsy, non-athletic individual can develop physical grace by walking more and doing it properly. Well walked muscles are less susceptible to aches and pains. Shakespeare's Henry VIII declared 'we'll walk a while and ease our legs.'

Walking makes the heart muscle stronger. An exercised heart can build up a reserve supply of capillaries which are vital in case of stress on the heart or heart attack.

The rich are literally conducting a class war against ordinary walkers. This comes from none other than that bastion of British establishment the Times. Class war wrecks ramblers' dream, goes the heading of its editorial page article by Richard Morrison in April 2000.

The article describes the joys of rambling in the countryside and points out how some millionaire estate owners seek to wreck the little joys. Millionaire Nicholas van

Hoogstraten bricked up a public right of way on his Sussex estate so that the 'riff raff' do not trample the grass near his mauseoleum-to-be built to preserve his remains for 5000 years.

Henry David Thoreau, the 19th century philosopher, in his celebrated essay on Walking, wrote with remarkable insight about the rich grabbing nature. He wrote 'At present, in this vicinity the best part of the land is not private property, the landscape is not owned and the walker enjoys comparative freedom. But possibly the day will come when it will be partitioned off into so-called pleasure ground in which a few will take a narrow and exclusive plesure only. Then fences will be multipled and man-traps and other engines invented to confine men to the public road and walking over the surface of God's earth shall be construed to mean trespassing on some gentleman's grounds. To enjoy a thing exclusively is to exclude yourself from the true enjoyment of it. Let us improve our opportunities then before the evil days come.

How remarkably true. Now whatever little public space, land accessible to us is being taken away and is being converted into golf courses, pleasure resorts, hotels, clubs and malls.

The phiolosopher, who with his simple living and civil disobedience, inspired Mahatma Gandhi, said 'I think I cannot preserve my health and spirits unless I spend four hours a day at least sauntering through the woods and over the hills and fields absolutely free from all worldly engagements.

This is remarkable because we are destroying nature, the very earth in our cities is being paved with concrete and we are losing touch with Mother Earth. The anti-automobile activist and author Jane Holtz Kay is very right to protest against the paving of the nation and her book is appropriately called the Asphalt Nation which represents a brutal attack on Nature for the sake of the automobile and the whole capitalist culture.

One of the greatest walkers, wanderers in India was the eminent Buddhist, Sanskrit scholar, historian and Marxist

Rahul Sankrutyayan. He walked through various countries in search of ancient texts and to study Nature and social life of people. And he wrote a book on wandering itself called Ghumakkad Shastra.

He wandered especially through Tibet and China, brought the local texts there into India and revived the study of Buddhism in India. Later, he participated in struggles of peasants and workers and wrote books on Marx, Lenin, Mao and Stalin.

He started his wandering at the age of 15 inspired by an Urdu poem which asked people to wander in the world and do it at an early age. His career as a wanderer is remarkable because traditionally Indian culture did not encourage going to other lands, going abroad. Even Mahatma Gandhi had to offer penance before orthodoxy when he returned from a visit to South Africa early in life.

Many foreign travelers have left vital accounts of their travel in India which are a very important source of knowledge for us about our own past, some times these are the only sources. Few of our travelers went abroad. Rahul was an exception. Another fine wandering scholar was V.K. Rajwade, a historian, who collected vast sources for writing of Maratha history. Among the people from whom he collected the vital manuscripts were princely rulers who had no idea of the importance of these documents. They did not care.

Prophet Mohammad too has stressed the importance of wandering through his famous statement 'go to China if necessary in search of knowledge.'

10

Bicycle - People's Vehicle

The bicycle was the vehicle with which Amartya Sen, the Nobel prize winning economist conducted some of his most important research early in his life. One was on the food shortage in Santiniketan district from 1975-77 and the other to collect data on rural socio-economic conditions. These two researches were central to his winning the Nobel prize and that is why his bicycle has been selected as an exhibit in the Nobel museum in Stockhom.

The bicycle had been gifted to Sen by his father in 1944.

Internationally-recognised agricultural innovator, scientist Anand Karve cycles daily 12 km to his farm near Pune and back. And this at the age of 70 He is the grandson of a pioneer in women's education Maharshi D K. Karve. He uses just an ordinary bicycle, the sort used by milkmen.

Unfortunately, there are few people like him in Pune a city once famous for its culture of bicycles and selfless social work. Much of the educated elite is now riding the bandwagon of globalisation. The use of bicycles is even less in other cities.

Bicycle use is being actively promoted by city governments in London, Paris and other cities and the bicycle is enjoying a great revival in many countries. But the Indian elite, still enamoured of the car, looks down on the bicycle.

The London Mayor Livingston's cycling adviser Jenny Jones has put the bicycle on top of the political agenda. London is now installing tens of thousands of self-service bicycles which anyone can pick up for a fee. The model has proved successful in Paris, Barcelona, Vienna and Lyon and is worthy of emulation everywhere. (stop engines with bike rental scheme. James Daley in Independent 4-9-07).

There is a similar picture elsewhere with some exceptions. The then Thane municipal commissioner Sanjay Sethi and Mayor Rajan Vichare rode bicycles to inaugurate five roads dedicated to bicycle riding on environment day, June 5, in 2005. What a sound contrast commissioner Sethi makes to bureaucrats who are obsessed with car riding.

There was this remarkable news item from Ottawa recently. In Canada work on a highway construction was stopped because it was felt that it would disturb eagles nesting nearby. If eggs or fledglings are found in the nests, construction will not resume until after they mature and leave the nests. Tourists and wildlife photographers come from all over the world to see eagles, an endangered species.

The highway is being constructed for the winter Olympics of 2010. When a pedestrian bridge was built on the Thames river in London in the year 2000 millions of pounds were spent to save a rare species of snails, the London Times reported. The bridge was inaugurated by the Queen of England.

We are so used to the dominance of the motor car on the roads that we think bicycles and pedestrians would be a hindrance for the traffic. This mindset has to change. It has changed tremendously in the West where bicycle is being given high priority. We cannot say that this cannot be done here because we are in India. We can do it if there is enough will and our politicians, bureaucrats and planners are properly briefed, educated on the issue.

Often even bicycle supporters adopt a defeatist attitude saying it is unsafe to ride bicycles on roads dominated by cars. The answer to this is that cyclists must become more assertive, use the road in larger numbers. Only then the risk will reduce, cars will learn their lesson and start respecting cyclists. If Adi Havewalla, a cycling champion in the forties, could ride several km in Mumbai at the age of 83, without much trouble there is no reason why younger and fitter people cannot do that. (IE 14-7-96).

There are as many bicycles in Mumbai as cars but there are no separate cycle ways or parking facilities. The bicycle is still seen in Mumbai as a poor man's vehicle, used mainly by delivery boys working in shops and pizza parlours. And since bicycles are much smaller in size than cars and do not make noise or threaten other road users, they are not noticed much. But at least planners should sit up and take note of the large number of cyclists and overwhelming number of pedestrians. Faizan Jawed, a young architecture graduate and winner of the Norman Foster travelling scholarship, has made an excellent film on the bicycle and bus rapid transit system in different countries. It has served to open the eyes of bureaucrats and engineers and planners to alternative ways of transport.

A survey conducted by Faizan and Colin Christopher in the upper class Bandra Khar area in Mumbai indicated a great potential for bicycle use in this area and the local residents' association headed by Anandini Thakoor is enthusiastic too. An entrepreneur Hemant Chhabria collects second hand bicycles, repairs them and gives them to tribal children in Thane district.

The bicycle is most environment-friendly, energy efficient vehicle. Besides, it is good for the health of the rider. It has proved to be a major instrument in bringing about women's liberation, giving enormous amount of freedom to women. It became useful in some other ways too, to fight American aggression in Vietnam, for example.

The guerilla resistance waged by the heroic people of Vietnam against the aggression was helped by bicycles. Americans with their sophisticated weapons could not defeat the more courageous, poor people who had a vastly superior morale.

The bicycle works best in guerilla warfare and especially in rough country. It was used by the IRA in Ireland during the war of independence against the English.

Between the two world wars the regular Irish army had a cavalry regiment mounted entirely on bicycles.

After the bomb blasts in the Underground railway stations and buses in London in 2005 there was a spurt in bicycle sales as many thought it was much safer to ride the bicycle.

On the other hand ignorant governments sometimes wield their clout against bicycles. Guangzhou, Shanghai, Ho Chi Minh city, Jakarta and Dhaka have all restricted bicycle use in response to gridlock created by the surge in motorbikes and motor cars. In Jakarta some 20,000 bicycle rickshaws were tossed into Jakarta bay in the 1980s and another 30,000 were confiscated in an official effort to rid the city of this 'backward' technology. In Vietnam the combined effect of municipal policies and increased prosperity has proved lethal for bikes, their share of trips dropping sharply since the 1970s, World Watch organization points out.

The bicycle is an ideal vehicle for policepersons. Walking would be the best so they can really stay in touch with people. But the bicycle would be the next best. You can weave through traffic and also remain in touch with people. Unless, you are in touch with real people, you cannot tackle crime.

Deputy commissioner Ajay Tomar of Ahmedabad police seemed to have realised this. He also had an additional reason to try to enforce use of bicycles by police personnel in the year 2005. They were growing too fat with bulging tummies. The bicycle also is better than a jeep to handle criminals, a jeep makes noise and may alert the culprits, while you are almost anonymous on a bicycle. Cops do not like bicycles because they are not viewed with respect in our society. Police say they cannot catch a culprit going in a car if they have bicycles. But prevention is much better than actually tackling crime and that is where the bicycle comes in. In the old days the district collector used to camp in rural areas in tents. If you have to administer an area you have to be right there, meet people, mix with them, serve them.

Americans drive cars for more than a trillion miles each year. Even if there is a slight shift to bicycles, the savings in costs would be tremendous, apart from dong away with air pollution, noise, parking and congestion.

Generally power is equated with big size. The bicycle challenges the concept of bigger is better. The idea came into consciousness with the publication of E.F. Schumacher's book in 1973 Small is beautiful. But America's popular culture has its fixations on seven-foot athletes, Rambo guns and the romanticized movie adventures of gigantic explosions and tough guys driving 18-wheelers.

Present China, while betraying the revolution of Mao is also reducing bicycle use and showing the same mistaken infatuation for the motor car as the United States. Bicycle was the main vehicle in China during the days of the revolution. The World Bank, the main source of urban transit investments in the developing world, published a report on the Chinese transport sector in 1985. It did not even mention the word bicycle. This is sadly typical of policy environment in which only motor vehicles are taken seriously.

Several cities in China began banning the use of bicycles by 2003. It was appropriately titled 'China's Leap Backward' in a heading in the Guardian (17-12-03). Isabel Hilton, a long time journalist in China, recalled the days of the sturdy bicycles called Flying Pigeon which could carry an entire family. Cars were rare. Only communist party officials traveled in cars, large green cars called Shanghai.

A combination of greed, corruption and bad planning have transformed many of China's cities into pollution dystopias, friendly neither to the bicycle nor to the human being. The old neighbourhoods of Shanghai were torn down to make way for motorways that soon became giant traffic jams.

In Shanghai, the Bund, the grand river front boulevard where lovers used to go to look at the Yangtze, where students would hang out waiting for a foreigner to practise English, one could idle away an hour watching the river traffic is now transformed into a deafening six lane highway.

But in Beijing, a lot of big roads still have wide bicycle lanes. Copehagen in Denmark is the bicycle capital of the world with citizens travelling one million km by bicycles each day, according to official statistics.

Japan makes extensive use of bicycles though it is a major car producing and highly advanced nation. So many Japanese commuters ride their bikes to public transit that the train stations need parking towers. The city of Kasukabe has a 12-storied bicycle park that uses cranes to park over 1500 cycles.

Bicycle parking at railways stations needs to be encouraged on a large scale in India but is sadly neglected. It is only only in the last few years that the Delhi Metro rail network has decided to set up state of the art bicycle parking facilities at new stations. (TOI 22-9-07).

Several European countries have thousands of km of bicycle tracks. In Netherlands 30 percent of trips are made on bicycle.

Some countries facilitate cycling by linking bicycles and public transportation which helps bicycles capture the short trips to or from a train or subway station. One key to establishing bike and ride link is adequate bicycle parking. Extensive bicycle parking facilities often with thousands of spaces are now standard at Dutch, Japanese, Danish and German train station.

It is much cheaper to provide for parking for bicycles than cars, besides there is the saving of space. No matter how good the infrastructure or how convenient the cycling, bicycles will not be used if the local culture does not welcome them.

The bicycle also greatly endeared itself to and inspired many writers. Bernard Shaw, the distinguished playwright who made so much fun of bourgeois foibles, exercised on a static bicycle installed in his home whenever he was short of inspiration on his typewriter, that was long before the era of the personal computer.

There is an interesting story about Shaw when he invited Bertrand Russel, the eminent philosopher, peace campaigner and humanist, to his place for the week-end. Russell was slightly bewildered at being told to alight at a station ten miles from Shaw's home. He was surprised to be greeted by Shaw on the station's platform, armed with two bicycles. We will ride the ten miles, Shaw said and Russel replied smilingly 'we will not.' Russell sat in the next train to Shaw's village and then Shaw cycled furiously from station to station arriving at the same time as the train.

The bicycle is a liberating force for women in many developing countries today. It emerges as a remarkable symbol in an Iranian film The Day I Became a Woman in which a woman director Marziiyeh Meshkini makes a debut. The film made in the year 2002 and shown in the women's film festival at Y.B. Chavan center in 2006 has remarkable scenes about women racing along on bicycles amidst spectacular scenery along the sea.

The women are wearing burkha and cycling is their way of asserting their identity. The husband of one of the participants Ahoo does not like this. He comes on horseback, asks her to refrain from riding the bicycle which he says is against tradition and when she refuses he instantly divorces her. But Ahoo keeps on cycling amidst much trauma, refuses to succumb to pressure from her father and other tribesmen but after they leave, she is finally vanquished by two others riding on horseback. They intercept her as she gets tired while cycling and take her away.

A redeeming feature of Salman Khan, film star, involved in road deaths and hunting of black buck near Jodhpur, is that he cycles a lot. 'I cycle about everywhere, I am not a fitness freak, it is just that when you are 70 or 80 year old you should be able to walk , cycle and run a little and in this cycling helps a lot. Film actor Arshad Warsi carries a folding bicycle to every location.

Two other film stars known for cycling are Anil Kapoor and Akshay Kumar. Salman inspired me to take up cycling, Kapoor says. It takes one hour for him to reach a shoot by car. On a bicycle, it takes just 10 minutes more. But he is disappointing on another score. Kapoor, however, disappoints by his recent decision to pour a lot of money into motor car racing. He owns with Atul Gupta the Indian franchise for A-1 grand prix. Action film director Tinu Verma regularly zooms past on his 18-gear bicycle from Amboli to Lokhandwala in Mumbai to the gym. He reaches in six minutes while previously his car took him 45 minutes. And it is much healthier too. He got the idea after seeing top personalities in the West taking to the bike. One wishes our planners, politicians and bureaucrats showed as much common sense.

Among the most delightful bicycling scenes in Hindi cinema is one in which Nutan rides the bicycle with other girls singing a song of joy Milke Panchhi Gaye Pyaraka Tarana (birds sing a song of love. In the film Anadi. Raj Kapoor is the hero).

Indian Institutes of Technology, premier institutions in the world, are known for cycling culture on their campus like campuses of European universities. Sadly, the culture is missing in several other educational institutions in the country. In the Mumbai university campus in Kalina I have seldom seen a bicycle but a lot of cars driven very rudely with honking disturbing one of the few peaceful areas in Mumbai.

One of the most thrilling sight on the roads is of cyclists in a race. The cyclists are so full of life, so determined. They are on their own, not slaves of the combustion engine. In comparison, the car race looks so artificial, despite all the thrills associated with it, the performance depends mainly on the kind of car a man drives. Cyclists are all virtually on par when it comes to the vehicle they ride, not so in car racing.

Vinod Punamiya, a Mumbai racer, raced ahead of the Mumbai Pune Indrayani Express train in December 2006 at the age of 49 and ahead of the Mumbai Pune Deccan Queen four months later.

Sadanand Agashe, a retired IIT professor in Mumbai, is using the bicycle for more than three decades and does not like to use even a scooter as it too causes air and noise pollution. That explains why I do not have a paunch, he says. The father of Jairam Ramesh, India's environment minister, used to teach in IIT Mumbai some years ago and used to ride a bicycle on the campus though he owned a motor car as well, recalls Sudhir Badami, an engineer. Jairam is also an IIT engineer.

On world nude bicycling day one sees pictures of nude men and girls on bicycles demanding better facilities for bicycles and protesting against high vehicular pollution.

Phulbarin Bai of Chhattisgarh state became a mother at 15 but went on in later life to organize women and taught one hundred of them to cycle. This women's empowerment brought her a Mini Mata award from the state governament. People used to laugh at us women when we first began cycling, but now we are accepted, she said.

Former American president George W Bush was known for his rides on the bicycle through a field of sunflowers on his 640 hectare ranch at Crawford, Texas. That is the positive side of the man who is entirely discredited because of his war-mongering and conservatism. In August 2005 White House released a photograph of his riding a bicycle with Lance

Armstrong who had just won the Tour de France for a record seventh time. Armstrong's was an amazing feat for anyone, particularly a former cancer patient.

Bush said he enjoys bicycling as the wind rushes past you. That is an experience you do not get while swimming, he says. Bush was also reported to have fallen quite a few times while bicycling on his ranch.

Bush spent more time with half a dozen cycling advocates in his Oval office in May, 2006, than he gives to some government leaders He praised cycling as a a way to chase that fountain of youth. During his official visit to China in 2005 Bush recalled that in 1975 he spent his 29th birthday in China riding on a bicycle. It was a fantastic trip. Everyone was on the bike. The Chinese were surprised to find an American ride a bicycle.

The People's Daily carried four pictures of Bush riding a bicycle during his official visit in 2005 dressed in shorts and a jersey.

But for many poor people in different parts of the world the bicycle is a desperate, basic need for their survival as for the worker in De Sica's classic film Bicycle Thieves. It is not an instrument of recreation or idealism for them.

In the heart of Los Angeles many poor people ride ordinary bicycles in search of work, bicycles the upper class cyclists would not touch shorn as they are of all engineering details and which would be considered by others to be unsafe, unenjoyable and unreliable. They remain invisible to most people as they are so unglamorous. The issue is put in focus in an excellent article L.A.'s invisible riders by Dan Koeppel in Bicycling magazine (14-7-06). He says it is easy for us to dream of a world of smiling cyclists, more bicycle paths, less traffic congestion and co-existing modes of traffic. For the poor cycling is not exactly an enjoyable exercise.

The average reader of the Bicyling magazine has four bicycles in the garage and has a high income. The ordinary worker has to think twice before buying a new bicycle. If we do not see the poor bicyclists on the road it is not because they are transparent, but it is because we are blind, says Koeppel.

The more affluent in LA have also begun ditching their cars and the city has started opening more bicycle lanes. Companies are holding cycling seminars and federal officials are pushing for tax incentives for bicycles. (LA Times 23-5-06). Los Angeles is right for cyling, the region is flat and the weather is lovely. Increasing number of people in suits are now seen riding bicycles. Riding a bicycle gives people confidence which is expressed in a slogan on a sweater 'on my bike, LA is mine.' You feel that the city belongs to you when you ride a bicycle, you are much closer to the city, the environment, the people. You feel there are no real boundaries. Of course sometimes, cyclists have to contend with attacks with eggs or slapping of the butt, even knocking down.

Cycling is low-priced, non-polluting, small and silent. But after a century of mass ownership the bicycle still raises quizzical eyebrows not only among urban planners, politicians, bureaucrats and selfish motorists.

OECD, organization of economic cooperation and development, says only five countries have comprehensive national cycling campaigns, Britain, Germany, Finland, Czech republic and Latvia. Of course, Netherlands and Denmark are way ahead of all these countries in promoting cycling since the last four decades. Poland, Spain are laggards. (IHT 6-5-06).

London, Paris, Chicago, Bogota and Seoul have embarked on major campaigns to incorporate the bicycle in the traffic system. In Bogota during the Mayoral term of Enrique Penalosa between 1998-2000 restrictions were imposed on cars during peak hours and bicycles were encouraged. Various other steps were taken. In the process millions of dollars which would have been spent on providing for car traffic were saved. No wonder Mr Penalosa is much in demand a consultant on urban issues in cities ranging from Dar-es-Salam to Jakarta and Mexico city.

London is one of the greatest successes in cycling thanks to the socialist mayor Ken Linvinstone known for his outspoken criticism of capitalists. Chicago's Mayor Richard Daley has prepared an ambitious plan for cycling for the city.

Popularising the use of bicycles is not easy. Even in the Netherlands, the heaven for bicyclists, there was tremendous opposition from politicians in the sixties. They complained of the nuisance of bicycles.

Surprisingly Netherlands and Denmark both great cycling countires have developed the cycling culture without any national cycling programme. It just grew out of people's interest and commitment.

There are thousands of km of bicycle tracks in European countries and senior politicians often ride the bicycle. Facilities for bicycles are built into policy framework of different countries.

Our politicians, bureaucrats and planners often visit Europe. Several politicians have now made so much money that they regularly go for a holiday abroad. Do not these fellows see the excellent facilities provided for cyclists? It is criminal on the part of these policy makers to completely ignore the excellent medium of the bicycle.

In fact, our police and municipal authorities regularly harass bicycle riders in cities. That is because these people are brought up on the slavish mentality that only cars have a right to the road. The police picked up the bicycle of Pradeep Joshi, a shop-keeper in Santa Cruz. It was worth about Rs 600. He was fined Rs 1200. Can one imagine such a huge fine being levied for doing something good to the society, riding a vehicle which causes no pollution, consumes no fuel. He paid Rs 600 which was pocketed by the police and he was not given a receipt Mr Narayan Alva, vice-president of the Indian hotels and restaurants federation, had a similar experience. (Kishore Rathod Westside Plus TOI 11-12-04)

As for encouraging cycling as a sport the Mahaashtra government's sports department sanctioned just Rs 1400 during the sports week organised by the government itself. In 2007. A similar meager amount sanctioned for the previous year was not even allotted to the Amateur Cycling Association of India for the 30 km race. (Westside Plus. TOI 2-1-07). But the Maharashtra government sanctioned Rs two crore for a private ATP Kingfisher tennis tournament with which the liquor baron Vijay Mallya is associated. After a series of high level meetings, the government gave the money from the contingency fund which is normally used only in emergencies like natural calamities. (Ravikiran Deshmukh. Mumbai Mirror 8-12-07).

Despite the apathy of governments towards bicycles people do need bicycles and have a big demand for them. So, bicycle production worldwide is consistently more than of cars.

The credit for improving the road system goes to bicycles, not motor cars. In the early days of the bicycle the bicycle required better roads with much smoother surface than horse-drawn traffic. Even the excellent French gravel roads of the day left something to be desired. So bicycle periodicals and organizations both in Europe and in the US began to agitate for improved roads, noted James Flink in his book The Automobile Age.

By the 1890s at least a dozen bicycle periodicals throve in France, the most important of which was the daily Le Velo. Cyclists were somewhat more successful about improving roads as the crest of the bicycle movement there coincided with the climax of several decades of agrarian discontent.

A number of the more important early automobile manufacturers were first bicycle manufactures – among others. Opel in Germany, Peugeot in France, Humber, Morris and Rover in England, Pope Peerless, Rambler in the US. A substantial proportion of engineering talent as well in the in the early automobile industry was provided by former bicycle mechanics including William Morris who initiated volume production of automobiles in Great Britain.

Cycling is excellent as a sport but it is more important to use the bicycle for transport. The U.K. won a large number of medals in the Beijing Olympics in 2008 but it used bicycles for transport much less than Germany, Sweden and Switzerland.

P Sainath, reputed journalist and rural affairs editor of the Hindu, has written about the way the lives of thousands of women, including Muslim women, in Pudukottai district in Tamil Nadu were transformed after they started riding bicycles. The drive was aided by the district collector Sheela Rani Chungat.

The star among cyclists in India was Jankidas, a national champion for several years in the 1930s and 1940s before he made his mark in hundreds of Hindi films and introduced Meena Kumari and Mala Sinha to the screen. He hoisted the Indian National Congress flag at the Zurich international cycling championship in 1946.

11

Fascism and Car

There is a close connection between craze for highways, speed, cars, fascism and dictatorship. There is also plenty of evidence of links between anti-democratic forces in India and the car lobby. And major American car companies had clear links with Nazi Germany.

Henry Ford, the founder of the Ford motor company and father of the modern assembly line, mass production, accepted the highest medal of fascist Germany, for foreigners, the Grand Cross of the German Eagle.

Henry Ford's pamphlet against the Jews 'International Jew – the world's foremost ; problem' brought him to the notice of Hitler in 1921 when he was chairman of the fledgling Nazi party. Hitler in his Mein Kampf condemned American Jew businessmen and singled out Ford for praise. He said Ford admirably kept his independence from Jews.

The Nazis lowered auto taxes and fees, simplified ownership rules and traffic laws, encouraged auto vacations, gave car designer Ferdinand Porsche the go ahead to develop a cheap and simple 'people's car' and inaugurated a crash programme to cover the countryside with a dense network of state of the art autobahns, points out Daniel Lazare in his book 'America's undeclared war.'

Car Busters magazine, a premier journal exposing the evils of car culture, shows further links between capitalism, fascism and car culture.

The Nazi autobahn project, which allowed rapid control of areas remote from the seat of power and not just in war time was duplicated in non-fascist countries in North America and Western Europe. Hitler believed that all strategic roads were built by tyrants from Roman times. These roads go straight across the country. All other roads wind like processions and are a waste of time, Hitler felt.

Hitler embarked on the autobahn project because this was essentially to create a huge monument, a demonstration of power and preparation for the war effort.

At the time the US and England had far more number of cars than Germany but it was Germany which embarked on the expressway because of Hitler's obsession with power and grandeur.

The war in Iraq is seen as the most vehicle-reliant war in world history. It shows the same American drive-through mentality as in normal times. In Iraq they operated mainly from closed, air-conditioned Humvees which isolated the American soldiers from the Iraqis unlike the former open jeeps in which soldiers could interact with local people.

Henry Ford, turned work into an endless repetition of tedious tasks and alienated the worker further from work as brilliantly shown by Charlie Chaplin in his film Modern Times made in 1936. The film, written, directed and produced by Chaplin specifically drew from Henry Ford's assembly line production methods which proved highly detrimental to workers.

The name Ford also became synonymous with anti-labour policies, spying on workers, stifling dissent and breaking unions. Citing the Ford motor company as the world's outstanding example of an industrial dictatorship, the New York Times in 1928 called Henry Ford an industrial fascist, the Mussolini of Detroit.

Ford allowed little time to workers to eat their lunch, go to the toilet or talk.

American car manufacturing companies also harmed people in their own country and in other countries in many other ways. In America they systematically contributed to the destruction or weakening of the public transport system, be it trams or buses. Increased car production also led to distorted town planning priorities. Due to the car American cities have spread out so far that many of them cannot be serviced economically with public transport.

Some years ago America's cities were walkable where more attention was given to the construction and maintenance of footpaths than of streets.

In pursuit of oil the US has also for decades overthrown governments which nationalized their oil reserves like the Mossadegh government of Iran in a CIA-directed coup in 1953. (Petro Bully by Michael Salman LA Times 29-10-07).

Big American companies exploring and refining crude oil have also created environmental havoc in some countries. Ken Saro-Wiwa an environmentalist opposing the degradation brought about by oil companies in Nigeria was hanged by his government.

Indian people's attention was drawn to the Movement for the Emancipation of the Niger Delta when Pandurang Tari, an engineer, working on a ship extracting oil in Nigeria was taken hostage and later released by the rebels who were friendly with him. (IE 2-11-07)

Nadine Gordimer, the Nobel prize winning writer, in an article in the New York Times drew attention to the oil politics in Nigeria and the atrocities committed by the Nigerian authorities against protesters.

The role of the oil giant Shell in exploiting the people of Nigeria and the hanging of protester Ken Saro-Wiwa was roundly exposed by PEN Center, a prominent international organization of writers. The problem in Nigeria is that its people have not benefited from the oil wealth unlike people in other oil rich countries.

Sauvik Chakraverti,, representing the view of free marketers, wants every Indian including the Nagas and the Garwhalis from the hilly regions to possess a car. That will make these states rich, he argued in an edit page article in The Times of India (March 27, 2001).

In another article he suggested that Rajpath, the broad avenue in New Delhi, be privatized and every government building be converted into shopping malls with, mark you, enough space for car parking..

But then even the Indian planning commission's deputy chairperson, the high profile Montek Singh Ahluwalia, wants to commercially develop Rajpath. The idea is strongly opposed by heritage experts including A.G.K. Menon.

On the other hand. Vaclav Havel, the renowned playwright and former Czech president, spoke out against expressways at the very beginning of his speech while accepting the Gandhi peace prize in India in 2003.

He said he had just toured Europe by car with his wife and was astounded by the senselessness of traffic on the expressways. Most of the vehicles consisted of huge trucks which exceeded speed limits and overtook one another without any warning. All that the transport system seemed to be doing was it gave Danish butter to an Italian or Italian butter to a Danish person. There was no logic to the whole thing except the blind logic of market forces.

He said we should blame ourselves too for the traffic mess because we travel alone in a car like thousands of others Paying rich tributes to Mahatma Gandhi he said had Gandhi been alive today, he would have warned us about the contemporary problems in the same way he had warned India about the Manchester textile mills or the railways. Without doubt, he would sound the alarm, his voice filled with compelling urgency, Mr Havel said.

There is a scene in the 1953 movie Roman Holiday, high up on nearly everyone's list of favourite romantic comedies. In the film a sheltered princess played by Audrey Hepburn steps out into a crowded city street for the first time in her life. She is both startled and exhilarated. The street is filled with all manner of people doing all manner of things, women carrying groceries, children darting about, men on bicycles and motor scooters, bakers with trays of dough balanced on their heads etc.

What makes it all so exciting especially for a member of a royal family is the sense of democratic order, the fact that everyone is engaged in something different yet in the final analysis are all busily doing the same thing which is utilizing the city as an arena and a tool.

Hitler's autobahns are providing a fascination for the new rich in contemporary China which has betrayed Mao's revolution imposing brutal working conditions on labour. Tens of thousands of Chinese tourists are traveling to Germany to drive powerful cars at upto 150 miles per hour on the autobahns despite fears by road safety groups.

The Germans, contrary to their love for the environment and widespread pedestrian-friendly culture, also love speeding. Few things are closer to the German heart than the freedom to drive like Michael Schumacher, the fabled Formula One champion. They consider speeding an inalienable right. (NYT 16-3-07).

Another example of the link between fascist tendency and automobiles is provided by the Maruti car project floated by Sanjay Gandhi, son of former Prime Minister Indira Gandhi.

Inder Malhotra, veteran journalist and biographer of Mrs Indira Gandhi, says in his book that Sanjay Gandhi wanted to become the Ford of India. According to other sources when Sanjay Gandhi was in England he frequently landed in trouble in his dealing with cars and the Indian ambassador had to frequently intervene on his behalf.

The Maruti scandal was exposed by the one-man inquiry commission of Mr Justice A.C. Gupta, a sitting judge of the Supreme court. All norms and procedures were flouted to give the car manufacturing licence to Sanjay Gandhi who did not meet any requirements for the project.

Bansi Lal, the then chief minister of Haryana, bent every rule to allot 300 acres of land at Gurgaon for the factory displacing a number of poor farmers and giving them just 10 per cent of the price for the land initially.

After Sanjay's death in an air crash, the Maruti car project was revived by the Indian government, led by Indira Gandhi, mother of Sanjay, in collaboration with Suzuki of Japan and interestingly it had much more democratic work environment than in other companies. The gap in the salary between the lowest worker and the top boss was very narrow, recalled R.C. Bhargava, a senior bureaucrat-turned Maruti chief. Every one ate in the same canteen and officers shared the open office with other colleagues. The first Maruti car rolled out on December 14, 1983, the birthday of Sanjay.

Sanjay's brother, Rajiv Gandhi, later Prime Minister of India also loved to drive fast cars. Rajiv's son Rahul, projected as a future Prime Minister in the dynastic ruling family, and his buddies had created a carefully camouflaged racing track 25 km from New Delhi where they drove fast motor cycles at breakneck speed. These so-called speed devils included Robert Vadra, brother in law of Rahul Gandhi.The story was broken by Bayas Anand of the Times of India July 20, 2005, but was not followed in the media.

In Mumbai too there are some car racing enthusiasts who go for races outside the limits of Mumbai, away from the sight of police. They communicate with each other on mobile phones through text messages. Companies have sprung up to modify cars for racing. Karan Shah of Ballard Pier has more business on his hand than he can handle and so is the case with Gautam Sachdeva of Colaba.

Of no less concern than flouting of all norms in the making of the Maruti car is the way VIPs behave on public roads. This is in typical North Indian tradition of 'might is right,' says Shatrujeet Kapur, an officer of the Indian Police Service, who has served as superintendent of Haryana highway patrol and road safety.

The disrespect shown to fellow travelers borders on contempt. No body seems to object to this blatant muscle-flexing. This may be because of the very feudal nature of the social milieu in which we live. Mayawati, the chief minister of Uttar Pradesh and champion of the downtrodden, has 350 policemen and 34 vehicles for her security. Wherever she goes, a curfew like situation develops, shops are asked to close down, traffic is stopped and people are asked to look the other way. A dedicated elevator lands in her chamber where the washroom is said to be like on in a seven star hotel. It is now proposed to acqauire land of the historic La Martiner college in Lucknow near the chief minister's house to set up a helipad so she can fly more than drive.

A private car of Vasant Davkhare, deputy chairperson of the Maharashtra legislative council, had its red light seized by the police and fined Rs 100 in Satara in 2008. It was by no means the first incident of its kind. (Lokmat 6-1-08).

Mr Deepak Pandey, ADC of former Mahaashtra governor Mohammad Fazal, made headlines in 2004. He was stopped by a traffic constable Vishnu Patil for talking on his cellphone while driving. An angry Pandey ordered the traffic branch to punish the constable and he, collapsed due to exhaustion and was admitted to a hospital.

Shiv Sena chief Bal Thackeray is an unabashed admirer of Hitler and has the same fascination for fast roads like Hitler. His political ally the Bharatiya Janata party too is obsessed with highways and one of its most ambitious projects during its tenure in Delhi from 1999 was the Prime Minister's Bharat Jodo Pariyojana linking all state capitals by four lane highways.

Prime Minister Vajpayee made highways a major but unsuccessful election issue in 2004, huge advertisements were placed in the media and his portraits were put up on the highways. These were pulled down after the defeat.

The project was mired in corruption and it came to the fore with the murder of Satyendra Dubey after he had drawn the attention of the Prime Minister's office to the rampant corruption in the highway project in his home state of Bihar. Dubey, an engineer working on the project, was honest and a product of the internationally renowned Indian Institute of Technology. The murder created revulsion among the bright products of IIT working in different parts of the world.

The authorities woke up after a public outcry. An online petition seeking in inquiry was signed by 16,000 people. Among those who sought justice was Narayan Murthy, a father figure on India's IT industry. What shocked people was that the Prime Minister's office was thought to have leaked Dubey's identity but it did not even respond to the killing of the honest engineer.

Subsequently in 2007 the Congress Prime Minister Dr Manmohan Singh made no secret of the corruption in road construction when he said it was spreading like cancer in every nook and corner of the city. He was inaugurating a two-day national conference on rural roads. It was because of corruption, he said, that newly repaired or constructed roads become unusable as soon as the rainy season begins.

Three years after the Dubey murder, Manjunath Shanmugham, a sales officer of Indian Oil Corporation, was murdered as he blew the whistle on a petrol adulteration racket in Uttar Pradesh.

There is total awareness that dealers indulge in adulteration either in collusion with or by coercing field officers, said IOC's former director of marketing P.K. Agarwal. (Indian Express 9-12-05).

Such is the obsession of the BJP with the highway and flyover culture that former Prime Minister Vajpayee and former deputy Prime Minister L.K. Advani released a book on the subject written by Nitin Gadkari, a former public works minister of the BJP in Maharashtra and a devout supporter of the automobile culture.

Gadkari has a slogan in his house extolling the Americans 'It is not because America is great that it has great roads but because America has great roads that America is great.'

Unfortunately, the much-trumpeted Mumbai-Pune expressway has for a long time proved to be a financial disaster, it just does not have enough traffic to recover the huge cost through toll. It has also proved to be a death trap with numerous vehicle crashes and many are using it as a racing track. Besides landslides are common during the monsoon.

The expressway has been sealed off from nearby villagers so that cars can have an unrestricted run. But a heavy price has been paid for this exclusivity. When motorists get injured, villagers do not come to know about the accident nor can they rush to their help.

It is true the expressway has cut traveling time and many people boast about how fast they can now reach Pune or Mumbai. The trouble is that such showpieces apart, there are traffic jams everywhere else.

Among the main beneficiaries of the expressway are real estate developers and land sharks who have made a killing by bringing Pune closer to the real estate investor class of Mumbai. This section wants to invest in the city because of its pleasant climate and good infrastructure so that Pune can become a colony to be exploited for Mumbai.

Genuine travellers prefer the train. Mr P.G. Patankar, a noted transport expert, says he always prefers to travel by train between Mumbai and Pune. It is pollution-free, reliable and fast.

It is odd that two-wheelers are not allowed on the expressway. It has just the rich do not want the 'show' to be spoilt by the presence of less privileged people. Jaideep Sahni, script writer of Chak De India.

It is sad that China is now embarking on massive motorisation, giving up its friendly image as a predominantly bicycle-riding nation. If the average person in China used as much oil as the average American, it will consume virtually all of the world's oil, says Walter Hook of Sustainable Transport after visiting China

Motorisation is taking a heavy toll of nature and the environment-friendly bicycle sector. New roads being built have led to the destruction of some neighbourhoods that are thousands of years old, destroying entire communities. The air has become less breathable. Bicycles have been banned from major city streets or pushed onto sidewalks. Man vs Machine on Beijing's streets is the apt headline of an excellent report in the New York Times of (4-8-04) by Philip Cunningham. In the report he shows how there are now two distinct classes in China, those who have cars and those who don't. The haves terrorise the have-nots. But the poor are fighting back.

In Shanghai traffic police punished 112,000 so-called jaywalkers and 347,000 cyclists in just three months in 2006 while motorists were easily let off which shows the severe bias against the common people in today's capitalism-driven China. (Sustainable Transport, July 2006).

The municipal office wanted to set up billboards with photographs of jaywalkers in a bid to shame them. Jaywalkers were also liable to go jail or lose their jobs and get reduced bonus. Can a system be more anti-people ?

During his election campaign President Clinton traveled by a train to attract voters . But the track on which he traveled had been abandoned earlier as part of the drive by the automobile and road lobby to kill railways. America is the only industrialized nation which refuses to subsidise rail travel.

We have our own motor bike maniacs with big bank balances, who else would spend Rs ten lakh on a two-wheeler, and with indulgent parents. But not all are crazy and with biceps. Dr Cyres Mehta, an eye surgeon from Colaba, Mumbai, says biking is an expression of freedom, the fun is in acceleration.

Surprisingly, India's commerce minister Kamal Nath has lobbied for the Harley, the popular American motor bike brand. In a letter to Prime Minister Manmohan Singh he urged duty on its import to 'rev ties between the US and India.' (IE 18-12-07). The brand has reported sluggish sales in America.

In Saudi Arabia, the citadel of Islamic conservatism, Saudi racegoers roam all night. They gather on the highways by 1 a.m. revving engines and deliberately spin out of control, skid, kill themselves or spectators. It is a collective scream of frustration, an empty life, full of boredom. (IHT 6-3-09).

It was the macho image of the motor cycle when a number of supporters of the ruling Communist party of India (M) in West Bengal rode to 'recapture' the embattled village Nandigram which had strongly resisted its land being used for a chemical complex in 2007.

A lot of tainted money is also used for buying luxury cars. Gutka baron Rasiklal Dhariwal manufacturer of Gutka, a tobacco product, gifted his grand-daughter Janhavi a Maybach car in Pune on her 21st birthday. Newspapers were quick to publish pictures of her showing off the car. It was later that Dhariwal's alleged links with the notorious underworld don Dawood Ibrahim were disclosed by the police.

The luxury car Rolls Royce had its first buyer in India in 2005 after many years when Pune's stud farm owner Yohan Poonawala bought one. Six chauffeurs were specially trained for driving the car by a representative of the company who was flown in from London. Previously princely rulers were the main buyers of these and other luxury cars. Among the first owners of a Rolls was the Maharaja of Gwalior whose family had an old record of being loyal to the British. So servile were several princely rulers that when the Prince of Wales visited India in 1921 they ordered Rolls to welcome him while the masses were protesting against the royal visit. The life style of many of the rulers was obscenely luxurious. Cricketer Ranji from the princely family of Gujarat had a fleet of cars.

The connection between America's empire building, militarism, feeling of insecurity and its aggressiveness and manufacturing of the monster vehicles, the sports utility vehicles (SUV) is well brought out by David Campbell in a lengthy article in the American Quarterly in, September, 2005.

The import or smuggling of the monster vehicles into India by our high and mighty and the glamorous society is relevant because this class thinks the SUV gives it greater security and power. The richer our elite becomes, the more insecure it feels and so its resort to such vehicles.

The SUV seen as the vehicle of the empire, a gargantuan capsule of excess consumption created by the Americans, partly to get over the insecurity arising out of the defeat in Vietnam.

President George Bush in his State of the Union address in 2006 finally admitted that America has become addicted to oil and something needs to be done about it. But he did not dare touch the automobile sector which consumes much of the oil. Actually, the American government is giving more subsidies and relaxing environmental restrictions on petrol-guzzling SUVs by giving them the status of light trucks. (the book High and Mighty. SUVs world's most dangerous vehicles and how they got that way by Keith Bradsher).

The oil addiction is such that it could only be satisfied by an international crime like the invasion of Iraq, says David Campbell, political scientist. The SUV is conceived by a para-military American culture which emerged after the defeat in Vietnam. It sought the remasculanisation of America with the glorification of Rambo and Rocky cults.

Look at the names of SUVs associated with aggression and abandon, Warrior, Navigator, Trail Blazer, Pathfinder and Escape. Owners of SUVs are crass and irresponsible, UK's minister for energy Malcolm, told the London Times (27-5-07) as the monstrosities consume more fuel and cause heavy pollution.

The Lamborghini Gallardo Spyder car with speed upto 314 km per hour, is advertised as stunningly brutal in its looks. Named after a fighter bull, it has pointy styling, sharp cuts and straight lines unlike the smooth and flowing lines of the Ferrari. (DNA daily 30-3-06).

The vehicle is thought to give the owners a feeling of security, a barrier, an urban assault vehicle in the homeland city at war. Your drive in it like a military figure, confronting others, posing danger to others but feeling secure in an increasingly insecure world.

With the televised invasion of Iraq, the monster Hummer vehicle became a best seller. The SUVs symbolize the arrogant owners; In Your Face attitude which says, get out of the way, we do not care for you. Hummer's name is derived from the US army's acronym for the vehicle High Mobility Multipurpose Wheeled Vehicle widely used in Iraq, Afghanistan and the gulf war.

The brutish car represents the ultimate arrogance of the political right-wing. Margaret Thatcher, the arch conservative, unabashed champion of personalized transport, and former British Prime Minister, refused to travel by railway, the real collective, public transport. (Martin Jacques, former editor of Marxism Today in the Guardian (5-6-08).

It is perhaps not surprising that the vehicle is feeding the appetite of businesspersons from Gujarat, the state which has sharply veered to the extreme right politically and Gujaratis make up a substantial NRI population in the US. Pharma barons including Sudhir Mehta and Pankaj Patel are buying up the car which costs more than Rs ten million.

Gujaratis are now willing to flaunt vehicles with novelty values, said imported car dealer Javed Desai. (TOI 18-11-06).

In reality, SUVs are not so safe. Because of their height, they have a tendency to roll over in case of an accident. The death rate for SUV occupants is higher than for other cars. In America more than 3000 SUV users die each year in accidents, the same number as those killed in the September 11 attack.

Advertisements of these aggressive vehicles create a fantasy world in which automobile owners enjoy tremendous freedom and gives them power. An advertisement for the U.K. Land Rover shows an eagle towering over the vehicle. The caption says, Go, spread your wings.

Several of the arrogant rich openly boast about their rash driving, how they drink and drive and how they learnt driving when as small as seven to eight years in complete defiance of rules.

The Bishop of London has done well to declare it sinful to contribute to climate change by flying on holidays or driving a gas-guzzling car Richard Charters will encourage vicars to preach more green sermons and warn congregations that it is now a moral obligation for Christians to lead eco-friendly lifestyles.

Some Christian leaders in the US declared some time ago that it is one of the great Christian obligations to use public transport as cars were damaging God's creation. They asked CEOs of General Motors and other companies to declare what steps they were taking to reduce pollution. (Benita Singh in Next American City journal, Oct. 03).

Why do people use monstrous cars with massive power engines when they cannot drive at those speeds on urban roads ? It is mainly about the brag factor, says Dilip Chhabria, car stylist who has renovated many cars for rich and influential clients. He says no one uses the full potential of the car be it a Ferrari or Porsche. But then cars are all about showing off, there is the smugness of knowing that people know you have a powerful engine under your bonnet. (Autocar magazine Dec. 2002).

Instead of seeking thrills in an expensive, mechanical device of the car, our young and rich could seek adventure in something inexpensive and environment-friendly, the skateboard which is becoming quite popular in Europe.

The whole ethos of the car creates anti-social feelings. A promotional write-up in the Times of India about Mercedes Benz S class says that with the car's luxuries everyone else will adjust to your pace. 'And if they don't, drive a stake through their hearts.' (TOI 21-7-06). Can anyone get more brutish ? Barbarity is accompanied by feudal values. The car is compared to a medieval castle, impregnable and invulnerable. It also shows the innate fear felt by the rich in a deeply unequal society.

Exotic cars are all about irrationality. The more irrational they are, the more attractive they become says Dilip Chhabria. The knowledge that you have an irrational car in your garage gives you a high that is difficult of match.

John Armitage and Phil Graham authors of Political Economy of Speed argue that intensification of speed in automobiles or war equipment is the negation of time. It is consumption and destruction of time rather than emancipation.

Car racing is among the most absurd outgrowths of our fascination with the car, argues Jonathan Dollymoore in an article in the London Review of Books. Drivers hurtle around in circles. Some lose control and end up as dead, mutilated, crippled. And yet, car racing is one of the most fanatically pursued sports. He also observes that nothing invites third rate sex psychology as cars.

The psychological consequences of accidents remain completely neglected. Twenty years ago you could see such fast driving only in the races. There is hardly anything more dangerous than racing with a one or two tonne car. We have made the automobile into a camouflaged means of expression of violence for potentially violent people. People release their aggression in cars. That is why cars become extremely dangerous. But this is seldom taken into account. In India because the rich are very influential they blame the victims rather than themselves for murders on the road. And the corrupt police often accept this version.

Car manufacturers and advertisers contribute to the deadly scenario with their constant glorification of speed and their creating the impression that there are wide open roads over which cars can be driven at a furious speed which the drivers can enjoy.

The city council of Paris has been contemplating for some time to ban SUVs in the city since the oversized vehicles are not meant for the city and they are a drag on the traffic. SUV owners could now be denied parking permits.

London's socialist Mayor Ken Livingstone has called SUV owners complete idiots

SUVs are now being targeted by protesters in Paris with deflating of tyres, the daily Liberation has reported. In the US a bright student in the California Institute of Technology was given a harsh prison term of eight years for firebombing 125 SUVs He was given additional three years in jail because of the new harsh US Patriot Act. His action was billed as domestic terrorism He belonged to the Earth Liberation Front which is regarded by the FBI as a terrorist organization though white supremacists and right-wing extremists are not classified in this category.

While violence is not easy to justify, one cannot forget that cars commit violence 24 hours year round and any act of resistance is extremely minor in comparison. A car may knock you down, cripple and kill you. But if you merely make a gesture of protest or just thump the car, your life could be in danger.

Some film stars have survived serious accidents only because their cars were very stable during accidents. Sanjay

Dutt, film star, known for his fast driving, fast life style and many brushes with the law, recalls driving at high speed in his Landcrusier with friends like film star Ajay Devgun from Mumbai to Bikaner. The car was being driven at nearly 140 km an hour when the tyre blew up and they survived because the car did not swerve. He started driving when he was 13.

The dark side of automobilism. Violence, war and motor car is the apt title of a scholarly article written by Kurt Moser in the Journal of Transport History (Sept. 2003). Aggressive tendencies generated by motor car and speed played a significant role in generating a collective mood that anticipated and prepared people for the first world war.

Psychologist Adler interpreted aggression of motorists on the road as a way of overcoming inferiority complex. Weakness is sought to be compensated by brutality.

The media, print and film, joins in glorifying brutal violence by cars and motorists. The Times of India car buyers' guide supplement gleefully describes a car chase in a film as 'malevolent, funny, audacious and downright evil. The villain stuntman Mike stalks four women in his car which is death-proof for himself. He then smashes into them at full speed, completely obliterating them. Alongside are big advertisements for car loans given by leading banks ICICI and HDFC.

Besides, fast cars are equated with progress while slower cars and other slow road users are seen to be impediments to progress.

Car racing is increasingly associated with greed, globalsiation and fascism. It has lost much of its charm of old. The daily Guardian has contrasted the utter lack of character in the centenary of formula 1 in 2006 with the centenary of Tour de France cycle race celebrated three years ago with a lot of festivities. This is because the cycling people have a real interest in the sport unlike people who run formula racing who are commercially-minded.

Motor racing is becoming more and more dull, mechanical and certain configurations required in cars have robbed formula of variety in technical matters that was among its glories, the Guardian has noted.

All through 90 years the sound of formula one was one of symphony of contrasting timbers with a wide variety of cars participating. Racing tracks also had more variety earlier. There used to be races in Casablanca and Tripoli. Monaco stands out because of its picturesque quality and an ambience that produces an unpredictable outcome. Modern tracks are all boring, very similar.

Greed is the culprit. In their desperation to capture new markets men running formula races have lost touch with the essence of their sport. (Guardian 19-7-06). Car racing is also marked by male chauvinism and has sought to discourage women drivers. 'A girl with big boobs would never be comfortable in a racing car. Can you imagine a mechanic strapping her ?', said noted racing driver Jenson Butt.

Nothing shows the world of car racing in poorer light than the sex orgy with prostitutes involving Max Mosley, president of the Paris-based international federation of automobiles, the governing body of motor sports. He has presided over the expansion of Formula One racing into one of the world's richest sports.

Moreover, there is a strong fascist connection. Max Mosley's father was the president of the British Fascist Union who secretly married the society beauty Diana Mitford in the home of Joseph Goebbels, the propaganda chief of Hitler. The orgy, whose tape was released by a tabloid, had a Nazi motif with the prostitutes wearing clothes of prisoners and Mosley speaking in German. (NYT 8-4-08). Immediately there were calls for his resignations from various quarters including four major car manufacturing companies, BMW, Daimler Benz, Honda and Toyota. The American Automobile Association demanded that the post demanded a high ethical behaviour.

It is sad that the Communist party of India (Marxit)-led government in West Bengal was keen to build a formula 1 race track at New Town in Rajarhat near Kolkata way back in

1998, had set aside 850 acres of land, even formed a motor sports council. Fortunately, the government of India announced that all cigarette companies were prohibite from sponsoring any sports event because of which global tabacco major BAT, the project sponsor, pulled out. (Rakhi Chakrabarty, Mumbai Mirror 11-11-06).

The Congress chief minister of Haryana, Bhupinder Singh Hooda made a trip to the Netherlands to sign an agreement for a race track in 2006.

The heavy toll of life taken by the automobile is sought to be justified by romanticizing death in accident as the death of fighter pilots, car racing drivers and bull fighters. A concept of sacred death is created.

At the height of universal concern over climate change in 2007 and demands for oil conservation, a section of the Indian elite was desperate to convert India's most famous road Rajpath in Lutyen's Delhi into a Formula one Race track. The Times of India enthusiastically welcomed the idea in an editorial saying the private sector must take this proposal forward through sponsorships so that auto-racing spurs auto business and inspires more Indian manufacturers and designers. It lauded the efforts of IIT (Indian Institute of Technology), the elite technological institute in Delhi, for working on a prototype for a racing car. (TOI 2-6-06).

Pushing the proposal were liquor manufacturer Vijay Mallya and former Andhra Pradesh chief minister Chandrababu Naidu. Racing champion Schumacher had a meeting with Delhi chief minister Sheila Dikshit on the issue. Imagine Raj Path, identified with India's unique democracy people, nationhood, being virtually privatized for the benefit of the racing and car lobby.

Andhra Pradesh is known for its poverty and suicides by hundreds of farmers but its chief minister Chandrababu Naidu had one big dream, to bring formula 1 racing to the state capital Hyderabad. He met formula 1 boss Bernie Ecclestone in

Hyderabad and then in Milan offering government support of nearly Rs 600 crore for the track. The infrastructure involved construction of a special road from the airport to the track, special customs counters at the airport to clear tones of heavy equipment and cars brought in by special Jumbo jets. Naidu had also planned to get exemption from the Central government on the ban on cigarette sponsorship for the races.

George W Bush, the invader of Iraq, listed car racing as his favourite sport The White House web site during his term showed a beaming Bush standing in the middle of the 2005 Nextel cup champion team and their car and another shows Bush in the Oval office with the 2006 Nextel cup champion Jimmie Johnson with him.

Car racing has been in the front line of capitalism with Fortune 500 companies sponsoring the races conducted by the National Association for Stock Car Racing (NASCAR) more than any other sport. It is also a big spectator sport with the racing telecast in 150 countries live. The sport is only behind National Football League in television ratings in the US.

Formula 1 is a waste of money. It is a vulgar, tedious, sexist, maddening trash with excruciating noise, says social analyst Mary Ann Sieghart. Vehicles go round and round with mind-sapping monotony on the same track for hours. One can't even see the drivers encased by protective clothing, helmets and cockpits. Nor do they do anything interesting with their bodies unlike gymnasts and athletes. It is true they are brave and quick witted but all this does not make the sport exciting. An what a waste of fuel, one car can only go four miles a gallon. And great swaths of land are dug up to build new tracks. The noise pollution is horrendous for miles around. It is a horribly macho sport and there is a special exemption to formula 1 from the ban on tobacco advertisements. (Times 21-3-08).

Cars are actually like moving cages, though advertisers talk of liberty and freedom brought about by the vehicles. The Americans have a great fascination for cars and guns, both responsible for many deaths, points out Eduardo Galeano, the top Latin American thinker and activist.

Advertisers have glamourised cars and created a false demand for cars by indulging in artificial images. Almost every other advertisement on television shows vast, empty roads in which the car has total freedom to move about. Paul Baran, the eminent American economist, analysed the advertising world very accurately when he wrote that advertising plays on status seeking, snobbery, social, racial, sexual discrimination, egotism, envy, gluttony, avarice, ruthlessness. Advertisements make use of these traits.

Monopoly capital teaches us to want what we really do not need. Advertising feeds on our irrationalities and drives us into debt.

In America they shoot animals while driving, there is also the phenomenon of drive-in marriages and of course drive-in theatres. In such a scenario automobiles have come to acquire more rights than human beings.

In poor countries, the money that goes into buying cars could sustain millions of bicycles and alleviate poverty.

Israel is practising a road apartheid with its policy of separate roads, roads for Israelis only and roads for Palestinians only. The Israeli military has blocked Palestinians even from driving on the main artery in what Israeli human rights groups say is a first step towards road apartheid.

The car lobby's hostility to common people, hatred for environment, progressive political issues is crystallized in the writing of Jeremy Clarkson in his column in the Times which is quite vicious and anti-poor.

He pours scorn on pedestrians and bicyclists saying they do not pay taxes, occupy so much road space and they should get lost. Clarkson says he wants to run down the cyclists asserting their claim to road space.

Clarkson apologized after branding British Prime Minister Gordon Brown as a one-eyed idiot during a press conference in

Sydney to publicise his TV show. Mr Brown had lost use of one eye in school while playing Rugby.

Several environment groups have demanded that Clarkson be banned from the BBC's widely watched programme on fast driving Top Gear. His antics have been criticized as thuggist.

In a society in which the upper class suffers from boredom because of collapse of human values, it is greatly attracted to the cult of speed and car racing. People cocooned by safety yearn for speed. Says Christina Odone, a noted journalist and atheist. Broken speed records, trashed cars, shredded tyres, is exciting stuff for some people. The image of a revving, roaring car tearing through the desert, away from rules and authority, rules bored minds. It is a brilliant con game in which the car is seen as a passport to freedom when in actual life it means wasting time in long traffic jams. Yet, millions of people buy such deceptive images and the car. says Chirstina Odone. (Observer 24-9-06). Besides the violence of speeding gives joy to certain people.

The BBC is thought to be doing such programmes of bogus thrill to attract the young who are increasingly switching off television and turning to more violent video games like Grand Theft Auto in which players pretend to be gun toting gangsters routinely shooting pedestrians.

The BBC programme sticks two fingers at the basic law of physics and biology that the faster you drive the more likely you are to kill or be killed. There is now a one in 17 chance of each of us being killed or seriously injured in a road crash because of the speed monsters, says Kira Kochrane who lost her little brother in a road accident. (Licensed to kill. Guardian 24-10-06).

Speed maniacs argue that the problem is not with speed but with bad driving that causes accidents. This is nonsensical. An effective punishment for speed maniacs would be to make them lose their licence. If their victims lose their lives, there is no reason why these guys should not at least lose their driving licence.

The car lobby and its motoring magazines see speed restriction as infringement of the rights of motorists to unlimited freedom.

The argument of the motor lobby that speed does not kill is likened to Hitler's propaganda technique that the bigger the lie it is more likely to be accepted. The most powerful argument against the fascist fascination for speed is made in the excellent book Murder Most Foul written by J.S. Dean, a former president of the Pedestrians Association, way back in 1947.

The spiritual home of British motoring interests is Nazi Germany, he argued. The Motor magazine in 1937 was high in praise of Nazi Germany for its political ideology and ruthless car culture. The magazine also ridiculed pedestrians, cyclists and speed limits as namby pamby.

The opponents of speed cameras argue that speeding drivers are normally perfectly nice people and so should not be punished for speeding. The cameras are also said to interfere with personal liberty. It is like saying we should let off wife beaters and child molesters because otherwise they are good people. (New Statesman 12-1-04) We strive to protect our children from paedophiles, child molesters, but ten times more children are killed by speeding vehicles. That should concern us more but does not. The car is a lethal weapon and they deserve to be hounded as mercilessly as housebreakers.

The lowering of the British national speed limit from 60 to 50 km infuriated the right wing motorist lobby in 2009. Motorists do not want to be prosecuted for dangerous driving but are quick to demand prosecution of cyclists, pedestrians and slow motorists. The world's most illiberal regimes have dangerous roads and the most liberal have strictest laws.

India's growing car industry and dependence on oil import force it to ally with the brutal military dictatorship in neighbouring Myanmar or Burma. A joint Indo-Myanmar army car rally was held in December, 2006. It seems deeply ironical considering the ruthless suppression of democratic protests by Buddhist monks and others in Burma in September, 2007. Ironically at the very time of the suppression a bigwig in India's petroleum ministry was in Burma seeking oil supplies.

The road and car lobby meet their Nemesis in the acclaimed novel Road by Cornac Mcarthy in which there are long lines of charred and rusting cars on the Interstate highway in a stiff gray sludge of melted rubber. That is when the world has been destroyed, turned ashen but a man, 40, and his son, 10, have still not lost hope and keep walking on the desolate road. (NYT 8-10-6).

12

Railways

The Indian Railways have very strict rules on how many live animals–cows, buffaloes, goats, donkeys etc. can be carried in a wagon of specified dimensions. Any breach of these rules is an offence punishable under the railways' own disciplinary action procedure as also under the Prevention of Cruelty to Animals legislations.

But no such rules govern the transportation of human beings. This was admitted by George Fernandes, railway minister, in 1990 in a Perspective paper titled Bombay Suburban Railway System. Need for New Initiatives published by Indian Railways.

Since then matters have got worse in the last two decades. It is not only that traveling conditions are more humiliating. There are long, depressing queues for tickets. And all this while the mobility for the rich increased tremendously with dozens of new brands of luxury cars flooding the market.

Mr Fernandes, who grew up on the streets of Mumbai as a fiery trade unionist, also led a historic nationwide strike of railway employees in 1974.

Though travelling conditions are worsening in the suburban sector in Mumbai and in fact throughout the country, there is little organised public resistance. People do react angrily sometimes by stopping trains but there is no organization which consistently and systematically campaigns on issues, challenges the authorities.

The cruelest part is that children sweep the trains during journey collecting money from passengers for the maintenance. Passengers routinely throw out their lunch packets and plastic bottles out of windows dirtying tracks throughout the country. The railways are also to blame as they do little to campaign for cleanliness.

Mr Laloo Prasad Yadav is being credited with financially improving the railways as railway minister since 2004. The man with his rustic charm has promoted privatization and he is a favourite with IIMs (Indian Institutes of Management). But the so-called railway reforms have failed to benefit the common people. The elitist policies continue.

The much lauded railway suburban network in Mumbai, the largest in the world, is actually very cruel to commuters who are denied basic facilities. The major terminus in Mumbai Churchgate station has just one toilet which is shabbily designed and dirty and where males have to stand precariously while urinating. Only sadistic incompetent engineers could have built such a monstrosity which continues for years.

Bad maintenance and filthiness is only a part of the problem. It is very badly constructed and designed and claustrophobic. It is the world's most used toilet with 200 men using the 37 spots every five minutes. The Western railway general manager R.N. Verma was himself not happy with the upkeep of railway stations during an inspection in 2009. This gives an idea of the callousness of the administration.

The new suburban trains introduced in 2008 are of substandard quality and immediately started rusting, point out Akshay Marathe, an engineering student, and Abhishek

Risbud, a management student, in a study submitted to the officials. And commuters agree that the quality is poor with sharp edges which hurt, the paint is wearing out, Handles which passengers hold for dear life are giving way endangering safety. And there have been frequent breakdowns of the new trains in 2009 made by Siemens, admitted P.C. Sehgal, managing director of Mumbai Railway Vikas Corporation.

Frederick Clairmont, makes some pertinent points in his book 'Rise and fall of economic liberalism'. He says railroad building in India by the British destroyed more occupational opportunities than it opened up.

It is true that the iron horse contributed immensely towards the opening of the American and Canadian West. The same is true of France, Germany, the United Kingdom and Japan.

However, in some cases the railways have even retarded balanced growth as is demonstrated in India and China and certain parts of Africa and Latin America.

The railways were intended to ensure supply of cotton from India to the textile mills of Lancashire and to break the cotton monopoly of the American South. Lancashire needed cotton and the Indian internal market and that is how the railway construction began with subsidies given by the government to private entrepreneurs. British investors were guaranteed a five per cent interest but the guarantee killed effort for economy, promoted recklessness and involved the country in liabilities much beyond what the people could bear. This was the main reason for the swelling of the Indian public debt. Private railway companies were prodigal in their construction cost because of the guaranteed returns. Enormous funds were squandered, reported former finance minister W.N. Massey.

Railways were given priority over the cheaper and more productive navigable canals. Testifying before the 1878 railways committee, irrigation specialist Sir Arthur Cotton stated that railways were no protection against famine. 'I am afraid we must reckon that out of the 40 million affected by the famine in Madras, Mysore, Hyderabad and Bombay, four or five million people have perished.

Despite the wide rail network India did not go through an industrial revolution because of British policies. All the other countries with a well-developed rail network like the US, Russia, Germany and to a lesser extent Canada and Australia benefited from the industrial revolution. The conception, promotion and launching of the railways in India were all British, as the eminent scholar Daniel Thorner points out. Dwarkanath Tagore, grand father of poet Rabindranath Tagore and wealthy merchant, offered to raise substantial capital to run a railway line but he died early and subsequently the role of other Indian businesspersons was thought to be passive.

The British did not train Indians for higher posts in the railways and the policy of buying only British equipment for the railways left little scope for growth of Indian industry.

Besides the rail network in India was not as extensive as was made out. The US and Germany, for example, had a much higher network per 1000 sq miles of land area.

The steel of the railways pierced the older India to the heart and the blood ran out. Millions of artisans in villages and towns found they could not compete with British-manufactured goods. The first 75 years of their history the railways destroyed more jobs in India than they created because the private companies running the railways were based in London and buiding India's economy was not on their agenda. On the contrary the Japanese used their railways to augment their economy.

As for the benefit from railways the Indians could only be said to have got a salesman's sample, Thorner has observed. incurring huge expenditure on railways and consequent heavy debt.

Credit, however, must be given to the genius of British engineers who built the railways. No less important is the contribution of thousands of workers who perished or were injured while doing the most difficult work in inhospitable conditions. The casualties run into tens of thousands. Workers died of epidemics, exhaustion and many possibly fell prey to wild animals. If panthers, driven from their geenery, attack humans in Mumbai to this day, one can imagine how vulnerable must have been the workers in the wilderness in those days. When we enjoy the thrill of railway journey we should not forget the humble men.

By the way, a car journey can never rival the train in thrill. The very arrival, departure and passing of a train is a treat to watch. As for the steam engine there is nothing like it. It is a pity the Indian railways have sold as scrap several steam engines and stopped running these though they have tremendous glamour. Instead, for very rich foreign tourists the railways run special luxury tours which obviously are running into heavy losses for the railways while denying basic needs of ordinary commuters.

It is fashionable to jeer at socialist concerns but the fact is that the early private railway companies treated the poorest passengers like savages, observes Bill Aitken in his book Exploring Indian Railways.

Bundled into cattle trucks, the door was locked on them. One cannot ignore the complaints made by Gandhiji and Nehru about the callous disregard the railways had for cramped and sweating legions battling to find a foothold on a rake drawn up for the privileged. As Vanderbilt, the proprietor of the New York Central Railway, in the early days of the railway said 'the public be damned.'

It was because of imperial arrogance and aloofness, the British built the railway terminals in Delhi as well as Howrah away from areas of power. The Britishers obviously did not want the natives to land by train too close to their seats of power.

The Mumbai suburban railway network is the biggest metropolitan rail system in the world carrying millions of passengers daily. Yet, year after year passengers are shabbily treated, humiliated. In the West metropolitan rail network is growing as there is increasing realization that it is economical and environment-friendly. It is heavily subsidized despite comparatively low response of commuters. Yet, in India despite high ridership, basic amenities are denied to people, like benches , toilets, overhead bridges. When such huge number of people travel, the scale of economy changes and obviously the cost of the railways goes down. Clearly, more questions need to be raised about the railway administration's claims that it makes losses on the passenger sector.

The suburban train motormen or drivers are overworked, have inadequate rest room facilities and they face the wrath of commuters if the system develops snags. When they threatened to go on a flash strike in 2007, the divisional manager of Central railway J.N. Lal reacted unsympathetically saying 'an ovestressed employee can leave the job.' (Mumbai Mirror 3-10-07).

A number of people fall to death from trains due to overcrowding though the railways would rather blame passengers, attributing the deaths to crossing of tracks.

What the railways cannot deny is that there are virtually no facilities for even first aid treatment, leave alone specialized medical care at railway stations despite rising deaths. This has become clear in hearings in the Mumbai high court.

Dr Sarosh Mehta, an orthopedic surgeon, is fighting a public interest litigation in the court to make the railways accountable for more than 3000 deaths on the tracks each year and take remedial measures. The railway authorities believe their job is only to run trains, not provide other amenities.

Worse, the railways refused parking facilities for an ambulance, officials used it for buying vegetables and ultimately forced an organization to withdraw its service from Mumbai. The ambulance Red Swastik, founded by senior IPS official T.S.

Bhal, had attended to over 8000 accident victims and rushed over 5,000 to hospitals between 2003 and 2007. The service was operated by Sameer Jhaveri, himself a railway accident victim who had lost both his legs in 1989.

Dr Mehta has suggested that there should be a doctor at every station and a paramedic in every train to help accident victims. A stretcher and primary equipment in the driver's cabin, a medically-equipped room and ambulance at each station are among his other demands. The gap between the train and the platform should conform to international standards and be not more than three inches, Dr Mehta says.

Jamshed Cama, a lawyer, produced before the court a video film as evidence which documents a person dying in a railway accident after laying on the track unattended as 15 trains pass by. The railways have thousands of sq km of space for commercial development near stations but not a few sq ft for parking of ambulances.

The Borivli-Virar stretch of 26 km on the outskirts of Mumbai is increasingly becoming more crowded as Mumbai is getting saturated and many people are settling in these periphery areas. These areas need not only more trains but also better walkways. But these elementary facilities are not provided while the government is doing everything to help builders to create a construction boom in this area.

It is a life and death struggle for commuters every day. When passengers lose their patience and go to the office of the station master's office to make a complaint, the police are called to 'take care' of the protesting public. The authorities may not be fascist, but they are certainly uncaring.

Another hazard commuters face is of stone throwing from the area near the railway tracks. There have been many cases of commuters losing their eye. Worse, the actor couple Dr Shreeam Lagoo and Deepa lost their teen-age son Tanvir when he was hit in the head by a stone a few years ago on the outskirts of Mumbai.

In desperation many people travel on roof of suburban trains endangering their lives and are often arrested by the railway police. But obviously there is an undeniable thrill in traveling on top of a train. This is exploited in the film Dil Se, film star Shahrukh Khan, Malaika Arora and a host of other dancers dance wildly on the roof of a running mountain railway singing the popular song Chhaiya Chhaiyya. Choreographer Farah Khan is quite proud of the dance and says it was actually done on top of a train.

A similar dance was performed in real life years later in a running train watched by railway minister behaving like a modern Maharaja. A troupe performed the dance not on top of a train, but on the flat surface of an open freight wagon attached to the Bikramganj-Sasaram train. Laloo addressed crowds at intermediate stations on the 41 km stretch lasting three hours. (TOI 12-12-06).

This was just a week after a major railway accident in Laloo's home state of Bihar when a bridge collapsed and crushed to death 35 passengers of the Howrah-Jamalpur express at Bhagalpur railway station in December, 2006.

Exactly 50 years earlier Lal Bahadur Shastri had resigned as railway minister in 1956 after a bridge collapse. The decision greatly enhanced the image of Mr Shastri, a clean politician, who later became Prime Minister.

The Bhagalpur bridge crash ceased to make news a day later because the deaths of ordinary people do not matter. Imagine if an airplane had been hit and some passengers had been killed. The media would have been hysterical for days.

The railways shirk all responsibility for people being killed on tracks. But the fact is most people have no option but to cross the tracks because proper bridges are missing.

Laloo Prasad's mania for speed, like the talk of reaching Pune from Mumbai in one hour, instead of the decades old time of 3.5 hours makes little sense because for ordinary passengers this brings little relief. On most routes trains are always late and overcrowded.

If one can escape injury on the train, one cannot escape humiliation of one kind or another. It is humiliating to wait in long queues to purchase railway tickets and miss a couple of trains. Nowhere are probably paying customers treated so shabbily. If one buys coupons to avoid standing in a queue for tickets, it is quite frustrating to insert them into the validating machine which do not function. One has then to go to the counter where a railway employee manually stamps the coupons. Trains are so overcrowded that one cannot get a seat even in first class at the starting point even at night, leave alone the peak hours.

Women in Karachi, Pakistan, have reacted with delight to the introduction of two buses exclusively for ladies. These buses give freedom from unwanted attention. Why did not anyone think of this before, exclaims feisty Mehreen Rehman as she sat in one of the buses. (Zofeen T Ebrahim in Business Line 26-11-04).

I do not have to bother about covering my head with dupatta, sitting like a statue and looking down, said the student of Rana Liaqat Ali Khan college.

The only snag with the exclusive buses is that the ticket is high, Rs 20 which is beyond the reach of poor women.

In Japan the main complaint of women commuters in trains is of groping by men. There are few reserved coaches for women and the incidence of groping is increasing. Many stations carry posters with the warning that molestation is a criminal offence. Women also complain of smell of alcohol and cigarettes on men.

Though by Indian standards Japanese trains are very comfortable and far from crowded, traveling apparently causes a lot of anxiety among the Japanese people. There is the same struggle to grab a seat in a local train as in Mumbai.

Railway stations even in Mumbai are badly constructed and maintained...the new Bandra terminus is a glass structure which is all right for cold, European countries, not for hot climate as in India. Moreover, a building built in glass cannot be comfortable without air-conditioning. Besides, ventilation is extremely poor in the Bandra Terminus as everything is closed and sealed and little air is allowed inside. The terminus at Kurla, catering mainly to less privileged passengers going to the relatively backward states like Bihar and Uttar Pradesh looks more worn down and with a very difficult, long, winding access which can be very confusing.

The worst callousness of the authorities pertains to failure to provide basic amenities like toilets, pedestrian bridges and benches at railway stations or to provide for their maintenance. Things are much worse for the handicapped and women. Even the entry and exit points at railway stations do not provide facilities for the handicapped. Even the able-bodied could trip and fall any time. It is much worse for the handicapped.

It is only in the last decade that special little compartments are reserved for the handicapped. And they are supposed to carry original copies of documents certifying them as handicapped. A college student Kaushik Morarji, 20, was fined for traveling in the special coach because he was found to be affected by polio to the extent of 30 per cent and not 40 per cent as stipulated. The railway defended the decision saying they were lenient and levied a fine of Rs 50, not Rs 500 in 2005, (Mumbai Mirror 15-11-05).

A study conducted by Shilpa Phadke, a college teacher, showed serious difficulties for women commuters. At Andheri suburban station the women's toilets were locked and after desperately running around it was found that the keys were not with the station master but with the shoe-shine boy who is far away. This running around has to be done in times of urgent need. The study was carried out for PUKAR (partners for urban knowledge and research).

This is not very much worse than days when long-distance trains did not have toilet facilities. People relieved themselves through the door or windows and died. In the morning trains had special halts to allow passengers time to go to the latrine, points out S.N. Sharma in his history of GIP Great Indian Peninsular railway.

Mumbai survives mainly because lakhs of people bear extreme hardship of suburban train travel. Occasionally, they lose their patience and stop trains. But the utterly callous railway administration, instead of addressing the problems, is now planning to subject commuters to surveillance.

The railway administration usually comes for praise from foreigners for running the world's biggest rail system quite efficiently. Only a part of the praise is deserved. It is all right to view the picture from the outside seeing how lakhs of people get in and out of trains day and night. It all looks so smooth. The fact is travelling is torturous and humiliating and lakhs of people put up with this year after year. It is true that the railways do a good job by and large. But there is also much callousness.

About 5,000 people are crammed in trains meant for 1800. This generates extreme discomfort and a high level of carbon di oxide. It was only in 2006 that the railway proposed to provide blowers to pump in fresh air and blow away the suffocating, polluting air.

Railway engineers and other high officers do not experience any of the discomfort because they never travel by suburban trains.There is often a demand that they should be made to do that so as to get some idea of the insulting conditions in which people travel.

Many commuters fall off trains due to overcrowding and die but the railways refuse to pay compensation to the victims. Many of these deaths are treated as accidents and wrongly attributed to the commuter's crossing of tracks. So the victim is accused of illegality in a travesty of justice.

Standing at the entrance in the overcrowded train to get a breath of fresh air actually constitutes an offence and people who fall down from overcrowded trains are often denied compensation. This drew a sharp rebuke from Justice A.B. Chaudhari in the Mumbai high court in 2009. The railways actually fined a student Rs 500 for traveling int the door of a suburban train (Loksatta. 2-2-05). Worse, a person killed in a railway accident is denied compensation if a train ticket is not found on his or her person.

As someone observed 'there is more condensed mass on the suburban train than the black hole.

Instead of providing basic amenities to the masses the railways are increasingly trying to provide more and more luxury to the rich and in the process incurring huge losses. The Palace on Wheels ultra-luxury train connecting the main tourist circuit for foreigners, Delhi, Agra and Rajasthan has run into heavy losses and so has the Deccan Odyssey launched by the Maharashtra government to attract tourists. The train mainly lies unused in the yard.

Now a luxury train Deccan Splendour covering the four southern States is being launched at a cost of Rs 36 crores with contributions from the states and the market. The railways are providing a free train and engine.

Railway minister Laloo Prasad Yadav got a feel of the hazards of train travel when he travelled like an ordinary passenger and not in the special saloon that he is used to. The stench in the toilet was so unbearable, I could not eat dinner, he said. He travelled from Kishanganj to Patna by the Capital express like any other passenger as his trip was originally not scheduled by train. It is not that he wanted to see or experience how ordinary people travelled.

Surely, our politicians should know that in Europe bigwigs regularly travel by cycle or underground trains. Our ministers can also easily pool cars or they can do even better travel by bus for cabinet meetings for example. After all, most of them live in the luxury of Malabar hill. They could easily take a bus to Mantralaya.

Why can't they do these things at least for a change ? I would feel suffocated if day after day I was taken exclusively in a car.

While the motor car has disrupted the city fabric, architecture and landscape, the railways have created some of the best pieces of architecture. The underground railway stations in Moscow have come in for universal praise. It cannot be denied that these are a shining achievement of Communist rule. The subway is considered the most beautiful subway system in the world. Each station is built with marble and other gorgeous stones. Each station is a palace for every day transit riders.

The Moscow Underground is far superior to the New York rail network. In fact, there can be no comparison, says Vladmir Paperny, a scholar who has lived in both the cities. The Moscow railways is a fairy tale underground space ornamented with mosaic, fresco, bas reliefs, attractive ceiling, all of which give the illusion of heaven and heavenly light. One can understand Indian suburban rail network could not be as good but why does it have to be so terrible, so lacking in even basic amenities like drinking water and toilets and upkeep of trains ? The Moscow Underground is cool in summer and warm in winter. It is so beautiful it seems marble benches grow out of the floors or walls and the signs and notices are in bronze frames as if they are pictorial masterpieces.

The Moscow Underground, originally named the Lenin Metro, with over 150 stations caters to most of the city and the trains take you through a parade of marbled, spacious, spotless stations which contrast totally with the grubby streets above ground.

For tourists it is a major sight seeing draw. Besides, it has an amazing array of art work on view. Mayakovskaya station in the city centre features mosaics, marble, brass chandeliers and 36 cupolas. The metro was perhaps the central element in Stalin's monumentalism that changed the face of Moscow for ever. The metro was to be a palace shining with the light of advancing victorious socialism and every screw was to be a screw of socialism.

The Tokyo subway system is truly efficient. I found that trains not only arrive right on time, they stop right on a platform mark so that passengers line up knowing exactly where the train doors will open. Train driving is a prestigious job

The Chicago train system offers great views of all the city's lively neighbourhoods. In Washington D.C. an old eleven km railway line has been revitalized.

Shamefully, a lot of rail network has been destroyed, neglected. But some of the best surviving landmarks belong to the railways. New Yorkers can still thrill on arrival and departure at the Grand Central terminal which is saved from burial by a Supreme court ruling and efforts of Jacqueline Kennedy. But another beautiful station the Pennsylvania was demolished to make way for Madison Square Gardens. It was an act of extreme cultural negation to demolish one of the finest works of architecture in the city, observes Anthony Tung, a noted conservationist. We used to stride into the city like emperors, recalled Daniel Patrick Moynihan. The railways had proposed to construct a 55-storey building above the Grand Central terminal.

By 1870 America had 50,000 miles of railway network which climbed to 240,000 miles by 1910. There were some parallel, duplicate routes run by competing private companies. Now there are only 572 railway stations for a population of some 300 million as compared to 59,000 stations in 1939. The Pennsylvania station in New York was pulled down in the 1960s. It remains one of the greatest crimes in American architecture history to have demolished a monumental gem and replaced it with a dehumanized space, observed eminent architecture critic Nicolai Ouroussoff.

Barrack Obama did well to revive a 50 year old tradition to travel by train from Philadelphia to Washington for his inauguration as president in 2009. Hundreds of thousands of people greeted him on the 135 mile route in freezing weather. The last US president to travel by train for his inauguration was Eisenhower. The train left an hour late as he was still writing his inaugural address. Obama traveled in a compartment made in 1939 when getting a job as a railroad porter was the highest aspiration for a black man in America and it was impossible to travel together with whites until the 1950s.

The Americans, in their craze for cars and air travel, are trailing in fast train travel. It is the longest train delay in history, the New York Times reported (19-2-09). We are 40 years behind high speed rail and missed the opportunity to lure drivers off choked roads and fliers away from delays at airports.

Engineers of Indian origin have played a big role in the running of New York's Metropolitan Transport Authority which runs the Metro railway system. MTA is the single largest employer of Indians in the US and the largest provider of mass transit in the West. Mysore Nagaraja, the head of a major company Capital Construction, is responsible for the restoration of the spectacular Grand Central station. (Chidananda Rajghatta. TOI 13-4-08).

13

Public Road Transport

Travel by public road transport buses is better than by private transport in many parts of India despite the government's negligence of this vital sector. State transport buses carry 65 million passengers daily. Yet, they do not have a strong lobby. They obviously suffer from numerous problems and deserve a better deal from the government. But look at the web site of the Association of State Road Transport Undertakings (ASRTU), an apex body of these corporations, and one does not get the foggiest idea. All that one gets are some dry statistics.

Vikram Gokhale, talented Marathi screen and stage actor, enthusiastically took up his job as ambassador of the Maharashtra State Road Transport Corporation but gave up soon in July, 2004, saying politicians did not want to make the undertaking profitable. They instead backed private transporters to raise funds for electioneering and contributed to the losses of the ST corporation. The undertaking can make profit if it is allowed to.

A former state transport minister Govindrao Adik, himself charged the government in 2005 with subverting the public sector body by promoting private vehicles. Similar is the story in several states.

With a little more imagination most states in the country could have had an excellent public transport system When land was easily available it could have been acquired for bus depots. But this was not done and now ST undertakings are desperately short of space.

Several of our burgeoning cities require scores of ST bus depots each but since these are not provided, passengers have to traverse long distances to reach far-off depots. No land use planning at all. There are constant media reports about new locations for a third airport for Mumbai. But no one bothers about the proposed inter state bus terminal for Mumbai which is pending for the past several years.

It would be sad if the public transport undertakings are subverted by corrupt politicians and bureaucrats because ST buses have become part and parcel of every day life for many people. The buses have given people a lot of mobility. An alternative to public transport means you have to travel in extremely crowded and hazardous conditions in jeeps which carry as many as 20 people or more, some hanging out precariously. This is a regular sight in rural areas.

ST buses have been literally the lifeline for many people. They have also provided a useful lunch carrying service between villages and towns benefiting the like of union agriculture minister Sharad Pawar and Mumbai's former police commissioner Dhananjay Jadhav in their school days.

Even popular tourist spots or wildlife sanctuaries are not easily accessible by public transport. The Ranathambhore tiger sanctuary is about 10 km from Sawai Madhopur railway station. But there are no buses and one has to depend on crowded jeeps.

In Maharashtra prior to the starting of the ST corporation in 1948 models of Ford, Chevorlet and Dodge were used for public transport. There was a craze among some people to enter the transport business, many sold their jewellery and other belongings to buy cars.

The Karnataka state transport corporation has done much better than other state undertakings. Gone are the days when it was known for its losses and inefficiency. It has been consistently making profits since the last five years.

It is setting up travel shops all over the state where buses will offer various facilities including reservation for travel from anywhere to anywhere. Bangalore city alone will have 109 of these travel shops.

In Bangalore some buses are run at reduced fares for poor people. The service named Atal Sarige after former Prime Minister Atal Behari Vajpayee was inaugurated by chief minister Yeddyurappa in 2009.

In Maharashtra as state bus services are being curtailed the plight of people waiting endlessly for a bus to arrive is best reflected in Achyut Vaze's Marathi play Chal Re Bhoplya Tunuk Tunuk. In the play one character shouts Bus Ali, Bus Ali (the bus has come, bus has come) and the other asks 'Kuthey Bus' (Where is the bus ?). The play is written in the style of the Theatre of the Absurd in the 1970s and it is a metaphor on the human condition also, apart from the actual frustration one goes through while waiting for a bus.

It is much like Samuel Beckett's famous Absurdist play Waiting for Godot in which two characters similarly wait in vain for Godot.

Mumbai has the best metropolitan bus service in the country. BEST in Mumbai has many shortcomings but it is far superior to the bus service in Kolkata and Delhi not to speak of several other cities which have no bus service of any kind. Yet, even the Mumbai buses are not very commuter-friendly, it takes a huge effort to climb the bus or get down as the step is too high from the ground.

The so-called luxury King Long Chinese buses introduced in 2008 proved to be a disaster in Mumbai. One caught fire and the door of another did not open trapping 75 passengers who had to get out through the driver's cabin.

In Pune the city buses are run-down but several bus stands are ideal, they provide excellent seating spaces and shade, something Mumbai should emulate. In Mumbai very often one is exposed to severe heat or rain as there are no bus shelters even in upper class areas and the new stainless steel, shiny ones are very badly designed, one cannot properly stand or sit down on or rest. Another hazard in Mumbai is the diesel generator at several stops meant to illuminate advertisement hoardings causing severe noise, unbearable odour and heat. Ironically a BEST stand outside Churchgate railway station illuminates an advertisement for Jet Airways. What a mockery of public transport by air transport.

The new bus shelters in Mumbai are an insult to citizens. They are so disgraceful, torturous, cribbed, cabined, confined. The irony is that they are constructed as part of making Mumbai a world class city. They are also expensive, ungainly, they obstruct a lot of road and footpath space. They only serve to rake in revenue through sponsorships to BEST. It is a torture to perch even for a while and one is pushed forward by two hideous steel bars which have no business to be there. The bus shelters on highways in the city, provided by the Metropolitan authority are more comfortable and more spacious. The shelters are designed in Paris, spare parts manufactured in Indonesia and Brazil and assembled in China, according to Milind Mhaiskar, joint metro commissioner.

Chennai is to have 500 so-called world class bus shelters at Rs 65 crore with facilities like coin vending machines, fans, dustbins, mirror, surveillance cameras to track pick pockets and eve teasers, according to transport minister K.N. Nehru. In fact, what citizens urgently need are minimum basic facilities, not gadgets.

Instead of providing basic facilities to commuters, BEST is bombarding them with commercial advertisements and vulgar Hindi film songs on screens in buses even as commuters hold on to dear life, hanging on to straps in overcrowded conditions.

For the disabled it is much worse. Following a public interest litigation the Mumbai high court asked BEST in March 2004 to introduce in four months 30 buses which could be easily used by the physically challenged. It has failed to meet the deadline several months later. A helpless lawyer Jamshed Mistry said there is no effective mechanism to monitor the implementation of PILs.

The BEST authorities have come up with a perverse scheme of leasing the space for shopping malls and such other fancy projects and car parking. The parking charge is a mere Rs 50 for a whole day. Actually, the BEST should not only hold on to its own space, it should be acquiring more land in the interest of promoting public transport and public interest. But for corrupt politicians and officers public interest is not on top of the agenda.

Compared to Delhi and Kolkata, bus transport in Mumbai is far better. BEST still has a monopoly of bus transport in Mumbai, unlike in the other two Metros. Because of greater realization that it should attract more passengers to remain in business, BEST is now a little more friendlier to passengers. Formerly, if one got in surreptitiously into a bus midway, not at the regular stop, the conductor was usually unpleasant and would make you get down. Not so now. Some buses now actually carry a board, you can get in anywhere you want. The bus will stop for you.

BEST's has lost some passengers and to allegedly illegal competition from auto-rickshaws. The BEST's air-conditioned service barely covers the cost of diesel as these have failed to divert people from their cars to buses.

Pune's buses are quite badly maintained and one should not be surprised to find a bus stranded on the road after the engine has caught fire. With all their faults, buses still are a far better option than taxies or auto-rickshaws. One bus has passenger capacity equal to 30 two-wheelers, 20 cars and 30 auto-rickshaws.

In the posh Seven Bungalows area in Mumbai, nearly 5,000 sq metres of bus depot space has been already leased to a developer for Rs 16 crore. The state government has allowed the builder to use as much as 60 per cent of the area against the normal 15 per cent. With such kind of developments where do citizens go? The state government, which has powers to check irregularities of civic and panchayat bodies, is itself promoting irregularities and congestion.

Nearly 10 years ago the Walkeshwar bus depot was partly leased out to a private developer leaving an awkward –shaped plot for the bus depot. Eventually the undertaking has now built a 15-storey building to house its officers on the remaining plot of land.

This leaves public transport shamefully neglected around Raj Bhavan and ministerial bungalows on Malabar Hill. No bus depot has been provided and narrow road space is used for two bus terminuses on Malabar Hill, one near Kamala Nehru Park and the other near Raj Bhavan. Buses have a hard time taking a U turn at the terminus on the narrow road. Most of the area is without footpaths which underlines the callousness towards the poor in this elite area.

Public interest is not high on the agenda of the government. The authorities are telling the BEST.

(Bombay electric supply and transport) undertaking to cut down its services on the Andheri-Ghatkopar route so that it does not compete with the proposed Metro rail link on this section.

There is more to it than meets the eye. Given the experience of the Delhi Metro it is clear that it is not viable because the number of commuters is far below capacity. The Metro is beyond the capacity of the poor. Actually, the very poor are prevented from entering railway stations in the first place. The real idea is to make the Metro accessible only to the better off sections whose number is swelling.

The BEST is the only means of road transport the poor can really afford. Now, the authorities want to attack it. That is the sad, if not the sinister, part.

The Metro is far too costly a form of transport. But the government is supporting it because it will help the car lobby. That will divert some bus traffic from road to rail. That means there will be more space for cars on roads and that is what the automobile lobby wants. The bus is the most efficient mode of road transport in terms of carrying capacity, use of road space, fuel consumption and pollution control. It should get priority over the Metro. But bus transport is gradually being subverted so that more space is created for the benefit of the car lobby.

Despite all the advantage of public transport, it is not exactly friendly to school, college girls and women. They face a lot of sexual harassment, men determinedly sitting and standing close to them. A study conducted by the Rambhau Mhalgi Pratishthan in Pune cites numerous cases of angry responses from girls. For many of them using a bus can be an unpleasant experience. Nearly three lakh women travel daily by Pune muinicipal transport and a survey showed that 86 per cent women complained of harassment from men, said activist-journalist Gauri Kanetkar.

In Maharashtra there are good bus depots right upto the village level. They are not maintained well but they are at least there. In many other parts of the country buses operate from small congested spaces and open grounds even in big towns. Several big towns do not have any kind of city bus service which is appallingly unjust to the poor.

I travelled by bus between Bhubaneshwar and Cuttack in 2005. I nor any other passenger was issued a ticket though the conductor collected the fare. This sort of privatization can only be considered criminal. Orissa chief minister Naveen Patnaik has dismantled most of the public transport and replaced it with inefficient private bus transport.

In the state known for hunger deaths I found signs of poverty even in the local bus in the state capital Bhubaneshwar. During on trip at least three people begged the conductor to reduce the fare, they simply could not afford to pay.

In Patna the magnificent Hardinge Park ground has been reduced to a station for haphazardly parked buses, milling passengers and yelling bus employees, points out Arvind N Das in his perceptive book The Republic of Bihar.

The construction of a bridge across the Ganga river in Patna triggered a sort of transport revolution in Bihar as it brought Patna much closer to North Bihar. There was a sudden proliferation of buses incuding luxury, deuxe and VDO coaches across the Ganga. The streets of Patna, Muzaffapur, Chhapra, Motihari, Darbhanga and others towns, which were built to cater to pedestrians at best horse-carts at worst, were choked with gaudy motorized monsters that multiplied daily.

Better off passengers get a seat inside the bus while the poor are pushed onto the roof. The bus owner and his employees are the bosses.

Public transport should be much better in the overpopulated, ailing, relatively backward state in central and northern India but it is the worst there. A little imagination and things can be turned round, as the district collector of Indore, the commercial capital of Madhya Pradesh showed in 2006. Unbelievably there were no bus shelters in this most advanced city in the state. Vivek Agarwal built several of them and introduced 53 low-floor, passenger-friendly, modern Tata buses, a great hit with commuters. The state capital Bhopal, I found, does not have a decent bus depot with any passenger amenities and buses operate from a crowded ground.

The state generally discriminates against public transport of all kinds all the time. In Mumbai More taxies are now seen cruising empty on the streets than ever before because they have nowhere to park. Though the number of taxies has gone up the parking spaces have been reduced. No new parking spaces have been created in the last six years, said A.L. Quadros, the moustachiod general secretary of the Bombay Taximen's Union. At the same time parking for private motor cars has increased sharply. (Mumbai Newsline, Indian Express (1-1-06). Regional transport authority commissioner G.T. Bandri said local residents usually object to taxi stands because they want to park their own cars in such spaces.

He said his office has stopped issuing new licences for taxies. So there curbs are being placed in vehicles for the general public while private cars are merrily allowed to proliferate.

Corporates have now entered the taxi trade and are maligning old taxis owned by ordinary people who cannot afford to buy new ones.

Taxies and auto-rickshaws face discrimination, inconvenience everywhere. For 18,000 auto rickshaws there is only one CNG gas station in Mira-Bhayandar on the outskirts of Mumbai involving a wait in a queue for over five hours.

It is interesting that Bhairavi Desai, a girl of Indian origin, is a major leader of taxi drivers of different nationalities, speaking numerous languages, in New York In 1998 the New York taxi drivers successfully went on a strike in support of their demands foiling the attempts of New York's Mayor Rudy Giuliani known for his anti-democratic character. She is the executive director of the New York Taxi Workers Alliance.

It is very courageous of her to do the work because taxi driving is a highly dangerous profession in America. A taxi driver is sixty times more likely to be killed while at work than an industrial worker, according to the International Labour Organisation. The drivers work in horrendous conditions as depicted in Clifford Odets's famous play Waiting for Lefty which provided a rallying cry for the labour movement in America in the thirties.

Bhairavi, who dresses in a Salwar Kameez, is the daughter of working class parents who migrated from Gujarat to the US in 1980. She is a graduate of Rutgers university and she formed the union as she found the working conditions of taxi drivers to be quite miserable with poor pay and long working hours. Most of them are immigrants from Asia, Africa and the Caribbeans. I saw working dignity, honesty, hunger and poverty while working among the drivers, she said. She looks like the girl next door but is a tough negotiator for the taxi drivers' demands. (Kalpana Sharma. The Hindu 20-3-02).

Biju Mathew, another leader of Indian origin of New York drivers, has authored a book Taxi ! Cabs and capitalism in New York city. The yellow cab is a striking metaphor of New York city but the drivers face many problems including harassment and paying heavy fines to the police for minor violations. They are treated like second class citizens.

South Asians make up a large number of taxi drivers in North America. Kinship between Punjabi speaking cabbies from India and Pakistan is greater than between Pakistani and Bangla Deshi cabbies despite their common religion. It is fun to hear the Punjabi drivers greeting each other in coarse Punjabi.

Some of them have done very well. Mohinder Singh, who came from Delhi in 1974, is a favourite with Senators. In contrast cabbies in India are reduced to a much lower social status. (Chidanand Rajghatta TOI 1-10-06).

The sighting of remnants of tram rails during road digging in Mumbai recently got the kind of attention in the media normally reserved for an ancient site. The tram service was unfortunately discontinued in the sixties. Melbourne is, apart from Kolkata, the only major city in the English-speaking world to have retained its network of trams.

Pop singer Elton John went shopping in Melbourne some years ago for souvenirs. He spotted one of the city's bright green trams trundling along the tracks and fancied one. He paid a large sum for one, took it home to England to set up in his garden as a teahouse.

Melbourne's public transport system also impressed a high-level team from Delhi during a visit for the Commonwealth Games in 2006 to prepare for the games in Delhi in 2010.

Mr M.S. Upadhyaya, additional commissioner of police for traffic in Delhi, said 'we practically saw no private vehicles in Melbourne. Everybody was using public transport which solves most of the problem.' (Indian Express 2-4-06).

The public transport scene in Pakistan is as bad as in India. Women complain of escalating fares, inadequate seating, rude conductors, corrupt traffic police, overcrowding, no consideration for children and the elderly who are made to get off and on while the bus is in motion. The menace of pressure horns, the interior of the bus with scores of mirrors, pan spittle, cigarette smoke, exposed nails and metal edges than often cause injury and tear clothes, men coming into women's compartment etc. That is the picture you have from Transport published by Urban Resource Centre, edited by Aquila Ismail and reviewed by Zofeen Ebrahim.

When a girl Bushra Zaidi was killed under the wheels of a bus in 1985 there were strong public protests and the troops had to be called. Today such accidents are routine.

Paris, headed by socialist Mayor Bertrand Delano, introduced trams on the boulevards in 2006, widened footpaths and added bus lanes slashing space for motor cars.

14

Gandhi and Railways

Nothing shows Mahatma Gandhi's passion for democracy and equality than his insistence on travelling by third class in the most harrowing conditions and his consistent championing of the cause of the third class traveller. This is well brought out in the book Mahatma Gandhi and the railways compiled by Y.P. Anand, former railway board chairman, with a foreword by noted history writer of modern India B.R. Nanda.

Gandhiji found that third class passengers were treated like sheep. Even in South Africa conditions were better with cushioned seats and sleeping accommodation. First class fare in India was five times more than third class. But third class passengers did not get one fifth or even one tenth of the comforts of first class passengers.

The turning point in Mahatma Gandhi's life came when he was thrown out of the train in South Africa in 1893 because a white passenger would not tolerate a coloured man traveling with him. This strengthened his resolve to fight racism and other forms of injustice. That incident was indeed a turning point in the life of the Mahatma.

In 2006 Indian Prime Minister Manmohan Singh made the same journey in South Africa traveling by a 124-year-old train with wooden compartments and pulled by a steam engine.

Gandhiji made a scathing attack on the inequities in the railways in India. He said railways came to India not for its development and progress but to help the foreign rulers to tighten the noose around the necks of Indians at an exorbitant cost to India and to help enrich the British at the cost of poor Indians. He was greatly influenced in this respect by the work done by Romesh Chandra Dutt and Dadabhai Naoroji in exposing how imperial Britain plundered India.

Till Gandhi had left for South Africa in 1893 his contact with railways in India was minimal, mainly for traveling between Rajkot and Mumbai. His real romance with the Indian railways started in 1915 and for the next 33 years till his death trains were his primary mode of transport. In this period he went out of India only once in 1931 to attend the Round Table conference.

In 1915 he went around India by train to understand the reality of the country on the advice of his political guru Gopal Krishna Gokhale. Gandhi writes that Gokhale himself gave him a tiffin box filled with laddus and puris for eating during travel.

After discovering the harrowing conditions of third class travel, Gandhi wrote that there is only one remedy for this awful state of affairs. Educated men must make a point of traveling third class and reforming the habits of the people as also of never letting the railway authorities in peace.

What shocked Gandhi was that people could not even buy third class tickets without being insulted and without having to pay bribes. Tickets were issued only a short time before the departure of trains causing a scramble and disappointment to many.

It was only in later life that the railways provided him special reserved compartments or travel.

Gandhi said that the railway management was criminally guilty in neglecting third class passengers. They are actually the most paying customers of the railways while first class passengers are practically a loss to the railways, he said while addressing a public meeting in Virudunagar in Tamil Nadu in 1927. Later he wrote that railway trains and steamers could become the best vehicles for practical education of millions of travellers in spotless cleanliness, hygiene, sanitation and camaraderie if proper facilities were provided.

He gently rebuked a station master at Patna station when he asked Gandhiji for permission to blow the whistle. He said the station master should treat all passengers equally and no special privilege should be shown to politicians and other interests. Gandhi also spoke out against ticketless travel and dirty habits of passengers.

He devoted a chapter in his autobiography highlighting the woes of third class passengers He describes how he travelled from Sahranpur to Hardwar in a roofless goods wagon grilled by the sun above and roasted from below by iron plates. On another occasion, traveling third from Lahore to Calcutta, the Mahatma had to pay a porter twelve annas to thrust him through the window of a compartment.

In contrast, ministers and railway bureaucrats in independent India travel in absolute luxury Imagine a whole coach compartmentalized into a bedroom, a living room, a dining area and a kitchen. Space for attendants including a cook and a bath. Expensive curtains and plush upholstery, teakwood chairs and fancy cutlery as Bhavna Vij Aurora wrote in the Indian Express some time ago.

The Indian railways spend aobut Rs 70 lakh on each saloon car about 10 to 15 are manufactured each year depending on the demand. Questions have been raised in Parliament and the comptroller and auditor general has objected to the expenditure on the continued manufacture of these coaches but railway officials vehemently deny the luxury angle. They call them inspection carriages to tone down the luxury part of it.

Most railway ministers have liberally used the saloons. It was only the maveric Mamata Banerjee who travelled overnight to a bomb blast site in Jammu in a sleeper coach with the security personnel while the general manager of Northern railway travelled in his own saloon attached to the same train.

When she proposed that officials emulate her the resistance she met was amazing. Officials wrote her long notes explaining how important saloons were to railway functioning and safety.

The British had made rules regarding the number of cattle which could be put into a carriage. No such limit existed for human passengers which means humans were treated worse than animals, points out G.D. Patwardhan, a veteran researcher in railway history.

Art Buchwald took up similar theme in a humour piece he wrote some years ago. The American system is notorious for neglecting the passenger traffic on the railways. He suggested that passengers be treated as freight so that they would receive better treatment from the railways. They could be carried in containers, insulated and air-conditioned. The big advantage, he wrote, is that once passengers are treated as freight they would improve the service. Also a way could be found to freeze people in refrigerator cars and then thaw them when they reached their destinations.

Buchwald has another interesting piece on motorists in France. 'It is safe to say that if a Frenchman has his choice between a car and a woman, he will in almost all cases take the car. For one thing a Frenchman has only one car, but he usually has access to many women. It is very unsafe to cross the street in France because motorists do not care for pedestrians. That explains why there are so many churches in Paris. Many go to a church to pray so that they can cross the road without being hurt or killed.

The railways are much worse off after privatization so much so that the prominent left-wing British playwright David Hare has made a devastating critique of it in his play The Permanent Way produced by National Theatre, London, in 2003. It is a docudrama which is based on real life characters and experiences.

We are presented with a mosaic of individual testimonies from 25 characters, both those responsible for running the privatized network and those at the sharp end of its failure.

The Socialist Review journal observed that the play has become a metaphor for what Britain has become. It has become a run-down society in which chronic under-investment in social infrastructure over decades has resulted in a country where nothing works properly. In sum the play looks at rail privatization as a symbol of the cultural, moral and political degeneration of British politics in general and of New Labour in particular.

15

Non-motorised Vehicles

In Bogota, Colombia, in Latin America, there was a severe pollution problem and traffic was so aggressive that nobody walked in the street. In 1986 Mayor Ramirez Ocampo started the Sunday cycle ways consisting of 80 km of avenues closed to motor traffic on Sundays for half a day. The response was enthusiastic and every Sunday more than half a million people went out on bicycles, rollers skates, skateboards and celebrated a public festival of joy and fun. Interestingly, this also made cycling attractive to the upper middle class and the lawyers and managers changed their black suits for T-shirts. Even the vainest yuppie would pose in the latest fashions alaong side the labourer from the slum on his bicycle. Suddenly people realized life could become enjoyable.

In India the upper class would use the cycle for exercise and physical fitness not for making a trip on the road. Hero has sold thousands of static exercise bicycles to hotel chains, health clubs and newly health conscious affluent urbanites from Mumbai or Kolkata, yet none of these customers would like to be seen riding a bicycle on the streets.

On the other hand in Japan, one of the most prosperous countries of the world, has introduced a very supportive bicycle policy. The 1981 Bicycle Law was specially aimed at improving safety and promoting proper parking. Most major cities have extensive bike and ride parking facilities and bicycle lanes are common in central business districts. The Japan Bicycle Promotion Institute is promoting the bicycle as a good and healthy form of transportation.

Delft is one of the most bicycle-friendly towns in Netherlands. Its train station has a parking area for 5000 bicycles.

In many developing countries, prices for bicycles are often too high though the price can be definitely brought down. In Bangladesh a bicycle costs twice as much as in West Bengal and in some African or Latin American countries bicycles are not available for less than 100 dollars which is very costly indeed.

Shanghai in China, which is being seen by the Indian elite as the role model for Mumbai, has completely reversed its pro-people transport policy. In 1986 it was essentially a city of walkers and cyclists.

Three-wheeler scooter rickshaws (TSRs) need to be given priority over private vehicles as this considerably saves fuel and space on the road and parking space, say two senior transport experts Dinesh Mohan, professor of transportation at Indian Institute of Technology in New Delhi and Mr Dunu Roy, environmentalist of Hazards Centre.

The TSRs should run on LPG or CNG gas or four-stroke petrol engines equipped with catalytic converters. Ample availability of these vehicles and taxies encourages non-ownership of private vehicles as traveling becomes much easier. Greater use of TSRs reduces need for parking places. A private car needs a minimum of two parking places, one at home and another at the destination whereas a TSR just needs one parking place in the city. It it makes ten trips in a day, it reduces the need for nine parking places.

A TSR is preferable to a car as it carries the same number of people on an average, takes one third of the parking area and half the space on the road as compared to the space occupied by a car. A TSR weighs a third of a car, it wears out the road much less has less tyre-rubber use and uses one third of the national resources to produce it. All this reduces indirect pollution. Since TSRs have a smaller engine they pollute much less per passenger than a car. Because of lower speeds and lighter weights, they are less threatening to pedestrians and bicyclists as compared to cars.

More spaces should be ;provided for parking of these vehicles. But far from doing so authorities are discouraging this. The Western India Automobile Association (WIAA), which lobbies for thousands of privileged motorists, has for years been demanding the removal of the taxi stand near its premises at Churchgate station where there is maximum demand. The stand is clearly in the public interest but the interests of the car lobby seldom coincide with those of the common people.

Auto-rickshaw drives are generally blamed for refusing trips, over-charging or bad behaviour but no one bothers to find out the social reasons for this. A training programme conducted for the drivers in Delhi has proved a step towards fostering socially responsible behaviour among the drivers, improving their information awareness as well as imparting dignity of labour to a profession that does not receive respect in Indian society, point out researchers Anvita Anand and Rajendra Ravi. In Delhi there are about 75,000 auto-rickshaws with permits. Considering that most of thee vehicles run on double-shifts, the number of drivers operating them shuld be nearly 1.50 lakh. Problems begin from obtaining a licence, often touts take away a lot of money.

Maligning the drivers is part of the growing trend towards treating all poor as criminals. Slums, for instance are seen as nurseries of crime. The poor are being pushed to the edge of illegality and invisibility, points out Dunu Roy.

The hand-pulled rickshaw are immortalized in Bimal Roy's film Do Bigha Zamin, featuring Balraj Sahani, and in the film City of Joy, featuring Om Puri, directed by Rolland Jaffe, and based on the novel of the same name by Dominique Lapierre. It is said that Balraj Sahani worked among rickshaw pullers to gain first hand experience of the work. He was a man of remarkable commitment who worked in Bhiwandi during the worst communal rioting in the seventies and for socialism for all his life. We cannot have another like him. He and Om Puri, another dedicated actor, worked hard on their roles and developed sores on their feet walking on the hot roads without any footwear. Balraj carried his wife and daughter in the vehicle while learning to pull the rickshaw, recalls Rinki Bhattacharya, daughter of director Bimal Roy. The rickshaws were outlawed by the West Bengal chief minister Buddhadeb Bhattacharjee in 2006.

Lapierre has struck a deep bond with rickshaw pullers in Kolkata and says they must not be removed from the streets. They are the greatest symbol of resilience in the face of tremendous adversity. (Tehelka 21-4-07).

The existence of these rickshawalas is proving to be embarrassing to the authorities in the city trying to win over foreign capital. Another reason is that removing the rickshaws will create more space for motor cars. There is also pressure from the automobile lobby which knows that the sales will not go up unless there is more space on roads for cars. So, all life is being subjugated to the interests of the car lobby and motorists at the expense of the poor.

Life is harsh for rickshaw pullers. They subsist on a frugal meal prepared on the roadside. It is a mixture of flour, salt and jaggery served in an aluminium plate with a lota of water. They become physical wrecks by the age of 40, they cough, spit blood and finally die on the street.

Why the crackdown on hand-pulled rickshaws in Kolkata? That is because it is easier to do this than tackle the city's real problems, says writer Ruchir Joshi. The pullers are poor, mostly Bihari, largely unorganized. They cannot hit back, unlike the cycle rickshaw walas who are more organized.

16

Sea Link

The Worli-Bandra sea link is the new showpiece, the new icon of Mumbai. The irony is that common people have no access to it though it is built with their money. The 5.6 km bridge across the sea is as an engineering marvel which people can see only from a long distance. Only motorists can use it.

Pedestrians and cyclists were completely barred. And BEST buses which carry millions of people were barred as well as they were refused exemption from paying toll for use of the bridge. This is completely against all tenets of social justice, modern transport practices, and India's own road transport policy.

Yet, the politicians confidently saw it as a major vote catching device. Mrs Sonia Gandhi, the Congress president, inaugurated the bridge amidst fanfare in June, 2009, and the previous night there was a spectacular display of fireworks. It was quickly decided at the function to name it after Mr Rajiv Gandhi, the former Prime Minister. What a great irony that it was sought to be sold as something of public interest.

The Shiv Sena and Bharatiya Janata party had launched the project and made the sea link as an election issue in

1999. So the centrist and right wing parties are no different on the issue of transport. The trouble is that even the established Left does not have an alternative vision.

So the ruling Communist party of India (Marxist) in West Bengal glorified Tata's Nano car by putting up posters of the car all over the state during the Parliamentary elections in 2009.

The party had rolled out the red carpet for Nano and blamed the opposition Trinamul Congress for driving the Singur car project from West Bengal through its agitation. The CPM had made the car project a prestige issue, forcibly acquired land from peasants at a low price and given it to Tatas, antagonised the poor, fired on them. Ultimately, it paid the price with a resounding defeat in the Lok Sabha elections.

So all the major political parties, Right, Left and Centre, have pursued car-centred policies while neglecting people's basic needs for transport even as the West is waking up to the threat posed by the car culture not only to the urban environment but to the earth itself and its climate.

The CPM as a leftist party in power continuously for 30 years in West Bengal in fact has a worse record than of other parties in urban transport and traffic. There are no traffic signals for pedestrian safety at the busiest junctions in Kolkata and vehicular pollution is so high the city is considered the capital of lung cancer. City police commissioner Gautam Mohan Chakrabarti admits the signal system is deficient and has asked additional commissioner K. Hariharan to improve it.

The government does not have a transport policy, it has a car policy, said leading journalist and environmentalist George Monbiot about Britain and it is equally applicable in India. Traffic planners in India always talk in terms of passenger car units and then plan to provide space to more and more cars. Pedestrians far outnumber cars but they are treated with contempt.

Nano is cheap only because of the heavy subsidy given to it by the government, argue Venu madhav Govindu of the

Institute of Science, Bangalore, and Deepak Malgham of the Indian Institute of Management, Bangalore.

The CPM posted Nano car pictures all over the state during the elections to remind the voters about the opposition's mistake of thwarting the state's indutrialisation. But the party had failed to produce an economic policy to help the poor, pointed out leading economist Prabhat Patnaik who is widely regarded as sympathetic to the CPM.

Two world famous bridges, Golden Gate in San Francisco and Sydney Harbour bridge provide free access to pedestrians and cyclists who throng there in thousands. The Sydney bridge even has railway tracks. The Bandra sealink would have been a great site for ordinary people if it had provided access to pedestrians and cyclists. It would have been so exhilarating to inhale fresh air and enjoy the breeze. With a little engineering this could have been easily done. A walkway does exist. It is for repairs. But it can be easily thrown open to the public. Even former deputy traffic police commissioner Harish Baijal agrees this can be done. The bridge design leaves one major lacuna. Motorists are unable to enjoy a view of the coastline of Mumbai as steel plates on the railings are put exactly at eye level and so block the view. So what should have been a visual delight is reduced to an aesthetic disaster.

Though suburban trains are the main mode of transport for people of Mumbai, the government is obsessed with flyovers and the sea link which mainly cater to motor vehicles. It is sad that the right of way has been given to motorised traffic since 1995 with the construction of flyovers, said Ajit Ranade, an economist.

17

Sachin Tendulkar

The complaint of cricket superstar Sachin Tendulkar in a way sums up what is wrong with the approach to traffic, architecture and development. Sachin Tendulkar complained some time ago that the developer who built his residential building La Mer, had not built the promised short-cut to the Bandra Reclamation flyover. Joining him in the complaint was film star Aishwarya Rai who then lived in the same building before becoming the Bachchan bride. Another prominent occupant of the building is the advertising executive and page three personality, the long haired and bearded Pralhad Kakar. Mr Kakar shocked many when he declared in a CNN-IBN television programme that the poor were to blame for sleeping on the pavements and being run over by a car as in the case of seven construction workers being killed at Carter Road in Bandra in 2006.

Few people are as mobile as Tendulkar, the star cricketer. He has a fleet of cars including the racing car Ferrari which was involved in a prolonged controversy with his seeking import duty exemption. But people like him want even more mobility while the poor are being increasingly immobilized. Pramod Mahajan, the leader of the right wing Hindu party the BJP, used his influence as union minister to secure the car tax exemption to Tendulkar who is rolling in wealth, yet sees it fit to seek such exemptions and other concessions.

Leaders like Mahajan are also obsessed with elitist schemes so that the upper class can have improved mobility. Mr Mahajan, who succumbed to revolver shots fired by his brother, told people in Bandra on the eve of the assembly elections of 2004 to vote for the BJP so that the Bandra-Worli sea link can be constructed faster.

The point is that while the mobility of the common people is being reduced the mobility of the affluent is increasing due to increased access to motor cars and more roads. Yet, ironically it is the powerful who are complainig and seeking to further improve their own mobility. At the same time they are not raising any voice in support of the disadvantaged. How can they? If you look carefully, it will be clear that it is the motorists, callous municipal officials and unsympathetic traffic police who are actually impeding the mobility of the poor.

I saw the area around Tendulkar's building and realized that the main problem is the absence of footpaths though the Mount Mary church is very close to Tendulkar's building and tens of thousands visit it during the annual fair. If the municipal body and traffic police have any sense, they should have given high priority for footpaths in this area.

But they do not even talk about it. Not far from Tendulkar's building is the old Bazar road, a lovely historic, old lane with single or double storey houses which is very nice to walk on. It would make perfect sense to make this an exclusive pedestrian road as is done all over Europe with wonderful results.

Yet due to utter lack of imagination and commitment of the authorities, this road is now as clogged with traffic as any other road and it has become worse because it is narrow and just cannot take so much traffic.

This kind of callousness is visible all over. The Shiv Sena has been in power in the municipal corporation in Mumbai for several years.

Those owning motor cars impose indirect costs on those who do not. As the number of motor vehicles increases, there is increased congestion and the cost is paid by others. Those using auto-rickshaws and taxies find that due to congestion caused mainly by cars, they have to pay much higher fare than they would have had to pay without congestion.

Many of the motor car users and motor-cyclists use their vehicles for fun, prestige and travel for the sake of travel rather than is actually necessary. It is mainly an ego trip. 'Daddy, shall we go for a drive ?' is a line from a television advertisement for a motor car which I always remember. The drive is supposed to be so enjoyable that the father forgets that his son has fared poorly in school examination.

There is also an insidious television advertisement for a two-wheeler which shows a bus depot full of parked motor cycles and the protagonist says 'Yeh public ka naya transport.' This advertisement is particularly insidious because it insults the common people who depend mainly on public transport. The implication is that buses can be done away with and the space can be used for parking two-wheelers.

In all enlightened societies there is more and more emphasis on public transport as it is most environment-friendly and also ideal for urban living and low-cost. But here we have an elite which looks down upon public transport.

Till a few years ago Tendulkar lived in a nice housing colony of writers called Sahitya Sahawas in Bandra (east). His father Ramesh was a sensitive poet and critic for whom the utterly commercialized advertising life of his son held little attraction. If Sachin Tendulkar ever cares to walk the not so long distance between Bandra (east) and Bandra (west) he would realize how very difficult life is for the common people and how inconsequential in comparison is his demand for a quicker access to the freeway. He is now building a big bungalow for himself in Bandra.

There is only one real link between the two sides of the suburb and that is the flyover and it is only recently that a footpath was built on it.

There are encouragiang reports recently of the dramatic improvement in public bus transport in Indore. On the other hand in Mumbai authorities are selling precious land of the BEST bus system, often cited as the best city bus service in the country. The land is desperately needed for expansion. But the authorities do not think so. They are simply auctioning the land to the highest bidder, selling the family silver.

This is outrageous by any reckoning. There is something sacred about public land meant for public amenities. Just as one would not give one's arm howsoever high the price, one must not give away precious land that is desperately needed for public amenities.

The collector of Indore Vivek Agarwal has put in place low-floor, comfortable, new buses and built bus stops. It is inexcusable that the city did not have bus shelters. What on earth were the politicians, the corporators and other citizens doing all these years ? There are no bus shelters at several places even in Mumbai, particularly along the highways. The two women, knocked down allegedly by Mr Bal Thackeray's assistant some time ago would not have lost their lives had there been a bus shelter to protect them.

During my visit to Bhopal, the capital of Madhya Pradesh and virtually the heart of India some time ago, I was shocked to find that the city was without a proper bus depot. It shows the hypocrisy of the ruling class that while it invites Charles Correa to design the state legislature building in Bhopal, it cannot think of constructing a proper bus depot. One wonders what the well-paid bureaucrats with enormous powers do if they cannot provide elementary facilities to the masses.

In Mumbai it is worse, existing facilities are being reduced if not eliminated as the dubious sale of BEST depot land and its use for car parking shows. Future generations will certainly not forgive the trampling of public transport and the pandering to the automobile lobby and land mafia. Even the richest nations are now promoting public transport and our ruling class is shamefully scuttling it even when there is increasing demand for it.

If BEST has so much surplus space, it can be used for setting up state transport depots. Each suburb in Mumbai is bigger in population than an average district town. If every town needs and has an ST depot there is no earthly reason why there cannot be one in each suburb. There is a big unfulfilled demand in Mumbai for such amenities. But then corrupt politicians won't be able to make much money there.

Everything is up for sale. Our politicians should be compulsorily made to read the famous statement of the Native Indian chief Seattle in response to the land colonization by the brutal whites colonialists in America. He said you will get dollars but what will you do with the dollars when with your form of development there will be no water to drink and no proper air to breathe.

Epilogue

Bus Rapid Transit

The spectacular success of the Bus Rapid Transit (BRT) system in Ahmedabad in just six months since its launch in 2009 shows results can be achieved with a strong political will. Chief minister Narendra Modi ensured that buses get priority over cars on the road. One can now have a pleasant ride by bus through a special reserved lane over 24 km. upto Ahmedabad's happening place, the Kankaria lake.

Similarly, in Delhi chief minister Sheela Dixit's drive in implementing the BRT in the capital is yielding results after a vicious campaign by the car lobby against it. Motorists are clearly not happy that ordinary people in buses travel ahead of them, much faster than them.

Mrs Dixit's son Sandeep Dixit, Congres MP, has set a good example by cycling to the Lok Sabha but is frustrated by lack of facility for bicycle parking in Parliament premises. Biju Janata Dal MP Bhartruhari Mahtab would also prefer to cycle to Parliament. Environment minister Jairam Ramesh has been urging officials to walk the short distance between various buildings rather than take cars.

The initiative taken by the city municipal commissioner I.P. Gautam helped in the success of the Ahmedabad project, said Abhijit Lokre, assistant professor in the Centre of

Excellence in Urban Transport University (CEPT) in Ahmedabad, and Madhav Pai, lead transport engineer for the Centre for Sustainable Transport in India. Dario Hidalgo, senior transport engineer of WRI Center for Sustainable Transport, and Pai have been among the strongest advocates of introducing BRT in India and have studied the system in various parts of the world.

Shivanand Swami, associate director of CEPT, who helped design the Ahmedabad BRT is acting as onsultant for BRT projects in Jaipur, Chennai and Surat. Bangalore is also planning a BRT system, according to the state's urban development secretary Subir Hari Singh.

Unfortunately, the authorities in different cities are seeking to curb the number of cycle rickshaws and auto rickshaws, the mode of transport of ordinary people, rather than the number of motor cas. Former chief justice of Delhi high court A.P. Shah has ruled that it was unfair to criminalise cycle rickshaws. Prashant Bhushan, leading lawyer, told the court in response to a petition filed by Madhu Kishwar, Manushi editor, that cars clog roads, not rickshaws.

The vicious campaign against the BRT in Delhi has been denounced by a number of scholars, planners and activists including Dunu Roy, Imrana Qadeer, Ravi Duggal, Jayant Pendharkar, Benny Kuruvila, Vinay Baindur, Ramaswamy Iyer, Sadanand Menon, Suman Sahai, Zoya Hasan, Praveen Pardeshi, Nandan Malushte, Kamal Mitra Chinoy, Sushil Khanna, Padma Prakash and Tapan Bose.

In Hyderabad the authorities are planning to expand roads causing destruction of several historic buildings, said Veda Kumar of the Forum for Better Hyderabad.

Mumbai is sadly lagging in democratising the transport scene. A technical report on the BRT has just been completed after five years and there is still no sign of any resolve to implement the system. Instead, the municipal corporation is giving lucrative concessions to builders to construct multi-storied car parks which no one is using and the BEST bus undertaking authorities want to give away the precious land of bus depots for helipads for helicopters for the affluent. Luckily, environment minister Jairam Ramesh put his foot down in March, 2010 against the proposal to construct helipads on top of buildings. The helipads would be extremely hazardous, said Ashok Kalbag, a senior IIT professor and engineer.

The air pollution caused by motor vehicles in Mumbai is now so serious and harmful that Mahesh Pathak, the secretary of the Maharashtra pollution control board, recently supported the campaign for a car-free day in the city. Maharashtra's joint transport commissioner Satish Sahasrabuddhe recently supported the demand for a congestion tax on vehicles. Socially conscious citizens of the upper class suburb of Bandra in Mumbai ensured a car-free Carter Road on the sea front in early 2010. It was supported by Congress MP Priya Dutt. But this needs to be extended all over and first the basics must be taken care of. In the adjoining posh Pali Hill there is no footpath anywhere on the busy zig zag roads.

The BRT system will have to be expanded massively in the country and this will take years. Till then, immediately relief ought to be provided to people by building decent, usable footpths and curbing car use throughout the country. This is the basic obligation of the ruling class to the people of this country.

Automobiles with their pollution are the biggest contributors to global warming and climate change. The damning verdict is official and scientific. It comes from a study led by Nadine Unger of the Godard institute of NASA in 2010, it shows how serious the crisis is and that shows how relevant is the title of this book . And how important it is to strengthen sustainable transport and curb the use of motor cars.

Index